Studia Fennica
Historica 15

THE FINNISH LITERATURE SOCIETY (SKS) was founded in 1831 and has, from the very beginning, engaged in publishing operations. It nowadays publishes literature in the fields of ethnology and folkloristics, linguistics, literary research and cultural history.

The first volume of the Studia Fennica series appeared in 1933. Since 1992, the series has been divided into three thematic subseries: Ethnologica, Folkloristica and Linguistica. Two additional subseries were formed in 2002, Historica and Litteraria. The subseries Anthropologica was formed in 2007.

In addition to its publishing activities, the Finnish Literature Society maintains research activities and infrastructures, an archive containing folklore and literary collections, a research library and promotes Finnish literature abroad.

Charlotta Wolff

Noble conceptions of politics in eighteenth-century Sweden (ca 1740–1790)

Finnish Literature Society • Helsinki

Studia Fennica Historica 15

The publication has undergone a peer review.

VERTAISARVIOITU
KOLLEGIALT GRANSKAD
PEER-REVIEWED
www.tsv.fi/tunnus

The open access publication of this volume has received part funding via
Helsinki University Library.

A digital edition of a printed book first published in 2008 by the Finnish Literature Society.
Cover Design: Timo Numminen
EPUB: eLibris Media Oy

ISBN 978-952-222-092-9 (Print)
ISBN 978-952-222-782-9 (PDF)
ISBN 978-952-222-781-2 (EPUB)

ISSN 0085-6835 (Studia Fennica)
ISSN 1458-526X (Studia Fennica Historica)

DOI: http://dx.doi.org/10.21435/sfh.15

Contents

Acknowledgements

When I was just finishing my doctoral studies, my senior colleague Pasi Ihalainen from the University of Jyväskylä asked me if I would join him in a new research project on the conceptual constructions of identities and loyalties in the eighteenth century. At the end of November 2004, when I defended my dissertation on the Swedish nobility's relations with France in the age of Enlightenment, we heard the good news: The Academy of Finland had decided to support our project during the three years to come.

The project "Enlightened Loyalties: The Conceptual Construction of National, Cultural and Political Identities and Loyalties in North-Western Europe, 1750–1800" ended in December 2007. Its members were Pasi Ihalainen, Jouko Nurmiainen and myself. Administratively, it was a challenge involving the bureaucracies of two Finnish universities. Intellectually, it was inspiring to the point that we would debate over the nature of concepts and historical processes until midnight during our quarterly meetings. This book is one of the three monographs produced by each of us during the project. My deepest personal gratitude goes to Jouko and Pasi for having read and commented on everything I wrote.

I am also grateful to Professor Henrik Meinander and the Ella and Georg Ehrnrooth Foundation for supporting my part in the research project at its very beginning, before the Academy funding started. I also benefited from the support of the Swedish-Finnish Cultural Fund in the form of free hotel nights in Stockholm during my archive trips to Sweden.

Research for this book was mainly carried out at the National Archives and the National Library of Sweden, but also at the Lund University Library, the Uppsala University Library, the Secret State Archive in Berlin, the University Library of Greifswald and the French National Archives in Paris. I thank the helpful staff of these institutions. In particular, I want to thank Professor Jens E. Olesen and Ivo Asmus for their most valuable and friendly assistance in introducing Jouko and me to the treasures of Greifswald.

I have enjoyed inspiring exchanges and friendship with my closest colleagues at the Department of History and the Renvall Institute of the University of Helsinki and the Department of History and Ethnology of the University of Jyväskylä. I also thank my friends at the Centre for Nordic Studies at the University of Helsinki, particularly Research Director Henrik

Stenius, for unending intellectual and conceptual challenges and great laughs. Many others also commented on various drafts and case studies during seminars and conferences. Thanks to all of you who bothered to read the manuscripts that preceded this book.

The path of this book from manuscript to print was made smooth and easy by the helpful, efficient and kind assistance of Professor Pauli Kettunen, Rauno Endén and Kati Lampela from the Finnish Literature Society. Thank you for welcoming my monograph to the Studia Fennica Historica collection and making publishing enjoyable.

As a person who takes a bizarre pleasure in foreign languages, I owe a particular debt of gratitude to Julie Uusinarkaus from the Language Services of our university for her intelligent and inspiring improvements to my style and for helping to find the right words.

Finishing this work at a very particular moment in Jouko's and my life also required some help from our parents. Thank you for always coming when we needed you most.

This book is dedicated to Elsa, as a tribute to her patience and curiosity.

Kirkkonummi, 27 November 2008
Charlotta Wolff

Introduction

This book is a study on political identity, loyalties and belonging in eighteenth-century Sweden. It deals with how political communities were formed and kept together by common practices of discourse, certain key concepts and common rhetorical arsenals. The study concentrates on the nobility, whose ambiguous relationship to monarchy and republicanism put its heavy mark on the era known as the Age of Liberty (1719–1772).

In Old Regime Europe, the nobility was part of the elite that retained political power in societies and regimes founded on a traditional social order with privileged estates and constituted bodies as intermediary powers between the rulers and the mass of subjects. During the eighteenth century, in Western and Northern Europe, the legitimacy of power through privilege was falling apart. This was partly due to the writings of radical thinkers attacking the very idea of noble privilege or wishing to extend the political influence of the third estate, and partly to the attempts made by the monarchical states since the fifteenth century to unify their administration, improve taxation and thus strengthen their central authority over the societies they ruled. Rival powers that were dismantled or diminished in the name of the *raison d'État* included local assemblies, estates and other "sovereign bodies in the state".[1]

A model for this development was the France of Louis XIV (1638–1715).[2] With the help of *homines novi* such as Colbert, the son of a merchant at Reims, Louis XIV had concentrated the aristocracy in the court, strengthened royal jurisdiction and broken the privilege of inheritance in civil and military offices by the creation of new officers directly subordinated to the government. Domesticated at the court and occupied with the attendance of the king and with various pleasures and festivities, the higher nobility was no longer in a position to raise an armed rebellion against the monarchy as it had done during the early years of the king's reign.[3]

---

1 Hagen Schulze, *Staat und Nation in der europäische Geschichte*, München, 1994. See also Robert Mandrou, *L'Europe « absolutiste ». Raison et raison d'État 1649–1775*, Paris, 1977.
2 The concept of model in this context is borrowed from Mandrou, *L'Europe « absolutiste »*.
3 Arlette Jouanna, *Le devoir de révolte. La noblesse française et la gestation de l'État moderne, 1559–1661*, Paris, 1989, pp. 390–399.

Noble opposition, however, did not disappear. During the eighteenth century, particularly its second half, the nobility resurged as a challenger to the French monarchical state. At the same time, the legitimacy of its very existence was strongly questioned by enlightenment philosophers and by the rising third estate. In France, immediately after the death of Louis XIV and during the regency of Philippe d'Orléans, the aristocracy formed by the high nobility, the highest court officials and civil servants, and especially the *parlements* (courts of appeals) and other sovereign courts of justice started looking for opportunities to restore its power. It formed a strong opposition during the whole reign of Louis XV (1715–1774) and partly satisfied its ambitions under Louis XVI (1774–1792), after the king, in an attempt to appease the growing opposition, restored the *parlements* that his predecessor had abolished. The liberal part of the court aristocracy eventually took part in the outbreak of the revolution and the outlining of an ephemeral new constitutional monarchy.

The classical absolutist rule of the Sun King begot many emulators among the crowned heads of Europe. In contrast, the opposition of the French *parlements* had an influence on how politics were perceived all over Europe. Their *remonstrances* (objections to laws made by the king) were printed and spread, and the struggle between the French king and his magistrates was reported in journals and gazettes read at every court, which thus influenced noble self-image. In a sense, noble opposition and the most subtle forms of it – including metaphorical rhetoric, libels and clandestine calumny pamphlets – had become part of the dynamics of court society all over Europe.[4]

Among the northern imitators of the French model was the prince elector Frederick William of Brandenburg, the *grosse Kurfürst* (1640–1688), who started to reduce the power of the nobility by making himself financially and politically independent of the Estates of Brandenburg, convened for the last time in 1654. He also began the work on a rational bureaucracy with the creation of a General War Commissariat.[5] His successor, Frederick III, who proclaimed himself as the first "King in Prussia" under the name of Frederick I (1688–1713), modelled his court on the French and developed a complicated court ceremonial. The perfection of the Prussian bureaucracy was achieved under his son Frederick William I (1713–1740). Unlike his father, the Soldier-

---

4   On the forms of noble opposition in court society, see, for instance, Daniel Gordon, *Citizens Without Sovereignty. Equality and Sociability in French Thought, 1670–1789*, Princeton, 1994; Bernard Hours, *Louis XV et sa Cour. Le roi, l'étiquette et le courtisan*, Paris, 2002; Charlotta Wolff, "Kabal och kärlek. Vänskapen som alternativ sociabilitet i 1700-talets hovsamhällen", *Historisk Tidskrift för Finland*, vol. 89 (2004:2), pp. 85–115; Robert Darnton, "An Early Information Society: News and the Media in Eighteenth-Century Paris", *American Historical Review*, vol. 105 (2001:1), pp. 1–35.

5   The commissar, *Komissar*, is a title borrowed from absolutist France, where it characteristically designated a revocable, specialised civil servant who had been chosen by the monarch to execute a special task described in his letter of appointment, the *commission*. By appointing *commissaires* instead of confining the same tasks to holders of regular, hereditary *offices*, the monarchy hoped to decrease the local power and corruption of its nobility.

King disliked unnecessary spending and courtly manners. He developed the army considerably, increased administrative efficiency and unified civil and military administration. Frederick William I devoted his entire life to the state and its service, and he expected his subjects to do so, too. If the Prussian nobility wanted to maintain its dominant positions as landowners, army officers and administrators, it had to cooperate with the Crown.[6] In a sort of contract with its nobility, the Prussian state had handed over local administrative and jurisdictional power in return for the noblemen's fidelity in the service of the crown. While the policy of Frederick William I had been very suspicious towards the nobility, his son Frederick II ("the Great", 1740–1786) outspokenly favoured his noblemen, giving them the exclusive right to civil and military offices and declaring the interest of the Prussian nobility to be the interest of the state. Hereby the king achieved an ephemeral balance that served his purposes of domination and satisfied the landed nobility, the *Junkers*, who dominated at a local level in the army and the administration.[7]

In both France and Prussia, the reinforcement of the monarchy was carried out effectively, but the nobility resurged and only reshaped its power. A rather different case is eighteenth-century Sweden, which has been chosen for this study on noble political identity and loyalty. In the late seventeenth century, royal absolutism also developed here. Charles XI (1660–1697) put the Senate aside, ruled with his private councillors and centralised the administration under his own direction. His rule became associated with the confiscation of landed property that had previously belonged to the Crown but had been given to the nobility as tokens of favour. These confiscations, called *reduktioner*, were most hated by the aristocracy and became the symbol of royal autocracy and sovereignty. They caused a permanent defiance towards the monarchy amidst the Swedish nobility throughout the following century.[8]

After the death of Charles XII (1697–1718), succeeded by his sister Ulrika Eleonora and in 1720 her husband, the prince Frederick of Hesse-Cassel, the nobility took its revenge. The new constitution of 1720 restored the power of the four-estate Diet and the Senate, and the nobility was granted extended privileges in 1723. The period from 1719 to 1772 was to be known in Swedish history as the Age of Liberty, 'liberty' referring to the freedom of the Estates and the absence of royal sovereignty, i.e. absolutism.[9] This Age of Liberty was dominated by the nobility to an extent that it has often been described as an aristocratic republic by both contemporaries and historians.

---

6   On Prussia, see E. N. Williams, *The Ancien Régime in Europe. Government and Society in the Major States 1648–1789*, London, 1999 (1970), pp. 292–365; Heinz Schilling, *Höfe und Allianzen. Deutschland 1648–1763*, Berlin, 1994, pp. 404–410; Robert M. Berdahl, *The Politics of the Prussian Nobility. The Development of a Conservative Ideology 1770–1848*, Princeton, 1988.

7   Schilling, *Höfe und Allianzen*, pp. 408–410; Walter Görlitz, *Die Junker. Adel und Bauer im deutschen Osten. Geschichtliche Bilanz von 7 Jahrhunderten*, Limburg an der Lahn, 1964.

8   Mirkka Lappalainen, *Suku, valta, suurvalta. Creutzit 1600-luvun Ruotsissa ja Suomessa*, Helsinki, 2005, pp. 40–44; Petri Karonen, *Pohjoinen suurvalta. Ruotsi ja Suomi 1521–1809*, Helsinki, 1999, pp. 289–324; see also Peter Englund, *Det hotade huset. Adliga föreställningar om samhället under stormaktstiden*, Stockholm, 1989.

9   On the concept of 'Age of Liberty', see chapter 2.

Profiting from the relative weakness of two German-born rulers, Frederick I (1720–1751) and Adolph Frederick (1751–1771), the Estates and particularly the nobility were able to dominate political decision-making at the Diet and in the chancellery. The high nobility also held the highest civil and military offices and had through its personal networks deep influence in nominations to civil and military employments.[10] The Estates and subsequently the nobility partially lost political power after the royal revolution of 1772, when Gustav III (1771–1792) re-established royal authority over the Diet, but the aristocracy remained influential at court, in culture and in administration.

Until the early 1770s, Sweden, like Poland, thus for some decades formed an exception to the tendency towards a reinforced monarchy in larger European states. Historians have sometimes tended to underline exceptionally "modern" features of Swedish political culture in the Age of Liberty, particularly with regard to the practices of the regular four-estate Diet and its parties, which have been compared to the early parliamentarianism that was developing in Great Britain. Regardless of whether this comparison is adequate or not, the republican features, social and political turbulences as well as the "revolutions" of Sweden were observed by contemporaries such as foreign diplomats in Stockholm, and make it interesting to take a closer look at Swedish political discourse and ideology and the changes that they underwent during the eighteenth century. The transition from royal absolutism to an Age of Liberty dominated by estate rule from the 1720s and back to royal authority from the 1770s as well as the social turbulences of the second half of the century and the radicalisation of political language could motivate a quest for a possible Swedish *Sattelzeit* – albeit that the finding of one may be more an intellectual game than the primary concern of this study.

The rivalry between the nobility and the monarchy undoubtedly put its marks on the self-image and identity of the leading estate and influenced political language and rhetoric. Another development that did the same was the transformation of estate society. During the second half of the eighteenth century, a new threat to the dominant position of the nobility was what has been called the *rise of the third estate*, the gradual social levelling of estate-based society, challenged by the growth of an educated bourgeoisie that did not benefit from any of the privileges gradually accorded to the old elites, the nobility and the clergy, no more than it identified itself with the rural masses.[11] Tocqueville, looking for the origin of the French revolution in his *L'ancien régime et la Révolution* in the early nineteenth century, saw a structural discordance between the centralising, egalitarian French absolutism and a society built upon privileges (what his generation would call *la feodalité*). By collecting taxes and imposing royal justice, the French absolutist

10 See, for instance, Charlotta Wolff, *Vänskap och makt. Den svenska politiska eliten och upplysningstidens Frankrike*, Helsingfors, 2005; Patrik Winton, *Frihetstidens politiska praktik. Nätverk och offentlighet 1746–1766*, Uppsala, 2006.

11 I am resigned to using the perhaps outdated concept of 'bourgeoisie' here to describe the educated urban middle class of teachers, lawyers, physicians, civil servants and artists that did not belong to the merchant burghers. For a critical analysis of the French concept of 'bourgeoisie', see Sarah Maza, *The Myth of the French Bourgeoisie. An Essay on Social Imaginary, 1750–1850*, Cambridge, Mass., 2003.

monarchical state was levelling the differences between classes and casting the ground of a democratic, i.e. egalitarian society. Still, according to Tocqueville, French society was dominated by the aristocracy, which stuck to its privileges and kept feudal attitudes alive despite the efforts of the monarchy to diminish them.[12]

In the meantime, the ideas of 'privilege' and 'estate' as well as their legitimacy were debated and questioned by changes in society.[13] In Sweden, where the formal basis of privilege and political representation was the division of the citizens into nobility, clergy, burghers and peasants, a new bourgeoisie that did not get its income from the traditional merchant activities which had defined the burghers' estate was being formed by the *ofrälse ståndspersoner*, the "non-noble persons of standing". This term, used by contemporaries and later on by historians, reveals the very contradictions of an estate that formally was not recognised as one, but socially and politically constantly reminded society of its existence. As the rise of a skilled middle-class elite continued, it gave birth in the late 1760s to a public debate over privileges and estate society in general.[14] In particular, the noblemen's rights to the highest civil and military offices were questioned with references to the constitution of 1721, which set merit and capacity, and not birth, as criteria for nominations to all public offices. There were also demands for new privileges for a new, large estate of commoners, the so-called *odalståndet* (approximately the "yeomen's estate", from Old Norse for free peasants), formed by the third and the fourth estates, the burghers and the peasants, possibly also those "persons of standing" who did not belong to any traditional estate.[15] The nobility eventually lost the cause in the debate over the right to offices at the Diet of 1771 and with the oath sworn by the new king, Gustav III. The following year, the royal *coup* sealed the defeat of the nobility by diminishing its political influence. This gradual process has been called the "levelling of the estates" (*ståndsutjämning*).[16]

The Swedish party elite of the Age of Liberty had been keeping up a very aristocratic political system, with its typical mechanisms of dominance and influence. In a gesture that has been seen as a symbol for the aristocratism

---

12 Alexis de Tocqueville, *L'ancien régime et la Révolution*. Préface, notes, bibliographie, chronologie par Françoise Mélonio, Paris, 1988.

13 On the debate on the future of the French nobility, see, for instance, Jay M. Smith, *Nobility Reimagined. The Patriotic Nation in Eighteenth-Century France*, Ithaca, 2005.

14 On this process and the debate, see the contributions in Marie-Christine Skuncke & Henrika Tandefelt (red.), *Riksdag, kaffehus och predikstol. Frihetstidens politiska kultur, 1766–1772*, Stockholm & Helsingfors, 2003.

15 In Sweden and Finland, the peasantry was free. The peasants' estate was formed by landowning peasants paying taxes to the Crown, thus acquiring their political rights. See Jouko Nurmiainen, "Gemensamma privilegier för ett odalstånd. Alexander Kepplerus som borgmästare och samhällstänkare", in *Riksdag, kaffehus och predikstol. Frihetstidens politiska kultur 1766–1772*, pp. 171–190.

16 On this process, see Sten Carlsson, *Ståndssamhälle och ståndspersoner 1700–1865. Studier rörande det svenska ståndssamhällets upplösning*, Lund, 1973; on the royal coup, see Peter Hallberg, *Ages of Liberty. Social Upheaval, History Writing, and the New Public Sphere in Sweden, 1740–1792*, Stockholm, 2003; Jonas Nordin, "Frihetstidens radikalism", in *Riksdag, kaffehus och predikstol. Frihetstidens politiska kultur 1766–1772*, pp. 55–72.

of the late Age of Liberty, the House of Nobility was closed to any new noble families in 1762.[17] The aristocratic "republic" of the parties and their senators – a monarchy without royal sovereignty – finally succumbed to party struggles and attacks from the lower estates. It was violently aggressed by pamphleteers requiring the abolition of noble privilege and the recognition of personal merit. In this situation, where the lack of legitimacy of the aristocratic system was obvious to the pamphleteers of a rising Swedish "third estate", it was a royal revolution, not a bourgeois one, that eventually absorbed the social discordance in Sweden.

Although the debates on the future of the nobility and of estate society more generally seldom deviated from the consensus that social differences had a functional legitimacy and that privileges should not necessarily be abolished but enlarged to other groups, the privileged estate was strongly challenged both by the monarchies and by social dynamics. The evolution towards stronger central administration during the second half of the eighteenth century required a re-orientation of noble identities and loyalties. Aristocratic political identity was traditionally built on the idea of privilege and liberty, on the perception of the nobleman as a sovereign and free citizen enjoying privileges that permitted him to be judged by his equals and to exercise political power alongside them inside their own estate, the aristocratic republic. In the Age of Enlightenment, new conceptions of state and community, based on other bounds of loyalty than personal ones or those attached to privilege, kinship and estate, challenged these traditional views and were also taken into account in the attempts to redefine society. It seems relevant to ask to what extent this evolution is perceptible in the political discourse of the nobility, the powerful group that had perhaps the most to lose.

Faced with the threat of effectively losing power, what attitude would the nobility adopt towards political authority in general and towards other political institutions and bodies? How did it see its own position? Should it be loyal to other political bodies or estates in the realm, to the king or other possessors of authority, and why? How did the nobility adapt to the slow transition from personal bounds of loyalty between the ruler and his loyal servants and vassals to the development of an impersonal contract between the subject and the state, manifested in bureaucracy and a standing army?

In order to answer these questions, we may look at the nobility's conceptions of political community, particularly of communities larger than its own estate, communities that supposedly could be the realm, the fatherland or something else. The recognition of this sense of community or belonging to a community larger than oneself is often followed by a perception of how common affairs should be ruled or of how the citizen should conduct himself in order to advance the public interest. It is subsequently possible to examine conceptions of loyalty, belonging and self by focusing on the relationship to state and society, mostly articulated through service and duty, but also by liberty and right, and particularly on the relationship to monarchy and to other estates. Concepts and rhetorical commonplace often serve as the social glue of such

---

17 Hugo Valentin, *Frihetstidens riddarhus. Några bidrag till dess karakteristik*, Stockholm, 1915, pp. 278–279.

14

communities as they articulate individual self-image or identity in relation to the shared values of the community.

In this book, these issues will be addressed as follows:

- since the political community could not exist without a common set of references, the first chapter will deal with the nobility's positioning on the question of the Swedish constitution in the eighteenth century;
- the second chapter will be dedicated to the concept of 'liberty' and its importance for the nobility;
- the third chapter will deal with how the nobility perceived citizenship and the duties the nobility attached to it;
- after these chapters on the common values and ideological framework of the Age of Liberty, the fourth and final chapter looks at the nobility's adaptation and resistance to monarchical restoration under Gustav III.

Conceptions of self, of loyalty or of belonging elaborated and used by politically active and influential noblemen can be investigated in texts written by the nobility on laws, political values, the monarchy and on the future of the nobility. Here, the choice has been made to study these conceptions through an analysis of the political language and the concepts used by the nobility. By examining several speech acts and political statements made at the Swedish Diet and elsewhere in the political sphere, we can ask whether any re-conceptualisation is perceptible, whether political change perceptibly influenced value systems and political conceptions, and how this was reflected in concepts and their use. Which were the concepts and values that articulated noble self-image? Eventually, what was the idea of nobility and how was it legitimated? Is this really a history of losers, or isn't it rather a history of an elite that successfully adapts itself? Before going into detail, it is necessary to make some remarks concerning the methods and sources chosen for this study.

Political concepts, conceptions and ideas

The history of political concepts or more generally conceptual history has gained much favour among historians in the last few years. As an interdisciplinary research strategy, it has been defined in almost as many various, sometimes rivalling ways as there are scholars practising it. Generally speaking, one could say that conceptual history studies the meanings or clusters of multiple meanings attached to a particular term from a historical perspective, in other words how concepts appear, are used and change in the course of history. A concept carries 'representations', which gives it a metaphorical function when compared to a simple word.[18] For some conceptual historians, concepts may even tend to become agents in history, or historical subjects in themselves. This may be a problem similar to the one that the history of ideas sometimes has been accused of: the ideas tend

18 The term *représentation* has been largely used by French historians since it was launched by the psychologist Serge Moscovici. An often-cited study on historical representations is Georges Duby, *Les Trois ordres ou l'imaginaire féodal*, Paris, 1978.

to become independent subjects under the pen of the historian. Another problem appears if this subject is erroneously considered as stable, while not only the words used, but also the sense of each term and concept change in the course of history.[19] Concepts are like shells or empty baskets which are loaded with different significations in different historical contexts or even situations ('speech acts'). Like ideologies, they are 'cultural artefacts'.[20]

While historical 'representations' studied by, for instance, the followers of the Annalist school are not always expressed in words, conceptual history, as a consequence of the so-called 'linguistic turn' in humanistic sciences, focuses explicitly on verbally articulated representations. Thereby the study of historical political concepts is closely related to the theory on speech acts applied by Quentin Skinner and the Cambridge school.

The method of approaching the concepts in German *Begriffsgeschichte* was defined by Reinhart Koselleck. In "Begriffsgeschichte und Sozialgeschichte" (*Vergangene Zukunft. Zur Semantik geschichtlicher Zeiten*) Koselleck defines conceptual history as a *quellenkritische* method that helps in understanding issues of social history, such as the transition from estate-based loyalties towards patriotic self-understanding, or the transition from aristocratic, kinship-based loyalties to royalist loyalty to the king, the state or a republican political community. *Begriffsgeschichte*, in practice, maps the meanings of words and concepts in their historical context and semantic field and interprets/translates them for the modern reader. As an example, let us take a term designating representative assemblies, such as the *Parliament/ parlements*: what does it mean in which context? The French *parlementaires* claimed to be the representatives of the Nation in order to legitimise their political ambitions, but their claims were based on privilege, not on a modern conception of political community based on direct submission to the sovereign and no longer on an intermediary or multiple authority.

In the tradition established by Koselleck, conceptual history has usually focused on the period that runs from the late seventeenth century to the middle of the nineteenth century, during which major changes took place in French and German, particularly Prussian, society, philosophy and political theory.[21] Particularly during the latter half of what has been called the

---

19 Cf. Bo Lindberg, *Den antika skevheten. Politiska ord och begrepp i det tidig-moderna Sverige*, Stockholm, 2006, pp. 36–37, and Melvin Richter, *The History of Political and Social Concepts*, Oxford, 1995, pp. 133–137.

20 Benedict Anderson, *Imagined Communities. Reflections on the Origin and Spread of Nationalism*, London & New York, 1991, p. 4, uses the example of nationalism as a cultural artefact. The significations of the concept define its sense and make up the very concept. Cf. semiology, which as a discipline comprises linguistics as only one branch of semiology, although the very concept of semiology could not exist without modern linguistics. Ferdinand de Saussure, *Cours de linguistique générale*, Paris, 1916, pp. 32–25.

21 According to Koselleck, these changes are particularly noticeable in German political concepts during the period 1750–1850. See Reinhart Koselleck, *Vergangene Zukunft. Zur Semantik geschichtlicher Zeiten*, Frankfurt am Main, 1979, and Reinhart Koselleck, *Preußen zwischen Reform und Revolution. Allgemeines Landrecht, Verwaltung und soziale Bewegung von 1791 bis 1848*, Stuttgart, 1967. The corresponding moment in France has been identified with the period 1680–1820, chosen by the editors of *Handbuch politisch-sozialer Grundbegriffe in Frankreich 1680–1820*. One can ask whether Paul Hazard's *La crise de la*

Sattelzeit, the period when a major re-orientation took place in Western European concepts reflecting political and ideological change, estate society was questioned and breaking up. This period corresponds to the establishing of Frederician Prussian absolutism and to the democratisation of Western society described by Tocqueville. Major conceptual changes that took place during this process of transformation have been the object of systematic studies, above all in the *Geschichtliche Grundbegriffe. Historisches Lexikon zur politisch-sozialen Sprache in Deutschland* and the *Handbuch politisch-sozialer Grundbegriffe in Frankreich 1680–1820.*[22]

An often quoted example is Prussia, where the nobility had lost its political power but the king still took advantage of a strictly corporative estate society to enforce the authority of the state.[23] The passage to a centralised state with loyal subjects directly subordinated to the absolute sovereign and monarch was made possible by the alliance between the Crown and its noblemen, who were given local authority in the king's name. Obedience and loyalty to the sovereign became a uniting factor, overriding the religious differences between a Calvinist king and his Lutheran, Catholic and Calvinist subjects. Contract, obligation and service were the keywords of Frederician state ideology. Loyalty to the Prussian absolutist state and king was formulated as a patriotic duty, as love to a common German fatherland taking up the role of a missing common religion.[24] A consequence of the building of an Enlightened Prussian state was the *Allgemeine Landrecht*, which has also been the subject of Koselleck's now classical study on how new ideals affect or do not affect political terminology and concepts.[25]

Another way of describing the process of philosophical change in the early modern Western world is the one adopted by the distinguished historian of political thought John Pocock. He has focused on the ideological turn that took place during the American revolution, in a process he calls a "Machiavellian moment". What Pocock terms as a "Machiavellian moment" is on one hand, "the possibility of a republic of equal citizens, enjoying the ancient liberty of ruling and being ruled", or the appearance of Machiavellian political thought (public interest prioritised over particular interest) in new forms of republican *raison d'État*. This ideal was clearly shared by the Swedish political elite of the so-called Age of Liberty. On the other hand, however, the term "Machiavellian moment" applies more particularly to the moment when the *res publica* is believed to be running towards its end (corruption undermining public virtue). A particularly interesting Machia-

---

conscience européenne 1680–1715, Paris, 1961, has influenced the temporal conception of the French *"Sattelzeit"*.

22 Otto Brunner, Werner Conze & Reinhart Koselleck (Hrsg.), *Geschichtliche Grundbegriffe. Historisches Lexikon zur politisch-sozialen Sprache in Deutschland*, Stuttgart, 1972–1997; Rolf Reichardt & Eberhard Schmitt, *Handbuch politisch-sozialer Grundbegriffe in Frankreich 1680–1820*, München, 1985–.

23 Frederic II was the author of *Anti-Machiavel* (The Hague, 1740).

24 For an overview, see, for instance, T. C. W. Blanning, *The Culture of Power and the Power of Culture. Old Regime Europe 1660–1789*, Oxford, 2002, pp. 194–232 ; a more extensive study on the concept of fatherland is Hans-Martin Blitz, *Aus Liebe zum Vaterland. Die deutsche Nation im 18. Jahrhundert*, Hamburg, 2000.

25 Koselleck, *Preussen zwischen Reform und Revolution*.

vellian moment, to which Pocock has returned in the third volume of *Barbarism and Religion*, is constituted by the end of the Roman republic, where *libertas* is threatened by the very *imperium* that it has given birth to.[26] It is possible to ask if the end of the Swedish Age of Liberty, as it was experienced by the nobility, should perhaps be seen as a Machiavellian moment in this second sense as well.

Pocock's metaphor could also be described as a transition of the political community and thus of the object of allegiance or belonging. In this process, personal loyalties towards a lord or family are replaced with loyalty towards the state, according to the new, "neo-Roman" republican ethos. This process parallels the transition from a society made up by sovereign, privileged bodies, inside which the citizens participate in common affairs, towards a society where the mass of free or equal individuals is directly subordinated to one, indivisible political authority, without intermediary levels of authority or privileged bodies within the sovereign state. Before the American and French revolutions, individual feelings of belonging were often based on kinship, estate or service, but not necessarily defined by citizenship or national identity as in modern societies. While the loyalties of the old world were personal and patriarchal, the modern ones have been popular and imagined or conceptualised in terms of 'class', 'nationality' , 'race' or even 'gender' and 'ethnicity'.[27]

The ideological turn of the end of the eighteenth century is also associated with the birth of sovereign nations as political entities. Ultimately, this implies a transition of sovereignty. On this basis it is possible to ask whether we can observe a change in how citizenship was experienced: was there a passage from loyal subjects to free citizens, from free subjects to loyal citizens, or even from free citizens to loyal subjects? Was the perception of who made up the political nation (e.g. the politically active citizens that defined themselves as the representatives of the nation) eventually affected? And what was the part of the nobility in all this?

In conceptual history, it has not always been fully acceptable to combine different national traditions of scholarship. Conceptual histories have rather been carried out as national projects, often inspired to some extent by the encyclopaedic and synthetic ambition of conceptual lexica such as *Geschichtliche Grundbegriffe* or the *Handbuch*. As a consequence, there are significant differences mainly between the Cambridge school, which does not acknowledge

---

26 J. G. A. Pocock, *The Machiavellian Moment. Florentine Political Thought and the Atlantic Republican Tradition*, Princeton, 2003 (1975), pp. 553–583; see also J. G. A. Pocock, *Barbarism and Religion*, vol. 3: *The First Decline and Fall*, Cambridge, 2003, pp. 309–310, 313.

27 Benedict Anderson's 'imagined communities', larger and stronger than those of the Old Regime, are examples of these new bounds of loyalty. See Anderson, *Imagined Communities*. Some social scientists tend to replace the politically incorrect 'race' with the more restrained 'ethnicity', which suggests an artificial return to societies split into different communities without a common, dominant ideology. However, the concept 'ethnic' (cf. 'ethnic nationalism') originates from a similar, organic understanding of human communities to the one that has given birth to the romantic idea of nationhood as it was articulated by Herder. See, for instance, Thomas Hylland Eriksen, *Ethnicity and Nationalism: Anthropological Perspectives*, London, 1993.

itself as conceptual history, and the German *Begriffsgeschichte*, but also between French, Dutch, Finnish or Swedish approaches to the history of political concepts. The methods of conceptual history tend to depend on the political context where it is elaborated and which it focuses on. However, a common feature in Germany, France and Great Britain, but also in the kind of conceptual history written by Finnish intellectual historians and political scientists, is the emphasis on the political, on political terminology and political representations.[28] No longer an auxiliary science of social history, as Koselleck defined conceptual history,[29] conceptual history has become something of an extension to the history of political thought and ideas. To some extent, this seems to apply also to Finnish and Swedish conceptual studies. The title of the Finnish *Käsitteet liikkeessä. Suomen poliittisen kulttuurin käsitehistoria* ("Concepts on the move. A conceptual history of Finnish political culture") is revealing in this respect.[30] In Sweden, the most important study of political key concepts in the early modern era is perhaps Bo Lindberg's *Den antika skevheten. Politiska ord och begrepp i det tidig-moderna Sverige*, which anchors the concepts and vocabulary in a larger philosophical and ideological context.[31]

This book, however, is not a systematic study of certain key concepts. Neither is it a study on eighteenth-century political theory. Its aim is to contribute to a larger reflection on the transformation of estate-based identities during the second half of the eighteenth century. Identity is primarily seen as the self-image of individuals and the ways this image is articulated. Individual identities, however, develop and are articulated in relation to other individuals and communities. This process takes place through conceptualisation and the use of language. Here, the history of concepts becomes a medium for the understanding of how identities and loyalties were articulated as it helps to estimate to what extent the concepts, metaphors and expressions were given commonly shared meanings, were being transformed or were simply arbitrary.

The sources and their context

The sources used in this study have been chosen on the basis of two criteria: a) they comment on politics, are rich in political terminology or have a political aim, and b) they have been produced by members of the noble estate or reflect noble political thinking or social identity. A first group of sources is formed by official, authorised papers, such as Diet minutes, memoranda or speeches. A second group is what we could call opinion papers, many of which were intended to be publicly spread: newspapers,

---

28 The most recent work in Finnish, which provides a general overview of the field, is Matti Hyvärinen, Jussi Kurunmäki, Kari Palonen, Tuija Pulkkinen & Henrik Stenius (toim.), *Käsitteet liikkeessä. Suomen poliittisen kulttuurin käsitehistoria*, Tampere, 2003.

29 Koselleck, *Vergangene Zukunft*, pp. 107–129.

30 Matti Hyvärinen, Jussi Kurunmäki, Kari Palonen, Tuija Pulkkinen & Henrik Stenius (toim.), *Käsitteet liikkeessä*.

31 Lindberg, *Den antika skevheten*.

pamphlets, but also memoirs, such as Count Axel von Fersen's *Historiska skrifter*.[32] Finally, a third group are private documents, such as diaries or correspondences, which often comment on politics and thus can be used to complete the picture in certain cases. As for the representativity of these sources, often understood as how largely shared the opinions expressed in them were, one could say that this is a minor problem when dealing with a social group that did not value democracy particularly highly but still was most influential in society. The sources chosen here were not always printed or largely spread, but they may still have influenced opinion or expressed opinions largely shared (correspondences reflecting Diet debates, for example).

A part of the sources are printed; another part consists of manuscripts. Using only printed sources would be unwise in a study on political language and thought in a period with no or very limited freedom to print. This problem becomes particularly obvious if we try to find traces of an oppositional way of thought or of speaking. Such thinking would probably not be found in officially authorised and printed texts – although censure never prevented authors from developing various ways of circumventing it and dissimulating subversive ideas in an apparently innocent discourse.[33] Manuscript sources such as unprinted or clandestine pamphlets, *libelles*, epigrams, songs and *nouvelles à la main* present several features that make them important, not to say inevitable, to a study on European political thought and language in the early modern period: conditioned by the existence of censorship but by definition not submitted to it, they can and to some extent must innovate more freely, which places them at the edge of conceptual change.[34] Also, official speech acts could remain unprinted – as a matter of fact, most of them were.[35]

Most of the sources used are in Swedish, but many are in French, the language commonly used by the European nobilities in informal and at times in confidential communication such as correspondence or diaries. The Swedish language of the second half of the eighteenth century was also strongly influenced by French and Latin vocabulary, particularly in political and economic theory.[36] It may thus be easy to perceive conceptual similarities between the language used by the Swedish aristocracy and that of, for instance, the French *parlementaires*. This points at the common European-ness of Swedish political culture, the study of which has often been confined to domestic political phenomena without a broader context. Still, similarities

32 [Axel von Fersen], *Riksrådet och fältmarskalken m.m. grefve Fredrik Axel von Fersens historiska skrifter*, utg. af R. M. Klinckowström, Stockholm, 1867–1872.
33 See e.g. Timo Kaitaro, "Klandestin filosofisk litteratur. Upplysande allusioner och nätverk", *Historisk Tidskrift för Finland*, vol. 88 (2003:2), pp. 216–224.
34 Henri Duranton, "Comment se diffuse l'information au XVIIIe siècle. L'exemple des *Lettres sur les affaires du temps* de Jacques-Élie Gastelier", in *Nouvelles, gazettes, mémoires secrets (1775–1800). Actes du colloque international, Karlstad, 17–20 septembre 1994*, dir. Birgitta Berglund-Nilsson, Karlstad, 2000, pp. 135–147.
35 For instance, the minutes of the Swedish Diet in the Age of Liberty (1719–1772) were systematically edited and printed only from the late nineteenth century onwards.
36 See, for instance, Gunnar von Proschwitz, *Gustave III de Suède et la langue française : recherches sur la correspondance d'un roi*, Göteborg, 1962.

are not the same thing as identical meanings or exact transfers. Although they might look the same or even share the same etymologic origin, concepts in different languages, countries or political communities do not always overlap each other, but refer to slightly different semantic fields and realities (*Bedeutungs- oder Erfahrungszusammenhang*). This has sometimes made it necessary, in this book, to make clear comparisons.

What might appear confusing to a Swedish- or French-speaking reader of this book is that the author has chosen to combine the diglossy of the sources with a third, narrative language other than the ones analysed. As an academic research report, this book is in English. In conceptual history, it might be an interesting experiment to use another language for the analytic narrative than the one(s) used in the historical discourse. Along with the problems of having to translate each concept – the loss of nuance or meaning, the need to use metaphors that do not always work – also comes a clear benefit: the researcher is forced to reflect on all the possible meanings of each term. Quite often, this also provokes a reflection on intention: are some concepts intentionally used by a historical author with a precise dimension of meaning in mind, or are they used only colloquially, without further reflection? A definite answer to these questions can only be given in rare cases, and we mostly have to confine ourselves to qualified guesses, but these questions are crucial to keep in mind if we wish to make an analytic study of how concepts and language have changed in the course of time.

The choice of an exterior, not to say neutral language (which, of course, is it not), should also reflect a wish to get away from a nationally confined "Swedish" history of Sweden. In many cases, it turns out that the politically active Swedish nobility, in its choice of terminology and rhetorical figures, was deeply indebted to a European and Latin heritage of classical republicanism. This has made it necessary to draw parallels to other countries and political discourses in order to point out common versus specific features. A comparative study reveals that "Swedish" political concepts were mostly Roman, French or generally European. To show this has been one of the primary concerns of the author. Although the main focus of this book is on the Swedish realm, including Finland and Pomerania, many of the conclusions concerning noble political identity in the Old Regime could apply to other European states.

The Swedish political elite of the eighteenth century did not live in an intellectual vacuum. As already has been mentioned, the early modern aristocratic identity was influenced by French court culture. Noble letter writing was outlined on the model of Madame de Sévigné's correspondence.[37] The readings of the social elite reflected a larger awareness of European philosophical and literary tendencies. The works of authors such as Locke, Pufendorf, Fénelon and Montesquieu were usually found in the private libraries of the nobility. The writings of, for instance, Carl Henrik Klick, a

---

37 See, for instance, Elisabet Hammar, *L'enseignement du français en Suède jusqu'en 1807. Méthodes et manuels*, Stockholm, 1980; Elisabet Hammar, « *La Française* ». *Mille et une façons d'apprendre le français en Suède avant 1802*, Uppsala, 1991; Jessica Parland-von Essen, *Behagets betydelser. Döttrarnas edukation i det sena 1700-talets adelskultur*, Hedemora, 2005.

rather modest Finnish-born nobleman who was to become one of the key figures of the so-called Anjala League during Gustav III's war against Russia, reveal influences from Raynal, Helvétius and Rousseau.[38]

Above all, the classics were central to an aristocratic upbringing, rhetoric and political culture. Young noblemen, the future representatives of their estate at the Diet and servants of the state, were trained in Latin rhetoric and eloquence at the universities. The importance of Latin in the Swedish political language in the eighteenth century has recently been thoroughly studied by Bo Lindberg.[39] Undoubtedly, Latin rhetoric and Roman political concepts and history also influenced if not political thought itself then at least the ways in which it was articulated.

With the classics thus came a certain amount of classical republicanism, with its commonplace references to Cato, Cicero and other authors of the Roman republic. Although it is difficult to measure how "republican" in a more radical sense the political values of its learned elite were,[40] the Swedish noble political discourse of the eighteenth century contains perceptible references to the Roman republic, ideals of common good and citizenship, and above all strongly negative attitudes towards monarchy as well as an idea of aristocracy as a morally good form of government based on honour and not on interest. This profound defiance towards royal sovereignty makes it particularly important to examine the attitudes of the Swedish nobility towards a royal power that finally tended to diminish the power of the Estates: did a Swedish "Machiavellian moment" in the stricter sense of the term take place before and with the royal revolution of Gustav III? We could argue that the end of the Age of Liberty was a crisis of the republic, confronting its limits and ultimately its dissolution. We could also argue that Gustav III defined a new republic by founding his political legitimacy on republican values and patriotic concepts, or at least that he took custody of the republic in a very Augustean way. Finally, it all happened again, with a new crisis of legitimacy and conceptual instability during the latter half of his reign, when the king, who no longer needed ideological legitimacy to reinforce his absolute power, disdained the republican arguments now accessible to the opposition.[41]

Most of the speech acts examined in this study were made by prominent members of the noble estate – in order to find the aristocratic way of thinking, it seems logical to look at the elite inside the nobility. During the Age of Liberty, the Swedish noble estate or the so-called House of Nobility no longer voted by classes (counts, barons and untitled nobility), but if we look at the power relations of the estate and the political parties, the front figures were mostly members of the titled aristocracy. However, it was not exactly the same old aristocracy as in the middle of the seventeenth century:

---

38 Bruno Lesch, *Jan Anders Jägerhorn. Patriot och världsmedborgare, separatist och emigrant*, Helsingfors, 1941, p. 88.
39 Lindberg, *Den antika skevheten*.
40 Republicanism has become an issue of research with the publication of *Republicanism. A Shared European Heritage*, edited by Martin van Gelderen and Quentin Skinner, Cambridge, 2002, 2 vols.
41 See Hallberg, *Ages of Liberty*.

absolutism had lifted some families, and when new men accessed the higher spheres of power, they also tended to receive higher titles. Particularly the elite of the Francophile Hat party, which dominated Swedish politics from 1738 to 1765, counted among them several members of younger nobility.

Among these, Count Carl Gustaf Tessin (1695–1770) was the grandson of an ennobled court architect. He studied to be an architect too, like his father and grandfather, but because of problems with his eyes he chose a diplomatic career and soon engaged in politics. A young critic of Arvid Bernhard Horn, Sweden's political leader of the early Age of Liberty, he was one of the actors of the rise of the Hat party at the Diet of 1738. By the middle of the century, we find him speaking to the Estates as a senator and Chancellery President (*kanslipresident*), i.e. prime minister. A younger politician promoted by Tessin and who also appears among the speakers was Count Clas Ekeblad (the Younger, 1708–1771), a civil servant and diplomat from a family with strong intellectual and cosmopolitan traditions. He studied in the Pietistic town of Halle in the 1720s, which seems to have made deep impressions on his style of writing and values. He in his turn was Chancellery President from 1761 to 1765 and again from 1769 to 1771. Another intellectually brilliant politician of the Age of Liberty was Count Anders Johan von Höpken (1712–1789), Chancellery President between Tessin and Ekeblad from 1752 to 1761, who was also known as a distinguished scholar of classics and Roman history, which is also very visible in his texts. Of the same generation, Count Axel von Fersen (the Elder, 1719–1794), one of the wealthiest men of the realm thanks to successful marriage strategies in the family, had studied law and history at the universities of Uppsala and Lund, but chose a military career.[42] His rhetorical abilities and talent for convincing made him Marshal of the Diet (*lantmarskalk*), i.e. speaker of the House of Nobility, at all Diets dominated by the Hat party from 1755 onwards. His speeches are often tributes to constitutional liberty, and it is not surprising that he would become one of the most prominent critics of Gustav III in the 1780s.

The opposite party, the Caps, also had very aristocratic front figures. Baron Matthias Alexander von Ungern-Sternberg (1689–1763) originated from a Livonian family and was a distinguished military officer and critic of the Hats' war against Russia in the early 1740s. He became Marshal of the Diet in 1742 and 1746. His speeches are marked by tradition. A younger, rising star of the party in opposition was Count Eric Brahe (1722–1756), also a military officer, and a personal friend of King Adolph Frederick. His family was of the highest aristocracy, with traditional ties to the Crown, and his wealth was comparable to that of Fersen, who was also his greatest rival in politics. His involvement in a plan to strengthen monarchy became fatal, and he was trialled by the Estates and beheaded with other members of the plot in July 1756. After the death of Brahe and Ungern-Sternberg, the leaders of the Cap party represented a more radical and less aristocratic tendency, with speakers such as Colonel Thure Gustaf Rudbeck (1714–1786), Marshal

---

42 On Fersen, see Johanna Ilmakunnas, *Aristokraattinen elämäntapa ja sen rahoitus 1700-luvun Ruotsissa. Carl ja Axel von Fersenin tulot, varallisuus ja kulutustottumukset*, Helsingin yliopisto, 2004 (unpublished thesis).

of the Diet of 1765–1766, who did not show the same astonishing degree of rhetoric brilliance, education and wit in his speeches as the others that have been mentioned here.

The Diet speeches that have been used here are, in addition to isolated speech acts on particular matters, above all speeches made by the Marshal of the Diet or by the Chancellery President, who formally spoke on behalf of the king, in front of either the entire noble estate or the entire assembled, four-estate Diet. By their very nature, these speech acts express a search for consensus and values that were largely shared or that the speaker wished to be shared by his audience. Persuasion was used to create an illusion of community. To achieve this, the speakers used both a conceptual substrate of tradition, with terms underlining the (pretended) long history of certain political values, and a more personal or innovative choice of significant concepts and terms referring to contemporary political choices. For instance, in the Sweden of the Age of Liberty there was a public consensus on the monarchical state of the regime (*monarchia mixta*), although in practice, it was very aristocratic. Still, the concept of 'aristocracy' remained very negative. Public political discourse would stress harmony, concord and a common striving towards public welfare as common values. At first sight, this makes it somewhat difficult to find texts that explicitly represent alternative ways of thought.

Also, the terms referring to contemporary politics pose problems, as the same concepts were recycled by different speakers but with slightly different meanings. One such central concept is 'liberty'. It is evident that this is done intentionally, which poses the problem of authorial intention.[43] A way to come closer to the author or to his understanding of a concept used in unusual ways is to look for honest opinions in less consensual writings such as private correspondences, although the dividing line between private and public can be very unclear here too since a letter could be publicly spread and read by dozens of people, which was something its author had to take into account. Consensus may also be an illusion: it is one thing to talk about loyalty and another to be loyal. In political consensus it also may be that once a thing has been stated, the speaker may feel free to do the opposite.

Not all political texts followed the official values of the realm. The short period of freedom to print in Sweden (1766–1772/1774), in combination with the spread of natural law and the radicalisation of natural law and Enlightenment ideals, encouraged political argumentation built on openness, critical reason and conceptual analysis. This tendency survived, *mutatis mutandis*, in manuscript pamphlets after the restrictions made in 1774 and was particularly strong during the first revolutionary years in France, which coincided with Gustav III's unpopular war against Russia in 1788–1789.[44]

---

43 Quentin Skinner, "Motives, Intentions and the Interpretation of Texts", *New Literary History* 3 (1972), pp. 393–408; see also Johan Svedjedal, "Textkritisk litteraturteori. Några linjer i svensk och anglosaxisk textkritisk debatt", in *Textkritik. Teori och praktik vid edering av litterära texter. Föredrag vid Svenska Vitterhetssamfundets symposium 10–11 september 1990*, red. Lars Burman & Barbro Ståhle Sjönell, Stockholm, 1991, pp. 42–78.

44 See, for instance, Annie Mattsson, "Kvinnliga tidsfördriv och manliga mätresser. Kön och sexualitet i smädandet av Gustaf III", *Historisk Tidskrift för Finland*, vol. 92 (2007:4), pp. 453–476.

The contemporaries also seem to have been aware of conceptual change, particularly at the end of the Age of Liberty and during the rule of Gustav III. In the pamphlet *Betracktelser wid Kongl. Svenska Ministerens Declaration, gifven Helsingfors den 2. Julii 1788* spread by the Russian court in Sweden, the author, after noting the restrictions made by the king on the citizens' freedom to speak and to write, analyses the terms in the Swedish declaration of war against Russia and describes a reconceptualisation of the vocabulary of political loyalty. He states that "Swedish ears [...] in the past 16 years [since the royal coup of 1772] have been used to some words having entirely other meanings than they had before".[45] In other words, this anonymous contemporary witness is describing the reign of Gustav III as a kind of *Sattelzeit* (of course, he does not call this process by such a name).[46] Conscious and intentional reconceptualisation, on the other hand, is visible in individual speech acts in the use of (fictional) etymologies to argue in favour of any conceptual interpretation, a proved trick that gives the argument an apparent erudite authority. This is the case in various pamphlets by rhetorically skilful anonymous authors, such as the *Johannis Magni, Upsala Erke Biskops Chrönica, öfversatt på Svenska*, where the tyrannical "King Östen" is told to have been called "Göstagh the third" because "Göstagh" is set forth as the "gothic" name for a person who "destroys and robs one's estates and possessions".[47]

This kind of document – oppositional pamphlets – which have been used in the last chapters of this book, presents a particular problem for the researcher. In the absence of the freedom to print, political debates took place in small, private circles. The texts are the products of this common, restrained sociability, these informal exchanges of ideas. The absence of the freedom to print increases the role of informal sociability in the propagation of politically daring texts. It also influences the form of the political pamphlets: these are often allegories and fables, not naming the political enemies by their name but by nicknames and metaphors. Even though the text was not printed and was circulated only as manuscript copies from hand to hand, the authors used the same tricks to circumvent censure as in manuscripts submitted to the censors for printing.[48] As a result, their lectures often, but not systematically, require keys to open up or at least gain insight into the historical context, not unlike small *romans à clef*.[49] One example is the *Riddare-Spel, hållit den 13 Augusti 1779*, which is a caricature

---

45 "Svenska öron, som på 16. års tid blifvit vande vid helt andra betydelser å vissa ord, än de förr haft", [Anon.], *Betracktelser wid Kongl. Svenska Ministerens Declaration, gifven Helsingfors den 2. Julii 1788*, KB, D 171:2.

46 On conceptual change during the Gustavian era, see also Mikael Alm, *Kungsord i elfte timmen. Språk & självbild i det gustavianska enväldets legitimitetskamp 1772–1809*, Stockholm, 2002.

47 "*sköflar och röfvar ens Gods och ägor*"; *Johannis Magni, Upsala Erke Biskops Chrönica, öfversatt på Svenska*, KB, Schröderheim, Historisk-politiska samlingar 4 (1789, 1792), D 171:4.

48 See Kaitaro, "Klandestin filosofisk litteratur. Upplysande allusioner och nätverk", pp. 216–224.

49 This type of material has been thoroughly presented in Darnton, "An Early Information Society: News and the Media in Eighteenth-Century Paris".

of the court and exists in several copies, another is *Min K[äre] Granne!*, a political satire from 1788 where the Sweden of Gustav III is described as a small parish with a new bailiff who changes all the rules to the general confusion.[50] In the same way as events that in a long-term perspective turn out to be of minor importance can have been perceived as very dramatic by their contemporaries, it may sometimes be difficult for the historian to distinguish a metaphoric allusion to a "big" historical event from a trivial anecdote, the queen from her maid, and the royal council from the tea party.[51] Nevertheless, these types of texts are products of the political culture of a court society without a modern public space and can as such be regarded as political texts, although they have not been central in this analysis.

50 *Riddare-Spel* is found at least in LUB, DelaGardiesamlingen, Historiska handlingar, vol. 22:12, and in KB, Schröderheim, Historisk-politiska samlingar 1 (1590–1707), D 171:1. *Min K. Granne!* in KB, Schröderheim, Historisk-politiska samlingar 2 (1788), D 171:2.
51 Examples of the satirical poems written by a central person at the Swedish court but without any apparent political content are Johan Gabriel Oxenstierna's *Caractèrer, portraiter och epigrammer*, published by Holger Frykenstedt, Stockholm, 1956.

Chapter 1: Definitions of a regime, or the ideal of mixed government

A central theme in this study is the relationship between the citizen and the state, the subject and the monarch. The theme is connected to the question of what kind of political system citizens would commit to and to which regime they would swear fealty and loyalty. Traditionally, the European nobility had tended to favour a mixed government, in other words, constitutions that granted the privileged estate political power and influence in public matters.[1] However, the question of the ideal constitution and its perfectibility was far from having a definite answer, particularly in countries experiencing considerable internal political changes or changes in their position on the European map of power during the eighteenth century. This was the case in Poland, famous for its unruly Diet and the *liberum veto* of the nobility that prevented most attempts to reform the constitution, but it was also true of Sweden.[2]

The ideal forms of government and the classification and definition of regimes had been the preoccupation of political thinkers since Aristotle, who divided the ideal forms of government into monarchy, aristocracy and constitutional republic, a partition that put its mark on political theory throughout the following two thousand years.[3] In *The Spirit of the Laws*, Montesquieu, although relying on Aristotle's main categories throughout his work, developed a slightly different classification and distinguished between the republican form of government (which could be either

---

1   See, for instance, the articles in Martin van Gelderen & Quentin Skinner, *Republicanism. A Shared European Heritage*, vol. 1: *Republicanism and Constitutionalism in Early Modern Europe*, Cambridge, 2002; Jouanna, *Le devoir de révolte*; Fredrik Lagerroth, *Frihetstidens författning. En studie i den svenska konstitutionalismens historia*, Stockholm, 1915.

2   See, for instance, Michael Roberts, *The Age of Liberty. Sweden 1719–1772*, Cambridge, 1986; Olof Jägerskiöld, *Hovet och författningsfrågan 1760–1766*, Uppsala, 1943. On Poland, see, for instance, Anna Greśkowiak-Krwawicz, "Anti-monarchism in Polish Republicanism in the Seventeenth and Eighteenth Centuries", in *Republicanism. A Shared European Heritage*, vol. 1, pp. 43–59.

3   Aristotle, *Politics*, III, 7 (the perverted forms are tyranny, oligarchy and democracy); see also II and IV. For a study on Aristotle, see, for instance, Fred D. Miller, *Nature, Justice and Rights in Aristotle's Politics*, Oxford, 1995.

democratic or aristocratic), monarchy and despotism.[4] Montesquieu's work was one of the most read political texts in the eighteenth century and still is today. Its classifications of regimes are constantly reproduced in perceptions of republics being the opposite of monarchies. This tendency to oppose the ideas of republic and monarchy is visible in eighteenth-century documents, for instance in foreign criticism of the Swedish regime, but it has above all become a characteristic of modern political thought. For its part, the famous balance of powers, which Montesquieu had borrowed from John Locke, influenced the draft for a new Swedish constitution of 1769 and the constitution of 1772, both the work of Count Carl Fredrik Scheffer, a former correspondent of the French philosopher.[5]

As philosophers, Aristotle and Montesquieu described *ideal* forms of government and how these would be perverted if politics became corrupted, illustrating their point with both historical and contemporary examples. Since the purpose was to demonstrate ideal constitutions, it would have been difficult to make specific states fit into the schemes. Montesquieu made references to ancient Rome, England and the republic of Venice, but for instance never commented on the Swedish form of government, although he mentioned Charles XII a couple of times. If we apply Aristotle's categories, Sweden could be – and was – described equally as a monarchy, an aristocracy (with its mighty Senate) and a constitutional government (through the freedom of its legislative Estates). By Montesquieu's criteria, the Sweden of the Age of Liberty would most probably be a monarchy with intermediate powers but no sovereign king. However, as a mixed government, Sweden would hardly have fitted very well into any of the modern categories developed by Montesquieu.

The concepts used by Montesquieu, however, were to a large extent the same as the ones used at the Swedish Diet. It is scarcely surprising that the terminology and concepts used and defined by the classical authors and used by the most read contemporary philosophers influenced eighteenth-century political language in Europe, at least as far as the learned aristocracy was concerned. Further, the old theories on corruption and on the danger of despotism that were present in and revived by Montesquieu's work become very interesting if we examine how Swedish contemporaries perceived the political evolution of their country.

Here, the aim is to analyse how the regime was conceived, conceptualised and described by the Swedish nobility in the eighteenth century. Particular emphasis will be laid on the classifications and the classical political terminology used in the descriptions of the regime, and on moments of constitutional transition or crisis such as the early 1720s, the 1750s and the revolution of 1772. How were the practical experiences of the regime and its crises expressed in classical terms? Was there any notion of ongoing political change? Further and in other words, did contemporaries of the Age of Liberty feel that the estate rule of the time was doomed to end by its very

---

4   Charles de Secondat, baron de Montesquieu, *De l'esprit des lois* (1748), II, 1.
5   Carl Gustaf Malmström, *Sveriges politiska historia från K. Carl XII:s död till statshvälf-ningen 1772*, vol. 6, Stockholm, 1877, pp. 67, 107–109, 391–393.

nature, as it was afterwards claimed by monarchists who saw in it only corruption and inevitable decay? These questions will be addressed not only in this chapter, but also in the following ones. More particularly, this chapter will present the political institutions and the power struggles that became symbols of the monarchic versus the aristocratic or republican features of the regime.

A moderate monarchy: the powerless king, 1720–1772

Like most European states of its size, Sweden in the Age of Liberty was formally a monarchy, but it was one where the power of the king was "moderated" by "intermediate powers", as Montesquieu put it.[6] These powers were the Council of the Realm (*riksrådet*), derived from the old royal privy council and called "senate" in foreign languages by contemporaries, and above all the Estates general (*rikets ständer*), comprising the nobility, the clergy, the burghers and the peasants, that assembled for the Diet (*riksdag*) every three years. Contrarily to the corresponding French and Prussian assemblies, the Swedish Estates had preserved their vitality and were in the eighteenth century developing towards a kind of early regular representative assembly, which is sometimes compared to the British Parliament.[7] Additionally, the free peasants were represented at the Diet by a fourth estate of their own. The balance of power between the king, the Senate and the Estates was regulated by the "fundamental laws" or constitutional documents of the realm (*rikets fundamentallagar, rikets grundlagar*), which had been rewritten after the death of Charles XII in 1718. During the Age of Liberty, the Estates and the Senate that they designated were clearly more powerful than the king. This came to a sharp change with the *coup* of Gustav III in 1772.

Before the Reformation, the king had been elected by the Estates, but since Gustav Vasa and the order of succession established by his son Charles IX, the crown had more or less automatically been hereditary. The early seventeenth century established a tradition of "mixed monarchy" (*monarchia mixta*), where the king did not rule alone as an absolute monarch, but together

---

6 Montesquieu, *De l'esprit des lois*, II, 4.
7 The comparison with the British Parliament, which has been recurrent in Swedish history writing after the works of Michael Metcalf and Michael Roberts on the Age of Liberty, needs qualification. Sweden had a four-estate Diet, which was not permanently assembled but was summoned by the king every three years or more often if needed. It was not a representative assembly in its full sense, since the Dietmen were not considered responsible to their electors. The House of Nobility was the only direct representative assembly, and this through privilege only, not universal right. Each estate had one vote, which made it possible for three estates to make a formal decision even if the fourth one, e.g. the nobility – which still dominated through its social capital and networks of loyalties in the lower estates – opposed. To the early forms of parliamentarianism belongs the idea of the senators being responsible to the Diet, although this responsibility was primarily individual. Thus there were no general votes of confidence, only dismissals of individual senators (*licentiering*). A primitive party system developed, in the form of factions distributing money but without any formal records of membership, and contrarily to the British Parliament, there was no formalised opposition sitting on particular benches.

with his council (*med råds råde*), and took advice from the Estates of the realm in matters of taxation.[8] Royal absolutism was introduced in Sweden at the end of the seventeenth century under the reigns of Charles X and Charles XI. Charles XI's harsh politics of reclaiming the crown estates that had been given away to the aristocracy during previous reigns provoked resentment in the nobility, which had previously been a reliable ally to the Palatinate dynasty, and turned the privileged estate against the power pretensions of the monarchy.

With the death of Charles XII and the extinction of the Palatinate dynasty, it became necessary to designate a new monarch. Frederick of Hesse-Cassel was recognised as king by the Estates after the abdication of his spouse, Queen Ulrika Eleonora. At the time of the death of the queen in 1741, the royal couple had no legitimate children, so the question of Frederick's succession became an urgent and central matter of deliberation at the Diet of 1742–1743. Eventually, after several turns and the interference of the Russian empress Elisabeth I, Adolph Frederick of Holstein-Gottorp was elected in June 1743. The following year, by the decision of the Estates, he married Princess Lovisa Ulrika of Prussia. The birth of several children from 1746 onwards settled the dynastic question for a couple of decades. Nevertheless, the fact that the Diet deliberately elected foreign princes that did not represent any diplomatic risk or showed apparent ambitions to power evidently weakened the political credibility of the king, whose prerogatives were already very limited through the new constitutions drawn after the death of Charles XII in 1718 and the abdication of his sister Ulrika Eleonora in favour of her husband (Frederick I) in 1720.

The constitution of 1720 strongly rejected all forms of absolutism and handed over the power to the Estates. With the end of absolutism and royal sovereignty began the period known in Swedish historiography as the Age of Liberty, a period of "estate rule" (*ständervälde*) that lasted until 1772. While the traditional royalist historiography of the nineteenth century perceived the Age of Liberty as an era of endless party struggles, division and political corruption, more liberal history writing usually would focus on its "modern" features of constitutionalism, early parliamentarianism and the beginnings of the freedom of the press.[9]

During the Age of Liberty, the form of government was defined by the constitution or the "instrument of government" (*Regeringsform*) of 1720,[10]

---

8 Nils Runeby, *Monarchia mixta. Maktfördelningsdebatt i Sverige under den tidigare stormaktstiden*, Uppsala, 1962. See also Petri Karonen, *Pohjoinen suurvalta. Ruotsi ja Suomi 1521–1809*, Helsinki, 1999, p. 197.

9 Royalist historiography was represented by Malmström, *Sveriges politiska historia från K. Carl XII:s död till statshvälfningen 1772*, 6 vols., Stockholm, 1855–1877; the rehabilitation of the Age of Liberty as a constitutionalist era was made in Lagerroth, *Frihetstidens författning*, and Fredrik Lagerroth, *Sveriges riksdag. Historisk och statsvetenskaplig framställning*, vol. 6, *Frihetstidens maktägande ständer 1719–1772*, Stockholm, 1934; the parliamentarian features have been stressed in Roberts, *The Age of Liberty*; on the press, see articles in Skuncke & Tandefelt (red.), *Riksdag, kaffehus och predikstol*.

10 *Regeringsform* is literally "form of government" in English. In modern English versions of Swedish constitutional documents, it is often translated as "Instrument of Government", a term which has its origin in the English constitution of 1653.

by the Diet Act (*Riksdagsordning*) of 1723[11] and by the oath sworn by each king on his accession to the throne (coronation oath, *Konungaförsäkran*).[12] Additionally some other legal acts such as the privileges of the nobility and the clergy of 1723 and the law on the freedom of the press of 1766 were considered "fundamental laws", i.e. constitutional documents that in principle could not be legally modified without altering the constitution. The restrictions on royal prerogative and the fundamental laws that regulated the field of authority of each body sharing political power – the king, the Senate and the Estates – made Sweden in the Age of Liberty what we would call a constitutional government. In eighteenth-century Sweden, this was called *lagbunden regering* ("law-bound rule"). The stress on law and legality is also very noticeable in the constitutional documents of the 1720s.[13]

The preamble to the constitution of 1720 stated that the aim of this legal document was to preserve the monarch in his highness (*höghet*), to support the authority (*myndighet*) of the Senate and to maintain the right and liberty of the Estates (*rätt och frihet*).[14] The order in which these three bodies were mentioned in formal documents derived from traditional theocratic perceptions of power hierarchies, but had little to do with their real prerogatives. In fact, during the Age of Liberty, sovereignty in the sense of 'supreme power' and 'empire' was not held by the monarch, but by the Estates. In the balance of power between the king, the Senate and the Estates, the Estates outweighed both the king and the Senate: the king could not rule without the Senate, and the Senate was responsible to the Diet.[15]

The term used in Swedish to characterise the status of the monarch was 'highness'. Its Latin correspondent, used in official Swedish documents up to the eighteenth century, was *maiestas*. This term had been deliberately favoured by Gustav II Adolph, who used it in the same sense as Jean Bodin, with all its connotations of monarchical sovereignty.[16] In European political theory, 'majesty' had often been positively associated or confused with 'sovereignty'. Derived from the Vulgar Latin term *superanus*, supreme, the French concept *souveraineté* designated from the thirteenth century onwards the supreme authority and power of the monarch holding the *imperium* (empire, lordship) in his own realm. This concept of the king's sovereignty permitted the French royal legists to circumvent the theory of the two swords,

---

11 *Riksdagsordning*, literally "order of the Diet" in the sense of "rules".

12 *Konungaförsäkran*, literally the "King's Oath".

13 Axel Brusewitz, *Frihetstidens grundlagar och konstitutionella stadgar*, Stockholm, 1916.

14 Preamble, Regeringsformen den 2 maj 1720, in Brusewitz, *Frihetstidens grundlagar och konstitutionella stadgar*, p. 23. See also Marie-Christine Skuncke, "La liberté dans la culture politique suédoise au XVIIIe siècle", *Liberté : Héritage du passé ou idée des Lumières ?* éd. Anna Grześkowiak-Krwawicz et Izabella Zatorska, Krakow/Warszawa, 2003, p. 32. Skuncke translates *höghet* (in French *altesse*) as *majesté*, which is semantically slightly different (cf. the difference between 'Majesty' and 'Highness' in royal titles, 'majesty' denoting a plenitude of power).

15 Regeringsformen 1720, art. 14, in Brusewitz, *Frihetstidens grundlagar och konstitutionella stadgar*, pp. 27–28.

16 Lagerroth, *Frihetstidens författning*, p. 117. See also Lindberg, *Den antika skevheten*, pp. 88–94, and Skuncke, "La liberté dans la culture politique suédoise au XVIIIe siècle", p. 32.

the spiritual *auctoritas* (authority) and the temporal *potestas* (power).[17] Jean Bodin, in *Les Six Livres de la République* from 1576, developed the theory of sovereignty and stated that the sovereignty of the state was best achieved in absolute monarchies.[18] According to Hobbes, this "sovereign power ought [...] to be absolute".[19] When Pufendorf's *De iure naturae et gentium* was translated into French by Barbeyrac, terms such as *summa potestas* or *summa imperium* were replaced with *autorité souveraine* or simply the short *souveraineté*, the term that we find in Montesquieu's works and in the Swedish concept *souverainitet / suveränitet*.[20] Swedish political writers also used terms such as *maiestas, summum potestas / imperium* and *imperium civile* to designate the sovereignty of the state.[21]

Because of the real amount of power given to the respective institutions, however, 'highness', despite its original associations with majesty and thus sovereignty, suffered a certain depreciation in Swedish political language during the Age of Liberty when compared to the "right and liberty of the Estates" or the "authority of the Senate". Perhaps also because of the awkwardness of Frederick I and Adolph Frederick in expressing themselves publicly, the 'highness' of the king tended to become a neutral, ceremonious and muffled term that could be associated with a certain passivity, and not, for instance, the more vigorous 'sovereignty' or 'majesty'.

In Swedish eighteenth-century political language, the concept of 'sovereignty' did not primarily refer to any positive popular sovereignty, but was associated with absolute power, autocracy and particularly royal absolutism. A small variety of terms were used to designate a concentration of power and the abuse of it. We can observe a group of frequently used terms formed on the old root *envåld*, the "power of one", "autocracy". These are *envälde*, which is the most used Swedish word for "absolutism", the tautological *envåldsvälde*, and the composed forms *envåldsmakt* (autocratic power) and *envåldsregemente* (autocratic rule). In the Swedish language, these were very strong terms, and they were easily associated with tyranny – the term would be frequently used in pamphlets against Gustav III after his second revolution in 1789.[22] They all derive from *våld*, which signifies not only power, but also violence.[23] It gives the terms a strongly negative connotation

---

17 This theory rested on the idea that while the spiritual *auctoritas* of the Roman church made the pope superior to kings and emperors, the emperor, as a special protector of the Roman church, had a kind of *auctoritas* over the other kings, who only detained the *potestas*. To be the "emperor in his own kingdom" and favour a national, Gallican theocracy was obviously a way to claim a share of the *auctoritas* for French kings such as Philip II Augustus, before the concept of sovereignty was developed under Philip IV the Fair in conflict with the pope Boniface VIII. The idea of two forms of power is present also in the terms used to define supreme power by Locke (supreme power, supreme authority); see Jean Ehrard, *L'esprit des mots. Montesquieu en lui-même et parmi les siens*, Genève, 1998, p. 147 ff.
18 Jean Bodin, *Les Six Livres de la République* (1576), book I, chapter VIII.
19 Thomas Hobbes, *The Leviathan* (1651), XX.
20 Robert Derathé, *Jean-Jacques Rousseau et la science politique de son temps*, Paris, 1995, p. 308; Ehrard, *L'esprit des mots*, p. 147; see also Petter Korkman, *Jean Barbeyrac and natural law*, diss., Åbo Akademi, 2001.
21 Lindberg, *Den antika skevheten*, p. 88.
22 See chapter 4.
23 Cf. the adjective *oväldig/owäldug*, which stands for "impartial" ("unforced").

due not so much to the idea of a single person invested with supreme power, but to the kind of abuse that the nature of this power suggests. In eighteenth-century Swedish historiography and national mythology, autocracy was regarded with all the more suspicion as it evoked war, national dissension and foreign oppression, such as the example of the Danish rule of Christian II "the Tyrant" before Gustav Vasa, who liberated Sweden from the Danish yoke and adopted the Lutheran faith in the 1520s.[24] For the nobility in particular, autocracy in more recent history was also associated with the reduction of personal liberty, wealth and power.

The legislators thus found it necessary to take measures to prevent a return to absolutism and autocracy. Article 14 of the constitution of 1720 stated that the Senate must prevent any attempts to oppress the Estates, to violate their liberty or to reinforce "the unlimited autocratic regime" (*det oinskränkte enväldsregementet*), and that any person conspiring to restore autocratic rule (*enväldsväldet*) was to lose his life, his honour and his possessions.[25] The constitution did not specify that *royal* autocracy in particular should be prevented. This was, however, explicit in the preamble to the constitution of 1720 as well as in the coronation oaths of 1720, 1751 and 1772, in which the king publicly declared "a legitimate dislike and a fair abhorrence of the unlimited royal autocracy or the so-called sovereignty" (*et rättvist misshag och en billig avsky för thet oinskränckte konungslige enväldet eller den så kallade souverainiteten*).[26] In addition to this, the oath sworn by King Frederick I in 1720 stated that were the king to yield to absolutism, he should be deposed.[27] The ban on autocracy was motivated by describing it as "harmful" and "contrary to the welfare of the fatherland", having "in many ways harmed, diminished and markedly weakened the realm". Those who promoted it were depicted as enemies of the king and of the fatherland and were to be judged as traitors.[28]

According to the constitution, the monarch could not rule alone, only together with the Senate, which was responsible to the Estates and had to

---

24 See Jouko Nurmiainen, *Edistys ja yhteinen hyvä vapaudenajan ruotsalaisessa poliittisessa kielessä*, Helsinki, 2009 (forthcoming), chapter III:1; see also Hallberg, *Ages of Liberty*, pp. 263–266; Jonas Nordin, *Ett fattigt men fritt folk. Nationell och politisk självbild i Sverige från sen stormaktstid till slutet av frihetstiden*, Stockholm/Stehag, 2000, pp. 224–225, and Lagerroth, *Frihetstidens författning*, pp. 44–60.

25 RF 1720, art. 14, in Brusewitz, *Frihetstidens grundlagar och konstitutionella stadgar*, pp. 27–28.

26 KF 1751, 1772, art. 6; 1720, art. 7, in Brusewitz, *Frihetstidens grundlagar och konstitutionella stadgar*, pp. 74–75, 85, 25; the formulation in the preamble to the constitution goes "*en billig osmak för det oinskränkte konungslige enväldet eller den så kallade souverainiteten*" ("a fair disgust at the unlimited royal autocracy or the so-called sovereignty"). Brusewitz, *Frihetstidens grundlagar och konstitutionella stadgar*, p. 23.

27 KF 1720, art. 7, in Brusewitz, *Frihetstidens grundlagar och konstitutionella stadgar*, p. 60.

28 "[...] *den så kallade souverainiteten eller det oinskränckte konungsliga enväldet, hvars värkan på mångahanda sätt har skadat, förminskat och märckeligen försvagat riket*"; "[...] *sådant förderfveligit emot landets nöije och välfärd löpande enväldsregemente*". Konunga-försäkran den 22 mars 1720, art. 7, in Brusewitz, *Frihetstidens grundlagar och konstitutionella stadgar*, p. 60; see also the oaths of 1751 and 1772, art. 6, in Brusewitz, *Frihetstidens grundlagar och konstitutionella stadgar*, pp. 74, 85.

account for its actions, if the Estates should ask it to do so.[29] Unlike in modern parliamentary democracies, there was no requirement that the ministers needed the majority's confidence, but if the Estates considered that a senator had lost their confidence, he could be dismissed by a procedure known as *licentiering* (cf. the French verb *licencier*, dismiss).

Indeed, real power lay in the hands of the Estates, which assembled for a regular Diet every three years. In his coronation oath, the king promised not to interfere with the Diet.[30] He was also bound by the constitution and his oath to follow the fundamental laws of the realm; should he fail, the Estates of the realm would no longer be bound by their oaths of fidelity.[31] The role of the king was mainly a representative one – a *decorum* – but as he did not have authority, he alone was actually not responsible to anyone, neither God nor the Estates.[32] This irresponsibility of the king was not without certain problems, as we shall see, as it remained unclear who controlled his *de facto* exercise of an authority that he *de jure* did not have.

The concept of 'sovereignty', as it appears in the constitutional documents and political speeches of the Age of Liberty, remained an ambiguous term. On one hand, it was used as a synonym for 'autocracy', the drawbacks of which were strong enough to suggest that, strictly speaking, even monarchy in itself was a suspicious form of government. On the other hand, the attentive reader may have noticed the reservation contained in the formula "sovereignty, or *unlimited* royal autocracy".[33] Would autocracy be more acceptable if it was "limited"? What would "limited autocracy" be? For the legislators writing immediately after the end of Caroline absolutism, emancipation from the conceptual apparatus of monarchical sovereignty was perhaps not an obvious matter. This ambiguity would later be exploited by Gustav III, when he in 1772 established a kind of constitutional absolutism.

Royal autocracy, *envälde*, "the rule of one", had its semantic opposite in the concept of *pluralitetsvälde*, literally "the rule of many". Originally, it seems to have meant the kind of representative (or, if we choose to use the classical but historically inappropriate term, democratic) rule exercised by the majority at the Diet, but as time passed and the Senate to an increased extent would exercise political power by delegation or in the absence of the Diet, the term was mostly used in the sense of *pluraliteten i rådet* ("plurality in the Senate") as an antonym for autocratic rule by the king. In a way, the concept of *pluralitetsvälde* was yet another way to express the *de facto* political sovereignty of the Estates. In the 1750s, the very idea of *pluraliteten* became a matter of conflict between the Senate and King Adolph Frederick.

---

29 RF 1720, art. 13 & 14, in Brusewitz, *Frihetstidens grundlagar och konstitutionella stadgar*, pp. 27–28.

30 KF 1720, art. 9, in Brusewitz, *Frihetstidens grundlagar och konstitutionella stadgar*, p. 61.

31 KF 1720, art. 22; KF 1753, art. 23, KF 1772, art. 23, in Brusewitz, *Frihetstidens grundlagar och konstitutionella stadgar*, pp. 65, 81, 90.

32 Lagerroth, *Frihetstidens författning*, pp. 203–206, 459–489.

33 My italic.

The authority of the Senate, ca 1752–1769

The term 'senate', used in Swedish and foreign Latin, French and even English texts on the Swedish political institutions of the Age of Liberty, was of course an obvious reference to ancient Rome. The term had a republican connotation – the Roman senate defended the republican regime at its end – and was also used in places like the republic of Venice and German towns to designate the governments of these free, self-administrating communities.[34] Nevertheless, it often contained a shade of aristocracy, as in republican Rome itself, where the senators formed the *nobilitas* and the first order of society.[35] It is characteristic that in monarchies such as Sweden or France, the concept of 'senate' was used by aristocratic republicans wishing to assert their right to rule by birth or privilege.

In France, after the publication in 1753–1754 of Louis Adrien Le Paige's *Lettres historiques sur les fonctions essentielles du parlement, sur le droit des pairs et sur les lois fondamentales du royaume*, which claimed that the *parlements* were older than the monarchy, the rebellious French *parlements* began to claim that they were the "Senate of France" and the "necessary council of the king". At the same time, the *Parlement* of Paris tried to aggregate the aristocratic peerage to itself, in order to constitute a privileged, truly political body (it is to be remembered that at least according to French royal political theory, the *parlements* were only administering and not making the law). The use of the term *sénat* was even perceived as partly legitimate by the royal officials, as the *parlements* administered justice like the Roman senate, but the *parlements'* claims to have any part in the political matters of the realm were dismissed.[36]

In Sweden, the use of the term 'senate' implied a direct link to the Roman institutions and provided a name for the privy council that did not refer to royal power and did not mention the king at all. It underlined the fact that the council was designated by and represented the Estates rather than the king, and that it was responsible to the Estates, not to his majesty.[37] The use of the term *sénat* instead of *conseil* in, for instance, the nobility's private correspondences thus seems to underline the well-cherished independence from sovereigns and the amount of republicanism present in noble political identity in eighteenth-century Sweden.

34 In Montesquieu's *De la liberté politique*, the Senate appeared as a republican organ: *"De là, il faut conclure que la liberté politique concerne les monarchies modérées comme les républiques, et n'est pas plus éloignée du trône que d'un sénat ; et tout homme est libre qui a un juste sujet de croire que la fureur d'un seul ou de plusieurs ne lui ôteront pas la vie ou la propriété de ses biens."*

35 See, for instance, Peter Garnsey & Richard Saller, *The Roman Empire: Economy, Society and Culture*, London, 1987, and Claude Nicolet, *Le métier de citoyen dans la Rome républicaine*, Paris, 1976, pp. 282–288.

36 On the use of the term *sénat de France* to designate the *parlements*, see "Reflexion sur le Parlement" in Chancellor Lamoignon's papers, AN, 399 AP 55, Chartrier de Malesherbes; on the *parlements* being the king's real council, see, for instance, Michel Antoine, *Louis XV*, Paris, 1989, pp. 573–581.

37 About the designation of the council, see RF 1720, art. 20; about its responsibility, see RF 1720, art. 14, and KF 1720, art. 9, in Brusewitz, *Frihetstidens grundlagar och konstitutionella stadgar*, pp. 27–28, 61–62.

Similarly, the king depended on the Senate and on the Estates. According to the constitution of 1720, article 13, the king could not rule without the Senate nor against it.[38] This was perhaps the most central point in the constitution, and its obvious purpose was to reduce the risk that the king would adopt autocratic and despotic rule:

> Kings have to rule their realms with and thus not without, even less against, the counsel of the Senate of the realm. And as Sweden's fundamental laws cannot be understood otherwise in this respect, everything that is declared, approved and established in one way or another against this is hereby abolished, changed and corrected.[39]

The Senate, in its turn, could not rule without the king, but it could act in the king's absence, if he was incapacitated through absence, illness or death. In this case, decisions could be made by the Senate by a majority of votes – *efter pluraliteten* – and signed by the council alone.[40] Formally, only the king could rule, since he alone possessed the 'majesty', while the Senate was 'counselling' and thus bound by law and responsible for its acts.[41] The Estates and the Senate could not share the immunities and sacred inviolability of the royal majesty and the royal person. The idea that the king was not responsible for his acts to anyone had its origin in older theocratic political theory – the idea of the king being *legibus solutus*, independent of the laws – but its practical significance during the Age of Liberty was that the king was not only without responsibility and inviolable, but also practically legally incapacitated, whereas the Senate, instead, possessed "authority" (*myndighet*). The expression *rådets myndighet*, as the choice of the term 'Senate' in translations, was related to the Roman concept *auctoritas senatus*, where *auctoritas* stood for a moral power larger than factual prerogatives, while "power" (*potestas*), or at least its legitimate source, was elsewhere. In Rome, it belonged to the people (*potestas populi*), in Sweden in the Age of Liberty to the Estates (*ständers rätt och frihet*).

Contrarily to the king, the Senate had responsibility, and its political duty to report to the Estates had become, in the constitution of 1720, something of a "constitutional guarantee against royal power".[42] The impression of a literally paralysed monarchy was only strengthened when the Senate in 1748 temporarily substituted the invalid king Frederick's signature with a stamp, which in time became a symbol for the paralysis of the monarchy. It was

---

38 RF 1720, art. 13, in Brusewitz, *Frihetstidens grundlagar och konstitutionella stadgar*, p. 27.

39 *"Konunger äger styra rike sino med och således icke utom, mindre emot riksens råds råde. Och som Sveriges fundamentallag icke annorledes häruthinnan kan eller bör förstås, så blifver alt, hvad häremot på ett eller annat sätt kan vara förklarat, gillat och stadgat, härmed aldeles upphäfvit, ändrat och rättat."* RF 1720, art. 13, in Brusewitz, *Frihetstidens grundlagar och konstitutionella stadgar*, p. 27.

40 RF 1720, art. 16; KF 1720, art. 16; KF 1751, art. 15, in Brusewitz, *Frihetstidens grundlagar och konstitutionella stadgar*, pp. 28, 63, 78.

41 See Fredrik Lagerroth, "En frihetstida lärobok i gällande svensk statsrätt", *Statsvetenskaplig Tidskrift för politik – statistik – ekonomi. Ny följd*, vol. 40 (1937), p. 196.

42 Lagerroth, *Frihetstidens författning*, p. 260.

reintroduced in 1757, after the worst crisis of the monarchy, and briefly reused in 1768.[43]

The formal tasks of the Senate, according to the constitution, were to advise the king according to the law and the interests of the realm, to assure that the fundamental laws were observed, but also to encourage the subjects to "faith and obedience" (*trohet och lydno*), to grant the majesty (*höghet*) of the king and the realm, the right and prosperity of the Estates, and generally to "counsel [...], but not rule". Of course, the Senate should prevent all attempts to attack the liberty of the Estates or to re-establish autocracy.[44]

These constitutional safeguards against excessive royal power had been made as a reaction against Caroline absolutism. The system had worked out relatively smoothly during the reign of the elderly Frederick I, since he ended up showing rather little interest in political decision-making once he had recognised his defeat against the Estates in 1720. With the return of a more self-confident monarch, there was the risk of an eventual conflict between the king and the Senate. That happened during the reign of Adolph Frederick, who regarded the royal task that had been given to him by a succession of coincidences as a choice of God, a view that was not far from traditional European theocracy but not very compatible with the extensive power of the Estates.[45]

Perhaps the most violent conflict between the monarchy and the aristocratic Senate representing the Estates broke out at the Diet of 1751–1752 and lasted until 1756. It originally concerned the king's right to choose the officials of the crown but developed into what the Secret Committee of the Diet called, through the pen of Bishop Johan Browallius, "confused conceptions concerning the form of government" (*Irriga begrepp rörande regeringsform*) and eventually "divergent conceptions of the right understanding of the fundamental laws" (*olika begrep[p] om grundlagarnes rätta förstånd*).[46]

According to the constitution, when new officials were appointed, the king was to choose one of three candidates suggested by the Senate. The method was regarded as satisfying the necessity of a balanced rule, which reduced the risk of a return to royal autocracy as well as the risk of the development of an aristocratic senatorial rule. The late King Frederick I had often tried to appoint other persons than those proposed to him by the Senate, but the Senate had mostly been able to vote down his suggestions. Adolph Frederick did not abide by the same kind of courtly favouritism but still intended to use his royal prerogatives politically. From the Diet of 1752

43 Malmström, *Sveriges politiska historia från K. Carl XII:s död till statshvälfningen 1772*, vol. 3, Stockholm, 1870, p. 326; vol. 4, Stockholm, 1874, pp. 267–268; vol. 6, Stockholm, 1877, pp. 80–81.

44 RF 1720, art. 14, in Brusewitz, *Frihetstidens grundlagar och konstitutionella stadgar*, pp. 27–28.

45 Malmström, *Sveriges politiska historia från K. Carl XII:s död till statshvälfningen 1772*, vol. 4, p. 136.

46 Lagerroth, *Frihetstidens författning*, p. 403; Browallius's memorandum printed in Malmström, *Sveriges politiska historia från K. Carl XII:s död till statshvälfningen 1772*, vol. 4, pp. 40–41; RA, Sekreta utskottets protokoll 1755–1756 (I), R 3045, ff. 127, 130v (15 and 17 December).

onwards, he tried to appoint officials that were loyal to the cause of royalty rather than to the ruling Hat party, the Senate and the aristocratic republicanism it represented. He did not care for the Senate voting his propositions down, neither for having promised in his coronation oath to follow the views of the Senate in such cases, but persisted in his pretensions to having the right, as a king, to appoint whoever pleased him. When the situation became inflamed, the king also started to absent himself from the meetings of the Senate and thus refused his signature to decisions made by the Senate.[47]

This prevented decisions from being executed and, in the words of the Diet's Secret Commission, dominated by the nobility and the burghers favourable to the Hat party, could lead to the "weakening, change and ruin of the constitution".[48] In addition, it seemed to transform the Senate into a drafting organ instead of a real council.[49] This continued for a couple of years, during which both the king and the Senate, dominated by the Hat party, tried to gain supporters, the Senate by using the press and the weekly *Ärlig Swensk* to defend the constitution publicly, the king and queen by forming a royalist party amongst court officials that had influence at the Diet and belonged mainly to the Cap opposition against the Hats in power.[50]

As soon as the Diet of 1755 opened, the Senate and the court attacked each other in different memoranda and declarations submitted to the Estates. In these political writings of both sides of the conflict, the eventual outcome of the situation was presented quite dramatically as either a return to royal autocracy (*envälde*) or the establishment of aristocratic senatorial rule (*rådsaristokrati*).

The king had defended his absence from the Senate and his refusal to sign decisions by pretending that it was his right to consider the propositions given to him by the Senate before he gave his consent. The Senate and the Estates perceived this as leading the country "into autocracy", since the vote of the Senate itself would thus be of no importance, contrary to the constitution, which stated that decisions in the king's council were to be made by a majority of votes (*efter pluraliteten*). If the king pretended that his authority was above that of the Senate by reserving himself the right to decide, the senators argued, there was a risk that his council would be reduced to one of a "sovereign lord" (*suverän herre*) and that the king would, *de facto*, have established autocracy. The king's misinterpretation of the fundamental laws could thus lead to the weakening of the constitution or the realm itself.[51]

---

47 Malmström, *Sveriges politiska historia från K. Carl XII:s död till statshvälfningen 1772*, vol. 4, pp. 80–126.

48 RA, Sekreta utskottets protokoll 1755–1756 (I), R 3045, f. 28 (6 November). The Secret Commission was the most important organ of the Diet. Its members belonged to the first three estates only, since the peasants were not considered able to deal with such important matters as e.g. foreign affairs.

49 Malmström, *Sveriges politiska historia från K. Carl XII:s död till statshvälfningen 1772*, vol. 4, pp. 80–126.

50 Malmström, *Sveriges politiska historia från K. Carl XII:s död till statshvälfningen 1772*, vol. 4, pp. 80–126.

51 RA, Sekreta utskottets protokoll 1755–1756 (I), R 3045, f. 28 (6 November). Malmström, *Sveriges politiska historia från K. Carl XII:s död till statshvälfningen 1772*, vol. 4, p. 135.

When the king answered the Senate with a memorandum to the Diet, the Senate stated with severity that the king himself had demonstrated all the perils of the situation, by not taking counsel of the Senate and leaving decisions unexecuted and the realm consequently without rule.[52] This view displeased the king, who answered with a declaration claiming that he had never opposed the principle of a majority of votes. He also complained that the Senate had exaggerated when it had described the state of the realm as "perilous". The Senate replied that it was indeed dangerous to leave the law unexecuted, because that could deprive the people of their freedom.[53] The Diet's Big Deputation gave its support to this view, strongly influenced by natural law: if a majority of votes in the council was not enough to legitimate a decision, liberty could not survive, and law was abolished; the king's conviction would become the law of the realm, and his conscience the security of his subjects.[54]

This was a most anti-absolutist and anti-theocratic way to put it. The Senate went even further in its comment on the king's memorandum. It stated that if kings were the defenders of liberty, it would not be necessary to restrict their prerogatives; if these were not restricted, there would be autocracy, and if there was autocracy, autocracy would replace the liberty of the nation, and it would then no longer make sense that autocratic rule had been abolished. The king's memorandum and the Senate's comment on it provoked extensive debates at the Diet and particularly in the House of Nobility, where the court had supporters. One of the leaders of the royalist party, Baron Erik Wrangel, even had a friend of his, Georg Wilhelm Leyonsteen, submit a counter-memorandum, in which he turned the Senate's argument the other way round by replacing "king" with "senate" and "autocracy" with "aristocracy". The Estates took this very badly, and Leyonsteen was even threatened with a trial.[55]

The final outcome of the crisis was violent. On the night between 21 and 22 June 1756, the preparations for an armed royalist uprising in the capital were dismantled. Arrests and interrogations, including the use of torture, followed. It soon became evident that the conspiracy was relatively large, including not only officers of the guard but also members of the highest nobility and the court, as well as the king and the queen themselves. From now on, the activities of the assembled Estates concentrated only on the investigation, and the Diet set up a commission to judge the conspirators suspected of complotting to restore autocracy. On 12 July, subversive pamphlets were found to have been spread in the provinces, among them *Swea Rikes tilstånd*, which was especially critical against the rule in place.[56]

---

52 Malmström, *Sveriges politiska historia från K. Carl XII:s död till statshvälfningen 1772*, vol. 4, pp. 137–139.

53 Malmström, *Sveriges politiska historia från K. Carl XII:s död till statshvälfningen 1772*, vol. 4, p. 141.

54 Malmström, *Sveriges politiska historia från K. Carl XII:s död till statshvälfningen 1772*, vol. 4, p. 142.

55 Malmström, *Sveriges politiska historia från K. Carl XII:s död till statshvälfningen 1772*, vol. 4, pp. 144–145.

56 *Swea Rikes tilstånd*, printed *s.l.*, 1756.

The revenge of the Estates on the royalist party and on the monarchy was merciless: on 23 July, four of the principal members of the conspiracy were publicly beheaded. Among them were the most distinguished leader of the royalist opposition, Count Eric Brahe, colonel of the mounted guard and former acting speaker of the nobility at the Diet of 1752, the court marshal Baron Gustaf Jakob Horn, and the captains Johan Puke and Magnus Stålsvärd. Four other conspirators of lower rank – an indiscreet innkeeper and three non-commissioned officers – were executed three days later.[57]

The king had not been as eager to support the revolution plans as the queen, and he even made a formal disavowal of the conspiracy when it was found out. Nevertheless, the royal couple were blamed. The Estates drew up a formal act, *Riksakten*, enumerating the offences committed by the king against the constitutions and his coronation oath but finally assuring that they were willing to forgive what had happened and renew their confidence in the king. The king could not but submit and seal the act; the following day, 24 August, he received a delegation from the Estates, declared that he would rule according to the law and recognised the legal authority of the Senate, which needed his confidence to work.[58] After the end of the Diet, in November, the king and the Senate ruled together, and the stamp was introduced again. The republican Hats had won the battle, at least temporarily. The monarchy had been humiliated, but royalism, nevertheless, was far from dead and would raise its head again some years later.

Sweden, an aristocratic republic?

The conflict between the king and the Senate is important since it concerns the question of whether the Senate could govern without the king or not, or whether the Senate was a republican or a royal organ. If we look at the constitution, it was neither. The constitution as well as political consensus had it that the "right and liberty of the Estates" as well as the majority of votes was the basis of the regime itself.[59] This seemed to indicate the possibility of a democratic element in the Swedish constitution. 'Democracy', however, was an extremely depreciated concept in early modern political terminology, and in the Swedish case, it was mostly used as a belittling or insulting word.[60]

Nevertheless, the "right and liberty of the Estates" was the most stabile and recognised one of the three elements upon which the Swedish regime in the Age of Liberty reposed. It was also the philosophical and ideological basis of Swedish eighteenth-century constitutionalism, regardless of how extensive the authority of the Senate could be. The expression "right and

57 Malmström, *Sveriges politiska historia från K. Carl XII:s död till statshvälfningen 1772*, vol. 4, pp. 198–218.

58 Malmström, *Sveriges politiska historia från K. Carl XII:s död till statshvälfningen 1772*, vol. 4, pp. 222–227.

59 *"Pluraliteten [...] grunden til Regeringssättet"*, RA, Sekreta utskottets protokoll 1755–1756 (I), R 3045, f. 110.

60 Lindberg, *Den antika skevheten*, pp. 195–197.

liberty" used in the preamble to the constitution of 1720 stated the Diet's independence from royal or ministerial interference and thus reflected a perception of liberty that could be defined as an immunity against the state (or any superior sovereign subject whatsoever).[61] The liberties of the estate assemblies of Old Regime Europe were generally considered that kind of safeguards, while modern parliaments are generally seen as being part of the state.[62] According to Fredrik Lagerroth, Swedish estate rule presented a more complex case, where 'right' and 'liberty' referred both to the privileges of particular estates and to the general common rights of the people, and applied both to the Diet in particular and to the realm more generally.[63] The particular rights of the Estates were, for instance, that all Diet members were granted physical immunity and could not be arrested by the officials of the crown during the Diet.[64] However, the constitution as well as the old law of the realm (*Landslagen*) declared that no free Swedish subject could be arrested without being trialled; thus physical integrity was not the privilege of Diet members only.[65] The deputies of each estate, the nobility, the clergy, the burghers' estate and the peasants, also elected their own speaker independently of the king's or other estates' wishes.[66]

As time passed, the liberty of the Estates became a synonym for their extensive power, while, at the same time, the Estates themselves merged with the state.[67] In the royal coronation oaths, the Estates were called *magtägande*, "detaining power", thus completing the *auctoritas senatus* with the *potestas populi*.[68] In 1760, when the power of the Estates was at its zenith, Carl Fredrik Scheffer, writing an interpretation of the Swedish constitutions for the heir of the throne Prince Gustaf, went so far as to translate the "right and liberty" of the Estates as the Latin terms *jus et imperium*.[69] The translation of *libertas* into *imperium* is all the more remarkable as classical political theory had argued over which one was the precondition of the other and to what extent they were antipodes.[70] By replacing *libertas* with *imperium*, Scheffer made a silent ideological statement of which one

---

61 See Quentin Skinner, "States and the freedom of citizens", in *States & Citizens. History, Theory, Prospects*, ed. by Quentin Skinner & Bo Stråth, Cambridge, 2003, pp. 11–25; Lindberg, *Den antika skevheten*, pp. 171–173.

62 Cf. Martin van Gelderen, "The state and its rivals in early-modern Europe", in *States and Citizens History, Theory, Prospects*, ed. by Quentin Skinner & Bo Stråth, pp. 79–96.

63 Lagerroth, *Frihetstidens författning*, pp. 93–94.

64 RF 1720, art. 46; RO 1723 art. 23, in Brusewitz, *Frihetstidens grundlagar och konstitutionella stadgar*, pp. 42, 247–248.

65 RF 1720, art. 2, in Brusewitz, *Frihetstidens grundlagar och konstitutionella stadgar*, p. 24.

66 RO 1723, art. 10, in Brusewitz, *Frihetstidens grundlagar och konstitutionella stadgar*, p. 236.

67 Lagerroth, "En frihetstida lärobok i gällande svensk statsrätt", pp. 185–211; see also Quentin Skinner, "States and the freedom of citizens", and Annabel S. Bratt, "The development of the idea of citizens' rights", both in *States and Citizens. History, Theory, Prospects*.

68 KF 1720, art. 6; KF 1751, art. 5; KF 1772, art. 5, in Brusewitz, *Frihetstidens grundlagar och konstitutionella stadgar*, pp. 60, 74, 85. See also Kari Saastamoinen, "Johdatus poliittisiin käsitteisiin uuden ajan alun Ruotsissa", in *Käsitteet liikkeessä*, p. 38.

69 Skuncke, "La liberté dans la culture politique suédoise au XVIIIᵉ siècle".

70 J. G. A. Pocock, *Barbarism and Religion*, vol. 3: *The First Decline and Fall*, Cambridge, 2003, pp. 276–277.

would precede. For Scheffer, liberty could be translated as "sovereign power" without using the very word. Scheffer also stated that this power was "completely unlimited" and absolute and belonged to nobody else in the realm. This power, according to Scheffer, was based on the fact that the Estates should be regarded as the nation itself, as, technically speaking, the subjects had delegated and transferred their political powers directly and completely to the Estates, which according to the ruling political doctrine were not responsible to their electors.[71]

Of course, there were several obvious dangers inherent in this view. One could reasonably think that royal absolutism had been replaced by a formal sovereignty of the Estates. In 1755, Baron Clas Wilhelm Grönhagen criticised what he called "the sovereign autocracy" of the Estates and was dismissed from the House of Nobility for having associated the free Estates with despotism.[72] The doctrine of the "right and liberty of the Estates", in its most extreme interpretation, thus seemed to open the way for a perilous kind of Machiavellianism, if the vital condition of liberty, that is *virtue*, was not granted.

One danger of aristocracy was the consequence of the concentration of power in a small circle. In an aristocratic government – as in a despotic one – the legislative and the executive mixed, and there could be no liberty when these powers were not separated, which was why there could be no liberty in an aristocracy.[73] As the historian Anders Schönberg put it, the Italian republics provided examples of how liberty had disappeared after a few had been too long in charge of defending the freedom of their fellow citizens.[74]

Another danger of an aristocracy was that the power held by the aristocrats would become hereditary. The conflict between the Swedish constitution and the hereditary privileges of the nobility, which granted the nobility the right to the highest offices of the realm, including those of senator and chancellor, pointed this out. When power became hereditary, aristocracy ceased to be a meritocracy and turned into an oligarchy. The republic then only existed inside the nobility. Since less competition was required, virtue would become more rare, and politics would corrupt into a state of "carelessness, laziness, abandon, which makes the State forceless and deprived of resilience".[75] In addition to being a threat to liberty, the rule of

---

71 Lagerroth, "En frihetstida lärobok i gällande statsrätt", pp. 188–189; see also Beth Hennings, *Gustav III som kronprins*, Stockholm, 1935, pp. 92–93; Marie-Christine Skuncke, *Gustaf III – Det offentliga barnet. En prins retoriska och politiska fostran*, Stockholm, 1993, p. 211; Alm, *Kungsord i elfte timmen*, p. 172.

72 Roberts, *The Age of Liberty*, p. 125, n. 42.

73 Montesquieu, *De l'esprit des lois*, XI, 6.

74 *"Uti de italienska stater ser man exempel, huru visse personer så länge åtogo sig at försvara sine medborgares frihet, at omsider frijheten var borta."* *Sveriges ridderskaps och adels riksdagsprotokoll från och med år 1719*, tjugosjunde delen 1769–1770, I, 22 april–24 oktober 1769, Stockholm, 1962, pp. 108–109.

75 *"Le grand nombre des nobles dans l'aristocratie héréditaire rendra donc le gouvernement moins violent ; mais comme il y aura peu de vertu, on tombera dans un esprit de nonchalance, de paresse, d'abandon, qui fera que l'État n'aura plus de force ni de ressort."* Montesquieu, *De l'esprit des lois*, VIII, 5 ; see also III, 3.

the few as well as that of one single person was perceived negatively because it promoted a particular interest rather than the common good, this *allmänna bästa*, public welfare, being the utmost priority of national politics.

The concept of *pluralitetsvälde*, which was meant to moderate the Senate, served as an efficient rhetorical arm against autocracy and against attacks on the free rule of the Estates, but it did not, however, provide protection against an aristocratic rule. On the contrary, because of the composition of the Senate and the power relations at the Diet, it affirmed the authority of the Senate and the power of the nobility. Paradoxically, the very strong power of the Estates gave the nobility a most considerable political position. The House of Nobility, with all the prestige that surrounded the place and with its developed rhetorical culture, was the centre of political life, and the aristocracy, with its networks of patronage and protection, also had great influence on political decision-making and on the construction of political loyalties in the lower estates.[76] By the terms of the nobility's privileges of 1723, only noblemen were made senators. In that respect, Sweden was a kind of aristocratic republic, moderated by the presence of not only one, but two commoners' estates at the Diet.

Officially, Swedish politicians unanimously condemned aristocratic rule, which was associated not with meritocracy but with oligarchy, no more positive than sovereignty. The suspicion towards oligarchy or the tyranny of the few was expressed in the constitution, which bade the Senate to counsel but forbade it to rule and to let personal interest, friendship or kinship outweigh the welfare of the Estates and the realm.[77]

'Aristocracy' was also frequently used as an insult when the Hats and the Caps accused each other of bad government. The party in opposition willingly depicted the Senate as an assembly of aristocrats, not only in the sense of an assembly of noblemen and Excellencies – which it actually was – but in terms of an oligarchic clique that ruled despotically, with reference to the concentration of power in a small co-opting circle. In this sense, 'aristocracy' was used as synonym for 'oligarchy', together with *envälde* as the opposite of *pluralitetsvälde*, representative rule based on the will of the majority and on consensus.[78] The concept of 'aristocracy' was given an explicit, anti-noble and radically democratic colour in its particular Swedish synonym *herrevälde*, "power of lords", once again formed on the root *-välde/våld*. It seemed to suggest that all types of unequal power were bad, an idea that was strongly rooted in the Swedish peasants' estate.[79] An official echo of this pejorative use of the concept of 'aristocracy' can be found in the *Riksakten* of 1756, the document by which the Estates and the king sealed their conflict. Among other things, it stated, with reference to the pamphlets spread by the opposition, that "the legal authority of the Senate has been

76 Roberts, *The Age of Liberty*, p. 69.
77 RF 1720, art. 14, in Brusewitz, *Frihetstidens grundlagar och konstitutionella stadgar*, pp. 27–28.
78 Valentin, *Frihetstidens riddarhus*, pp. 90–91.
79 On the peasants as political actors, see Karin Sennefelt, *Den politiska sjukan. Dalupproret 1743 och frihetstida politisk kultur*, Hedemora, 2001.

regarded as an aristocratic authority, leading like the autocracy to the oppression of liberty".[80]

The question of the prerogatives of the Senate and of the king was raised again at the Diet of 1769. At that moment, the Hat party was making its comeback after a short period of Cap rule from 1766 to 1768, but this time, the Hats did not take the role of the defenders of aristocratic republicanism. On the contrary, they interpreted the constitution in a sense that was more favourable to the monarchy and accused the Cap administration of having violated the constitution. The Cap Senate, fearing a return of the Hats, had been reluctant to summon the Estates for 1769. In December 1768, the king, now increasingly supported by former Hat politicians, abdicated in protest, leaving the Senate with no other alternative than to summon the Estates, as bade the constitution. The Diet opened with reflections on whether the Cap Senate had formed itself into an aristocracy trying to rule without the king, thus offending the fundamental laws of the realm.[81]

In critical pamphlets against the Senate, the executive was accused of "ministerial aristocracy", a very hard accusation, since this "aristocracy" was associated with strong iniquities such as "illegal constraint and domination", "servility and villain submissiveness".[82] These gloomy perspectives also lurked behind the concept of herrevälde, "rule of the lords", the lord being, in the popular imaginary, the feudal Danish one who flagellated the peasant, imposed taxes and used violence.[83] The accusation had an even stronger signification of not only political but also social injustice at a time when the nobility monopolised higher offices and when the nobility's pretended exclusive right to these offices was strongly questioned.[84]

The Swedish defiance towards concentrated power thus not only concerned monarchs, but ministers and court aristocrats too, as well as arbitrarily ruling persons in general, as in the invocative despotisme ministériel used by the French parlements to designate the extensive power of the royal administration, an echo of the despotism of the executive defined by Bolingbroke.[85] The

---

80 "Personers förseelser uti ämbeten, grundade eller uppspundne, hafva blifvit afmålade såsom regeringssättets fel, rådets laglige myndighet ansedd för en aristocratisk myndighet, lika ländande till frihetens förtryck som enväldet, och den enfaldigare förledd att räkna för en förbättring af RF., hvad som tjente att öka konungens makt med förlust af ständers rättigheter och följakteligen med minskning af nationens fri- och säkerhet." Quoted in Brusewitz, Frihetstidens grundlagar och konstitutionella stadgar, pp. 185–186.

81 Cf. RF 1720, art. 45; RO 1723, art. 3–4, in Brusewitz, Frihetstidens grundlagar och konstitutionella stadgar, pp. 40–42, 233–234; Sveriges ridderskaps och adels riksdags-protokoll från och med år 1719, tjugosjunde delen 1769–1770, I, 22 april–24 oktober 1769, utg. Sten Landahl, Stockholm, 1962, pp. 21–126.

82 "At afsäga all trälagtig och neslig undergifwenhet, både af utländska afsigter, och inhemskt olagligt twång och ofwerwälde, til förekommande af Ämbetsmanna Aristocratie." Tankar Huru en Riksdags-Man Bör Utöva Sina Öma Pligter Emot Medborgare och Fädernesland. I anledning Af en utaf Trycket nyss utkommen Skrift kallad: En Ärlig Riksdags-Mans Syldigheter [sic], på Urtima Riksdagen 1769, Stockholm, 1769, p. 2.

83 Cf. Sennefelt, Den politiska sjukan.

84 See, for instance, several articles in Marie-Christine Skuncke & Henrika Tandefelt (red.), Riksdag, kaffehus och predikstol.

85 Skinner, "States and the freedom of citizens," p. 17. Bolingbroke had a great influence on Montesquieu and on French parliamentary thought.

corresponding Swedish term *ämbetsmanna aristocratie* was used by the Hats at the Diet of 1769 when referring to the Senate that had been nominated by the Caps at the previous Diet of 1765–1766 and the dominance of their friends and relatives in the administration. The Hats also voluntarily answered the old, popular fears with arguments that could be read as partly populist and partly reflecting a philosophical perception of politics such as the *rikshistoriograf* (royal historian) and member of the noble estate Schönberg's statement that "the aim of all political rule is the general welfare of the people and not that of certain persons".[86]

When the House of Nobility, at the beginning of the Diet in April 1769, voted on whether the short-lived Cap Senate had tried to rule without the king and thus violated the constitution, this view received a majority of the votes at the House of Nobility. Suddenly, the king, who in 1756 had been accused of crimes against the fundamental laws of the realm, appeared to be the one who had protected the constitution and "the liberty of the nation", as one of the members of the noble estate, Leonard Magnus Uggla, put it.[87] The idea that the Senate could not rule without the king, although present in the constitution of 1720, was now underlined in a newer, royalist interpretation of the law, and together with the exploitation of popular fears of aristocracy it would eventually pave the way for Gustav III and his remodelling of the Swedish political discourse.[88]

What is remarkable is that the elite in power itself recognised the frailty of its position and the legitimacy of the criticism. A former Marshal of the Diet, Baron Matthias Alexander von Ungern-Sternberg from the Cap party, had stated during the debates on the publication of *Ärlig Swensk* in 1755 that it could be dangerous to let the people, who feared for aristocracy and *herrevälde*, know that the king's decision depended on the will of the Estates and the Senate:

> One knows what impression the public has and which long may prevail amidst the Swedish nation; namely that the King detains power on everything, and that commonly a Rule of Lords or an aristocracy is feared for. Should the Public therefore learn from the humble answer of the Estates of the Realm that the King's decision depends upon the majority of votes in the Senate, the old impression might rouse dissatisfaction and all kinds of opinions against it.[89]

86 *"Afsikten med all politisk regering är folckets väl i allmänhet och icke vissa personers"*, *Sveriges ridderskaps och adels riksdagsprotokoll från och med år 1719*, tjugosjunde delen 1769–1770, I, 22 april–24 oktober 1769, p. 107.

87 Quoted in *Sveriges ridderskaps och adels riksdagsprotokoll från och med år 1719*, tjugosjunde delen 1769–1770, I, 22 april–24 oktober 1769, p. 126.

88 See chapter 5.

89 *"Man wet hwad* impression *hos allmänheten finnes, och hwilken hos Swenska* nationen *länge torde bibehållas, neml. at Konungen är magtägande i alt, och at i gemen fruktas för et Herra Wälde el.* aristocratie. *Skulle derföre Allmänheten af Riksens ständers underdåniga swar få se, at Konungens beslut* dependerar *af* pluraliteten *i Rådet, så kunde den gamla* impressionen *deremot wäcka missnöje och allahanda omdömen."* RA, Sekreta utskottets protokoll 1755–1756 (I), R 3045, f. 127v–128r (15 December).

In other words, that the king was not sovereign was something that should wisely be concealed from the common people. What we have here is a proven consensus on political rhetoric. The same kind of consensus, even more largely shared, was the one on the power of the Estates. To circumvent the consequences of the extensive powers of the Estates dominated by the House of Nobility, the political elites of the Age of Liberty would use rhetorical strategies emphasising consensus, national concord and the common good as antonyms for the unequal distribution of powers. The most important element in this consensus, however, was the concept of 'liberty', by which all forms of oppression and abuses were exorcised, as we shall see in the next chapter.

Chapter 2: Under the rule of liberty

As we have seen, the Swedish form of government, during the Age of Liberty, was neither an absolutist monarchy, nor entirely an aristocratic republic, despite many features of aristocratic rule. Officially, the regime was based on the notion of the "right and liberty of the Estates" (*ständers rätt och frihet*) mentioned in the preamble of the constitution. To preserve this integrity of the Estates, freedom and balance of power, it was necessary to maintain the fundamental laws (i.e. the constitution). This necessity was systematically stressed in official political discourse, solemn speech acts and papers produced by the Diet, with explicit references to "the laws". The consensus on the value of the laws also meant that royalty striving to enlarge its prerogatives, as well as aristocratic senators, would be attacked with constitutionalist arguments. The result was an apparently republican discourse, in fact a conceptual assimilation between 'law' and 'liberty', which manifested a legalist view of the rule by the Estates in the spirit of old aristocratic constitutionalism influenced by newer political theory.[1]

In the conflict between the Senate and the king concerning the king's powers and prerogatives in 1755–1756, what had been at stake, according to the Hat-minded legislators and the periodical *Ärlig Swensk*, was the liberty of the people and of the nation. This may sound fairly "modern" or radically republican, but it was not necessarily the case. Certain concepts may have been chosen in order to exacerbate the conflict and make the situation uncomfortable for the monarchy. What was then the larger significance of such concepts as they were used in more ordinary political contexts? And how did the noble idea of liberty develop during the century?

The objectives of this chapter are to understand the meanings of the concept of 'liberty' as it was used by the nobility in Diet papers; to show how 'liberty' was instrumented in political discourse, and finally, to reflect on what and whose liberty Swedish eighteenth-century politicians were talking about. Was it a liberty from oppression, a liberty given by law, a natural liberty or a liberty linked to security?

---

1 On this substrate of aristocratic constitutionalism, see Lagerroth, *Frihetstidens författning*.

The absolutism of Charles XII had awakened a hatred towards arbitrariness, lawlessness and all forms of sovereignty, i.e. autocratic rule.[2] The new political discourse would focus on liberty and legality.[3] The authors of the constitutions of 1719 and 1720 thus found it necessary to base the new regime on law and to grant liberty through the new fundamental laws. According to Sten Lindroth, these authors – aristocratic jurists and politicians – were so impregnated by natural law and English, republican political theory that the constitution of the Age of Liberty could be regarded as a kind of social contract put to paper.[4]

This basis, the political liberty of movement of the Estates as founded on the absence of monarchic sovereignty and the freedom from inner and outer oppression, gave birth to the concept of 'the Age of Liberty' and the particular political culture and political ideology that characterised this period in Swedish history. The rule of the Estates and the party system that developed at the Diet make it possible to consider the Sweden of the Age of Liberty a republic, although it was a very aristocratic one. The central place given to the concept of 'liberty' allowed rhetorical allusions to the Roman republic and other, modern states without ruling sovereigns. In consequence of the hatred of sovereignty, a very strong ideology of liberty developed in Sweden as a counterweight and safeguard against monarchic absolutism, which the defenders of liberty perceived as their greatest enemy. The connections to the classical republican heritage were underlined by the long-lasting influence of Latin on the Swedish political language.[5]

As 'right', 'rights' and 'liberty' became central and common concepts and political language was influenced by natural law, it was possible to develop, in a new way, ideas concerning constitutional law, rights and the rule of law. In the constitutional discourse of the Age of Liberty, liberty was also often associated with law and rights. In this respect, in addition to classical political terminology and theories of natural law, the conceptions of liberty were also founded on a mediaeval, Scandinavian heritage, which emphasised the law as a precondition of legitimate rule.[6]

Here, the intention is to examine how the concept of 'liberty' was used in solemn speech acts at the Diet and to show how it was connected to notions of 'rights' and how this connection received new meanings at the end of the Age of Liberty and the beginning of the Gustavian era. The quotes and

---

2 Lagerroth, *Frihetstidens författning*, p. 281.
3 The different streams in the political discourse of the Age of Liberty, among them the constitutional discourse, have been presented by Martin Melkersson in *Staten, ordningen och friheten. En studie av den styrande elitens syn på statens roll mellan stormaktstiden och 1800-talet*, Uppsala, 1997, p. 21.
4 Sten Lindroth, *Svensk lärdomshistoria. Frihetstiden*, Stockholm, 1978, pp. 532–533; see also Per Nilsén, *Att "stoppa munnen till på bespottare". Den akademiska undervisningen i svensk statsrätt under frihetstiden*, Lund, 2001, particularly pp. 114–117. See also Erik Fahlbeck, "Studier öfver frihetstidens politiska idéer", *Statsvetenskaplig Tidskrift*, vol. 18 (1915), pp. 328–329. Fahlbeck's article continues in vol. 19 (1916), pp. 31–54, 104–126, and is a criticism of Lagerroth. Despite his intention to bring more contrast to the picture, Fahlbeck himself repeats the monarchistic, Gustavian historiographical theses; cf. vol. 19, pp. 120, 126.
5 On Latin and Sweden as political idioms, see Lindberg, *Den antika skevheten*.
6 Lindberg, *Den antika skevheten*, pp. 176–177.

examples have above all been chosen from the ceremonious speeches made by the Marshals of the Diet to the nobility, the assembled Estates and the king. Although not as consensual as the speeches made by the Chancellery Presidents, these speeches both aim at a sense of community and express ideological and partial positions. The last decades of the Age of Liberty, the 1750s and 1760s, are particularly rich in examples; one could say that the notions were then crystallising. During these decades the concepts seem to have become more ideologically coloured, where they had earlier been consensual.[7]

In what follows, liberty will first be analysed as a regime, then we shall look at the relation between liberty and law, and finally, at the connections between liberty and rights.

The state of liberty and liberty as a regime

For the republican politicians of the Age of Liberty, both Hats and Caps, liberty was intimately associated with a free constitution. The abolition of royal absolutism was manifested in the continuous celebration of liberty in Swedish political rhetoric, official speeches at solemn occasions as well as in normal, everyday Diet sessions. After 1718, the hatred of sovereignty – the domestic absolutism of foreign oppression – was so strong that the preservation of liberty became the utmost purpose of Swedish politics and one of the most common *topoi* in the political discourse. After Charles XII's death and the transition to estate rule, Swedish politicians started, at some point, to call the new regime an 'Age of Liberty'. The oldest example of the term mentioned in the authorative and often cited dictionary of the Swedish Academy is from the middle of the 1750s and refers partly to any epoch during which a people would rule itself and partly to the period in Swedish history between 1718 and 1772. In the first sense, the term was used in 1755 by Baron Anders Johan von Höpken ("Rome's Age of Liberty", *Roms frihetstid*), but in the second by the same Höpken as early as in 1751 and by Niclas von Oelreich in *Ärlig Swensk* in 1755 ("our present Age of Liberty", *vår nu warande Frihets-tid*).[8]

It is, by the way, no coincidence that the same concept was used by Höpken with reference to the Roman republic as well as to the Swedish regime after 1718. In the education of his generation of Swedish politicians, Latin and Roman history was still very important, and Rome and the classical authors were natural models for Swedish political orators. Höpken himself was particularly familiar with the Roman antiquities, but a classical influence is also perceptible in more French-styled speakers such as Carl Gustaf Tessin and Axel von Fersen.[9]

---

7 Fahlbeck, "Studier öfver frihetstidens politiska idéer", *Statsvetenskaplig Tidskrift*, vol. 18 (1915), p. 331, states that the ideas were "ripening"; see also Nordin, "Frihetstidens radikalism", pp. 61–62, 64.

8 "Frihetstid", *Svenska Akademiens ordbok* (SAOB), http://g3.spraakdata.gu.se/saob/.

9 On the importance of Latin, see, for instance, Lindroth, *Svensk lärdomshistoria. Frihetstiden*, pp. 572–586; Tore Frängsmyr, *Svensk idéhistoria. Bildning och vetenskap under tusen år*.

It is not insignificant that the dictionary of the Academy dates the term to the 1750s, although the dictionary does not claim to have found the first occurrences. Later historians both in Sweden and Finland have used this reference to date the appearance of the concept to the 1750s.[10] Peter Hallberg, however, has found earlier occurrences, the earliest of which is a speech by Olof Dalin from 1749 ("our Age of Liberty", "our blessed rule of Liberty").[11] The expression 'Age of Liberty', in its Swedish form, may be even older. It can be found, although not in the definite form, as early as in 1747 in a speech by the Chancellery President, Count Carl Gustaf Tessin, to the assembled Estates in *pleno plenorum* at the State Hall (*Rikssalen*) of the royal palace of Stockholm on 31 March 1747, in the middle of the ongoing Diet. In this speech, intended as a political vindication of his own acts, Tessin first used expressions such as "the use of our blissful Liberty" and "the fruits of our liberty" before he stated that he had received his first Diet commission from Charles XII and thereafter had participated in every Diet "from the earliest age of our regained Liberty" (*ifrån wår första återwundne Frihets tid*), where *Frihets tid* appears as a false compound. Finally, Tessin also used the expression "our freedom and security", where security could be interpreted as associated with the absence of domestic and foreign oppression.[12] If the concept 'Age of Liberty' was created at the end of the 1740s only to reappear in *Ärlig Swensk* in the mid-1750s, this coincides with the weakening of the monarchy during the last years of Frederick I, the skillful orators Tessin and then Höpken being raised to the office of Chancellery President, and the beginnings of the struggle for power between the Senate and the king after Adolph Frederick's accession to the throne. The application of the concept of 'the Age of Liberty' to one's own regime can then be seen as a manifestation of a generally more polarising political discourse.

Since the "time of our regained Liberty" was used by Tessin as a clear antonym to the precedent Caroline era without any further explanation, we cannot exclude that the formula *frihets tid* or *frihetstid* as a compound had

Del I: 1000–1809, Stockholm, 2004, pp. 116–118, 223–224; background in Bo Lindberg, "Latein und Grossmacht. Das Latein im Schweden des 17. Jahrhunderts", in *Germania latina – Latinitas teutonica*, hrsg. Eckhard Kessler & Heinrich C. Kuhn, München, 2003, pp. 679–692, more in Lindberg, *Den antika skevheten*. On Höpken, see Jonas Nordin, "Anders Johan von Höpken. 'Sveriges Tacitus'", in *Drottning Lovisa Ulrika och Vitterhetsakademien*, red. Sten Åke Nilsson, Stockholm, 2003, pp. 63–89. On the Ancients and the Moderns in Sweden, see, for instance, Lindroth, *Svensk lärdomshistoria. Frihetstiden*, and Outi Merisalo, "The *Querelle des Anciens et des Modernes* at the Academia Aboensis in the Eighteenth Century", in *Germania latina – Latinitas teutonica*, pp. 751–768.

10 See, for instance, Juha Manninen, *Valistus ja kansallinen identiteetti. Aatehistoriallinen tutkimus 1700-luvun Pohjolasta*, Helsinki, 2000, pp. 108–109; Alm, *Kungsord i elfte timmen*, p. 132; to some extent also Lindberg, *Den antika skevheten*, p. 186.

11 *"vår Frihets-tid"*, *"vår välsignade Frihets-regering"*; Hallberg, *Ages of Liberty*, p. 55. Hallberg translates Dalin's *"Frihets-regering"* as "government of Liberty".

12 *"wår hugneliga Frihets bruk"*, *"wåra frihets frukter"*, *"ifrån wår första återwundne Frihets tid"*, *"wår frihet och säkerhet"*; [Carl Gustaf Tessin], *TAL, Til Samtelige Riksens Högloflige Ständer, Af Herr Riks-Rådet, Cantzli-Rådet, Öfwerste-Marskalken och Academiae Cancelleren, Höfwälborne Grefwe CARL GUSTAV TESSIN, Tå Riksens Ständer in Pleno Plenorum uppå Stora Riddarhus Salen woro församlade, then 31. Martii 1747*, Stockholm, 1747.

been used before Tessin's speech and with reference to the rule of the Estates after 1718. With reference to a political situation and to the new nature of the regime, the concept 'liberty' alone was already used. This was the case in a speech by Count Charles Emil Lewenhaupt from 1734, where he dated the beginning of the state of liberty to Queen Ulrika Eleonora's accession to the throne.[13] This could be representative of the associations given to the concept of 'liberty' until the end of the 1740s.[14] As a state, 'liberty' was fairly static.[15] In this sense it was also used by Tessin in 1738 ("our well-acquired Liberty").[16] It can be noted that whereas Lewenhaupt still gave the concept a historical continuity by associating it with the graceful queen, Charles XII's sister, Tessin saw liberty as having been actively acquired by the Estates. *Frihet*, liberty, with its antipode, *självsvåld*, generally translated as "licence" (from the Latin concept of *licentia*), although a more exact translation would be "arbitrariness" (literally, *självsvåld* is close to "self-will"), were also the slogans of the attacks directed at the Diet of 1738–1739 by the rising Hat party against Count Arvid Bernhard Horn, the leading figure of Swedish politics during the first part of the Age of Liberty.[17]

Although Fredrik Lagerroth, at the beginning of the twentieth century, endowed the Swedish ideal of liberty and eighteenth-century consitutionalism with mediaeval roots, the absence of oppression was described by politicians of the Age of Liberty as an entirely new regime and the beginning of a new era, a "new age in government" (*en ny regements tid*). This was how Tessin's rival and opponent, Count Eric Brahe, put it when the Diet was closed on 4 June 1752 after the early tensions between the king and the Estates had been temporarily overcome: "We thus continue, with immaculate consciences, to begin a new age in government, as licence has not caused loss of liberty [...]."[18] Hereby Brahe underlined that Sweden was still living under the rule of liberty and rejected all suspicions of royalist licence, these being no longer of any concern.

Liberty was thus celebrated not only by the more republican of the aristocrats. We can note, however, that Brahe, who in the early 1750s increasingly appeared as one of the leading figures of the emerging royalist court party, used moralising expressions such as "conscience" – also used

13 "*Et wid anträdet af Eders Kongl. Maj:ts Regering uti en skiälig frihet försatt Folck* [...]", [Charles Emil Lewenhaupt], *Til Hennes Kongl. Maj:t Wår Allernådigste Drottning, Af Grefwen och LandtMarschalken Högwälborne Herr General Majoren CARL EMIL LEWENHAUPT, Uppå Samtel. Riksens Ständers wägnar håldne Tahl wid Riksdagen A. 1734*, Stockholm, 1734.
14 See Ingemar Carlsson, *Olof von Dalin och den politiska propagandan inför "lilla ofreden". Sagan Om Hästen och Wår-Wisa i samtidspolitisk belysning*, Lund, 1966, p. 222.
15 See Lindberg, *Den antika skevheten*, p. 194.
16 "*vår wälförwärfwade frihet*"; *Landt-Marskalkens Högwälborne Grefwe CARL GUSTAF TESSINS Tal, Hållit til Ridderskapet och Adeln Wid Landt-Marskalks Stafwens emottagande Den 17. Maii 1738*, Stockholm, 1738.
17 Carlsson, *Olof von Dalin och den politiska propagandan inför "lilla ofreden"*, p. 222.
18 "*Wi fortfare med ofläckade samweten, at så börja en ny Regements tid, thet sielfswåld ej gifwit anledning til frihets förlust* [...]." [Eric Brahe], *Öfwerste-Lieutenantens Högwälborne Grefwe ERIC BRAHES TAL, Hållit på Riks-Salen I Stockholm, När Riksdagen slöts then 4. Junii, 1752*, Stockholm, 1752.

by King Adolph Frederick during the conflict with the Senate, as we have seen – and implied that liberty could be lost through excessive freedom and licence. Brahe also seems to have emphasised the meanings and limits of liberty in a way slightly different from Tessin's, for instance by associating liberty not only with the law but also with the mildness and grace of the monarch later in his speech.[19]

In the political discourse of the Age of Liberty, it was rather common to talk about the grace of the monarch. Not only was it part of the traditional political formulas of reverence, but it was always a way to disarm monarchy rhetorically and thus underline the power of the Estates and the House of Nobility. One out of many examples of this is Count Axel von Fersen's speech to Queen Lovisa Ulrika on 19 October 1755, where Fersen, as Marshal of the Diet, mentions "the mild government of our most gracious King, who shelters the law and protects liberty" (this was half a year before the royal couple attempted their *coup*).[20] More remarkable is that Brahe in the above-mentioned text both emphasises the royal grace and alludes to the dangers and limits of liberty, that is licence, and to the legalism that thereby seems necessary.

The recurrent dualism of liberty and licence referred to the tension between the two latin concepts for 'freedom': the virtuous *libertas* and the negative *licentia*, unrestrained freedom, licence and self-will. The conception of a fragile liberty which risked degenerating into licence was part of the universalia of Western political theory. During the eighteenth century, it can be found in Montesquieu's works – which were most influential at the moment when the consitution of 1720 was abolished – as well as in several Swedish Diet allocutions.[21] In classical political theory, the survival of republics, i.e. free governments, depended on the political virtue of the active citizen. If there was no virtue, liberty and the state would easily perish as the rulers would yield to arbitrariness and abuse of power.[22] To put it as Axel von Fersen did when speaking to the House of Nobility on 22 April 1769 at the beginning of the Diet that had then convened at Norrköping:

> The inestimable benefit of being free thrives badly on abuse, and it is abused when the Law of Conscience does not confirm the application of the Laws of the Realm, and when love and reference for God and the

---

19 "Wi lemne med trygghet wår wälfärd uti en Mild Konungs Hand, som afstått medfödd rättighet, at therigenom förwärfwa Sitt folk allmän säkerhet och befästa Rikets landamären. Som Som uti Sina undersåtares lagbundne frihet finner sin hjelp, uti theras sielfkrafde tilgifwenhet sin styrka, och uti fägnades, at hafwa giort theras wäl. Sin skatt." [Eric Brahe], Öfwerste-Lieutenantens Högwälborne Grefwe ERIC BRAHES TAL, Hållit på Riks-Salen I Stockholm, När Riksdagen slöts then 4. Junii, 1752, Stockholm, 1752.

20 "vår nådigste Konungs milda regering, som hägnar lag och beskyddar frihet"; [Axel von Fersen] Til Hennes Kongl. Maj:t, Landt-Marskalkens Högwälborne Grefwe AXEL FERSENS TAL, Tå han, med Ridderskapets och Adelens Deputerade, aflade theras underdåniga Hälsning then 18 Oct. 1755, Stockholm, s.d. [1755].

21 Montesquieu, De l'esprit des lois, VIII, 2. On these two concepts in Sweden, see Skuncke, "La liberté dans la culture politique suédoise au XVIIIe siècle".

22 See, for instance, Quentin Skinner, The Foundations of Modern Political Thought. Volume 1: The Renaissance, Cambridge, 1978, pp. 42–44. Montesquieu, De l'esprit des lois, VIII, 5; see also III, 3.

Authorities as well as an unfeigned *Patriotic* zeal do not guide the
Deliberations and consolidate the Decisions.[23]

"Patriotic zeal" corresponds to what Montesquieu calls political virtue, *vertu
politique*, with reference to the *virtus* or the merit that characterises the good
citizen.[24] The "patriotic zeal" of course also belongs to another central semantic
field, which is that of the love of fatherland, which also was emphasised only
a few days later in the sermon made by Bishop Anders Forssenius on 26 April
1769 as part of the rituals of the opening Diet.[25] That was hardly a coincidence
during the period of political discord and party struggles that the Swedish
political community experienced during this spring of 1769.

Liberty was considered to degenerate particularly easily in aristocratic
regimes, where the republic so to say "existed only within the nobility", in
other words, only the nobles were merited citizens, and where hereditary
positions diminished competition and made virtue less necessary and thus
more rare. The rulers could then more easily become lazy and careless in the
affairs of the state.[26] This form of irresponsible arbitrariness and political neglect
was also one of the meanings of the Swedish concept for licence, *självsvåld*.

For the most part licence was evoked as a casual, indirect accusation
against (unnamed) political opponents and as a warning to the listeners,
independently of the political sympathies of the speaker. *Självsvåld* as a
political insult had been taken into use by the opposition against Count Horn
when criticising the ruling party and was used in the same way throughout
the Age of Liberty by both Hats and Caps, particularly during the political
crises of the 1750s and 1760s. It was also used by Count Fersen in the
speech mentioned above, at the beginning of the Diet of 1769:

> Zeal for Liberty must therefore never degenerate among Us, which
> nevertheless would happen if Liberty was transformed into lawlessness,
> if only the name remained, and was used to the detriment of the Realm
> and private security, and to promote foreign ambitions, and if the Law of
> the Realm became a cover for vengeance, Conceit and the lowest desires.[27]

23 *"Den oskattbara förmån at wara fri, wantrifs i missbruk, och då missbrukas den, när intet
Samwets-Lagen styrcker Riks-Lagarnas tillämpning, och när intet kärlek och wördnad för
Gud och Öfwerheten och en oförfalskad* Patriotisk *nit leda Rådslagen och fästa Besluten."*
[Axel von Fersen], *Landt-Marskalken, Generalens, Riddarens och Commendeurens af Kongl.
Maj:ts Orden, Högwälborne Grefwe Herr AXEL FERSENS Hållne TAL Wid Landt-
Marskalks Stafwens Emottagande Den 22. April 1769*, Norrköping, 1769.
24 On the concepts of virtue, see J. G. A. Pocock, *The Machiavellian Moment*, pp. 37, 75–78;
on Montesquieu and virtue, see also J. G. A. Pocock, *Virtue, Commerce, and History.
Essays on Political Thought and History, Chiefly in the Eighteenth Century*, Cambridge,
1985, pp. 37–50.
25 See Pasi Ihalainen, "Lutherska drag i den svenska politiska kulturen i slutet av frihetstiden.
En begreppsanalytisk undersökning av fyra riksdagspredikningar", in *Riksdag, kaffehus
och predikstol. Frihetstidens politiska kultur 1766–1772*, pp. 85–89.
26 Montesquieu, *De l'esprit des lois*, III, 3, VIII, 5; see also Skinner, *The Foundations of
Modern Political Thought. Volume 1: The Renaissance*, p. 59.
27 *"[…] nit för Frihet bör derföre inom Oss aldrig wanslägtas, hwilket likwäl då ske skulle,
om Friheten förwandlades uti Laglöshet, om blotta namnet wore quar, och nyttjades Riket
och enskylt säkerhet til förfång, och främmande afsigter til befordran, och om Rikets Rätt
blefwo en täckmantel för hämnd, Högfärd och nedriga begjär."* [Axel von Fersen], *Landt-*

When Fersen here spoke about the degeneration of liberty, it was obvious that the vicious enemies were, firstly, the Caps, who were losing power in the Senate and were being accused of having tried to make Sweden an aristocracy. At the same time, the allusion to "foreign ambitions", "vengeance" and "the lowest desire" was a rhetorical trick that allowed the aristocratic Hat politician to partly prevent criticism from the court party against the aristocratic rule of both Hats and Caps in the Senate and the House of Nobility, and to partly address a warning to the less trustworthy persons among his own party's sympathisers.[28]

A more philosophical and erudite view of the inherent threats on liberty can be found in a statement made by Anders Schönberg. His statement from the same weeks of April 1769 contains no less criticism against the outgoing Senate, dominated by the Caps since 1766, which was accused of having delayed the summoning of the Diet when it had become apparent that the party would lose its power.

> It is not to defend the nation against autocracy, when one objects to the summoning of those who constitute the only and reliable defence of liberty. In the Italian states we see examples of how certain persons assumed the defence of their fellow citizens' liberty for such a long time that eventually liberty was gone.[29]

Apparently, Schönberg had been reading Machiavelli and referred to Florence under Savonarola and the Medici, possibly to the aristocratic rule of Milan and Genova, and perhaps also to the developments in the aristocratic republic of Venice in previous centuries. The transition from republic to monarchy in the Italian cities of the Renaissance constituted an efficient historical warning of how liberty could be obliterated when the delicate balance between aristocratic republic and oligarchic tyranny was disturbed.[30]

Thus the notion of licence and the corruption of liberty was particularly well suited for criticism against any "aristocratic rule of lords" (*aristokratiskt herrevälde*) and oligarchic tendencies. At the end of the 1760s it was particularly used by the court party, which was gaining ground at the expense of the Hats. The supporters of the court claimed that the liberty of the Estates, under aristocratic rule, was corrupting into licence.[31] Intimations of indolence,

---

Marskalken, Generalens, Riddarens och Commendeurens af Kongl. Maj:ts Orden, Högwälborne Grefwe Herr AXEL FERSENS Hållne TAL Wid Landt-Marskalks Stafwens Emottagande Den 22. April 1769, Norrköping, 1769.

28 Only some months later, there were fissures inside the Hat party. See Malmström, *Sveriges politiska historia från K. Carl XII:s död till statshvälfningen 1772*, vol. 6, pp. 141–144.

29 "*Det är icke at försvara nationen mot enväldet, när man afstyrcker deras sammankallande, som äro frihetens endaste och säkraste försvar. Uti de italienska stater ser man exempel, huru visse personer så länge åtogo sig at försvara sine medborgares frihet, at omsider frijheten var borta.*" *Sveriges ridderskaps och adels riksdagsprotokoll från och med år 1719*, tjugosjunde delen 1769–1770, I, 22 april–24 oktober 1769, pp. 108–109.

30 On the Italian republics, see Pocock, *The Machiavellian Moment*, pp. 83–330. On Schönberg, see Gunnar Kjellin, *Rikshistoriografen Anders Schönberg. Studier i riksdagarnas och de politiska tänkesättens historia 1760–1809*, Lund, 1952.

31 See Skuncke, "La liberté dans la culture politique suédoise au XVIIIe siècle", pp. 38–40.

arbitrariness and abuse were given moral undertones of all kinds and would during the following century develop into stereotypes such as the decadent aristocrat depicted as cruel, unscrupulous and greedy for power.[32]

Above all, the accusations of licence, directed against the political elite of the Age of Liberty and, as time passed, against the estate rule itself, would be frequently repeated by the monarchistic Swedish history writing during the rule of Gustav III and the nineteenth century.[33] According to Gustav III's political propaganda, Swedish liberty had been lost explicitly because of licence and aristocratic rule, which the king solemny declared to his guard right from the first moment of his *coup* on 19 August 1772. To re-establish the "right", "true", "good" or "durable" liberty after the rule of the Estates was what Gustav III saw as his task.[34]

But let us return to the conceptions of liberty in speeches from the Age of Liberty. Tessin, in his above-mentioned speech from 1747, had declared the danger of licence to be irrelevant. Tessin's speech was intended as a vindication of his own acts, for which reason Tessin did not use the theme as an accusation, but rather regarded it as necessary to deny any inherent menace against liberty. Instead, he pointed at Sweden's free constitution as a model for the rest of the world:

> May the world thus discover that an unlimited licence is not a danger associated with the noble Liberty! And may the Countries and Peoples, which, like we, enjoy its sweet fruits, always have in us worthily esteemed participants and an edifying example![35]

To put forward the moral example and the virtues of a free government was a way to build a defence against licence and degeneration. In order to keep up the political credibility of the regime on a domestic and international level and to exorcise different threats, it was necessary to underline the moral superiority of republican states or states with a free constitution. This moral superiority consisted of the natural frugality, honesty and noble-mindedness

---

32 On the vicious aristocrat in Swedish political discourse and historiography in the eighteenth and nineteenth century, see Carl Arvid Hessler, "Aristokratfördömandet. En riktning i svensk historieskrivning", *Scandia* 15 (1943:2), pp. 209–266. The idea of the supposed immorality of the aristocrat is close to the perceptions and fantasies analysed by Michel Delon in *Le savoir-vivre libertin*, Paris, 2000.

33 See, for instance, Hallberg, *Ages of Liberty*.

34 *"Jag försäkrar härmed, at Mitt enda upsåt är, at åter sätta lugnet i Mitt Kära Fädernesland igienom sielfswåldets förtryckande, Aristocratiske magtens afskaffande och then urgamla Swenska Frihetens uplifwande, samt Sweriges gamla Lagars återställande, som the före 1680 warit."* [Gustav III], *Kongl. Maj:ts Nådiga Försäkran, Til Thess Lif-Garde, Artillerie och samtelige trogne undersåtare här i Residence-Staden Stockholm, Gifwen then 19. Augusti 1772*, Stockholm, 1772. See Alm, *Kungsord i elfte timmen*, pp. 130–153.

35 *"Werlden röne således, at et tygellöst sielfswåld ej är en, then ädla Friheten, widhängande fara! Och the Länder och Folk, hwilka, såsom wi, thess liufwa frukter nyttia, äge städse uti oss wärdt aktade deltagare och et upbyggeligit efterdöme!"* [Carl Gustaf Tessin], *TAL, Til Samtelige Riksens Högloflige Ständer, Af Herr Riks-Rådet, Cantzli-Rådet, Öfwerste-Marskalken och Academiae Cancelleren, Höfwälborne Grefwe CARL GUSTAV TESSIN, Tå Riksens Ständer in Pleno Plenorum uppå Stora Riddarhus Salen woro församlade, then 31. Martii 1747*, Stockholm, 1747.

or magnanimity (*ädelmod*) of free citizens (the classical concept of *virtus* also included magnanimity). These virtues were required for the survival of free societies. The classical models were, in this respect, Sparta and the Roman republic.[36] In Sweden of the eighteenth century, speakers and writers also willingly underlined the good "state of nature" – with its innocence and integrity – in which they considered their own country to have remained in, while more "civilised" states further south were seen as decaying.[37] To boast about Swedish liberty and set it as an example for other peoples was rather commonplace in festive political speeches.[38]

Among the advocates of liberty, Fersen was one who successfully earned a martyr's crown during the following decades, since he contrarily to many other former Hat politicians did not join the supporters of Gustavian rule but rather became an incarnation of the aristocratic opposition so odious to the Swedish monarchy. One of the more remarkable tributes to liberty in the solemn Diet speeches was his speech on 21 October 1756. As the Diet, during which the court had tried to reinforce monarchy, was ending, the Marshal of the Diet, Count Fersen, spoke to the House of Nobility in an exalted, preaching tone, announcing to Sweden and the world what we could call a gospel of liberty:

> It has been and it is our duty to consolidate, with almost unbearable concern, the foundations laid by our in eternal memory honourable and praiseworthy Fathers to the development and happiness of the Fatherland; to protect our glorious laws from violence and infringement; to acquire the confidence of the public for the statutes of the Estates of the Realm; to make liberty a daily and hourly subject of thanksgiving; to propagate the love of it and make this the innate inclination of the entire Society; to defend the sovereignty of the Law; and through such a happiness of Sweden's Inhabitants arouse, in the rest of the world, astonishment at our happiness and respect for our constitutions.[39]

---

36 See, for instance, Skinner, *The Foundations of Modern Political Thought. Volume 1: The Renaissance*, pp. 84–101.

37 See descriptions of the fatherland in Wolff, *Vänskap och makt*, pp. 307–316.

38 Several examples, among them Fersen's speech on 18 October 1755: "*Wördnad och trohet för Öfwerhet och Fädernesland, laglydnad och ömhet för then ädla friheten, hafwa i alla tider, på ett för andra folkslag lysande sätt, utmärkt Swenska Mäns frägd, och befästat thet ährenamn, the sig therigenom, med så mycken billighet förwärfwat.*" [Axel von Fersen], *Til Hans Kongl. Maj:t, Landt-Marskalkens Högwälborne Grefwe AXEL FERSENS TAL, Tå han, med Ridderskapets och Adelens Deputerade, aflade theras underdåniga Hälsning then 18 Oct. 1755*, Stockholm, s.d. [1755].

39 "*Oss har ålegat och åligger at nästan med odrägeligit bekymmer, stadga then grund, wåre, til ewärdeligit åminne, heder[-] och tackwärda Fäder, lagt, til Fäderneslandets upkomst och sällhet; at skydda wåra härliga lagar från wåld och intrång; at förwärfwa Riksens Ständers författningar, allmänhetens förtroende; at giöra friheten til et dageligit och stundeligit tacksäjelse-ämne; at fortplanta thess kärlek och giöra then samma til hela Samhällets medfödda böjelse; at fäkta för Lagens enwälde; och at genom en sådan Sweriges Inbyggares sällhet upwäcka hos then öfriga delen af werlden, förundran öfwer wår lycka och högaktning för wåre författningar.*" [Axel von Fersen], *Landt-Marskalkens högwälborne Grefwe AXEL FERSENS TAL, Hållit Til Ridderskapet och Adelen Wid Landt-Marskalk-Stafwens afgifwande then 21 October 1756*, Stockholm, 1756.

It was no exaggeration to talk about an "unbearable concern" since the Diet had been exceptionally difficult because of the surprising, abortive royal coup, which the Estates suspected had been planned with the support of Prussia.[40] "Violence and infringement" was an explicit reference to these events, which were perceived as an attack on the constitution and the liberty of the Estates. The winners, the radically constitutionalist Hats, still needed to secure public opinion and convert the hesitant to a firm belief in and love for liberty – as Ungern-Sternberg had pointed out the previous year, the broader masses were generally faithful to the king.[41] The tone had become almost religious. After the bloody end of the abortive revolution, the positive speech of the Marshal of the Diet and the final Diet service in the cathedral became a means to, if not reconcile, at least formally patch up and bless the "new" order, in this case the same, old aristocratic system, but ideologically more radicalised, with a stronger grip on power. In addition to the service and sermon that typically ended the Diet, Fersen here took up the part of a kind of chief priest of the republicans, proclaiming thanksgiving and the gospel of liberty after liberty had received its bloody sacrifice.[42]

If we compare Fersen's speech to, for instance, Brahe's from 1752, the ideological escalation appears clearly: where Brahe emphasised the "innate right" of the king, Fersen spoke about the "innate inclination of the entire Society" towards freedom. In one case what mattered was the prerogative of royal authority, in the other the vocation to liberty of the "entire Society".[43] The conception of the origin of law and of the legitimacy of monarchic power thus appears rather divergent in these two examples. Particularly

40 On the events, see Malmström, *Sveriges politiska historia från K. Carl XII:s död till stats-hvälfningen 1772*, vol. 4, pp. 122–236.

41 "*Man wet hwad* impression *hos allmänheten finnes, och hwilken hos Swenska* nationen *länge torde bibehållas, neml. at Konungen är magtägande i alt, och at i gemen fruktas för et Herra Wälde el.* aristocratie. *Skulle derföre Allmänheten af Riksens ständers underdåniga swar få se, at Konungens beslut* dependerar *af* pluraliteten *i* Rådet, *så kunde den gamla impressionen deremot wäcka missnöje och allahanda omdömen.*" RA, Sekreta utskottets protokoll 1755–1756 (I), R 3045, f. 127v–128r (15 December).

42 Bishop Olof Osander's final sermon on 21 October 1756 was, with regard to the circumstances, very unpolitical. [Olof Osander], *Christelig Böne-andakt, Såsom et förträffeligt Wälfärds Medel för alla Swea Barn, och hela Swea Rike, I anledning af Apostelens Pauli Förmaning I Tim. 2:1, 2. Under Hans Kongl. Maj:ts Och Samtelige Riksens Högloflige Ständers närwaro, Wid Riks-Dagens slut den 21 Oct. 1756, Uti En Christelig Predikan I St. Nicolai eller Stockholms Stads Stor-Kyrko, förestäls Af Olof Osander, Biskop i Wexiö*, Stockholm, 1757. On the conservative conceptual apparatus of the sermons, see Pasi Iha-lainen, "Parlamentspredikningarna som medium för officiell politisk teori i England, Holland och Sverige på 1700-talet", *Historisk Tidskrift för Finland*, vol. 88 (2003:2), pp. 225–241; Pasi Ihalainen, *Protestant Nations Redefined. Changing Perceptions of National Identity in the Rhetoric of the English, Dutch and Swedish Public Churches, 1685–1772*, Boston & Leiden, 2005, pp. 74–85.

43 "*Wi lemne med trygghet wår wälfärd uti en Mild Konungs Hand, som afstått medfödd rättighet [...]*"; [Eric Brahe], *Öfwerste-Lieutenantens Högwälborne Grefwe ERIC BRAHES TAL, Hållit på Riks-Salen I Stockholm, När Riksdagen slöts then 4. Junii, 1752*, Stockholm, 1752. The conception that the king himself could have rights had been rejected in a statement by Mindre Sekreta Deputationen, *Betänkande om irriga begrepp rörande regeringsformen*; see Malmström, *Sveriges politiska historia från K. Carl XII:s död till statshvälfningen 1772*, vol. 4, p. 41.

remarkable is the constitutionalism that appears in Fersen's speech, with the reference to "our glorious laws", the constitution that must gain the confidence of the public, and the paradoxical, very striking expression "the sovereignty of the law" (*lagens envälde*; a more elegant translation could be "the supremacy of the law"). For Fersen, the emphasis on legalism was not only a way to stress the illegality of the abortive coup. More than that, it was the very core of his perception of liberty, a view that he shared with many other politicians of the Age of Liberty. The word 'liberty' alone or the enthusiastic proclamation of its gospel could not grant the absence of oppression and abuse. On the contrary, Fersen argued at the Diet in 1769, the term 'liberty' was often used as a cover for treason. As the Polish case had shown, the word alone did not create freedom; only the security of the laws gave liberty its strength.[44] Many aristocratic constitutionalists of the late Age of Liberty would repeat that the letter of the law became a surety for liberty, which was expressed in the all the more common terms "law-bound liberty", *lagbunden frihet*. There was nothing new in this.[45] But the re-emphasising of lawfulness and adherence to the law in the late 1760s may indicate an increased feeling that the constitution was under threat, a fear of anarchy and licence, which also appears in other contemporary sources.[46]

Liberty by law

That liberty should be based on the law was one of the most important political conceptions that were largely shared in Swedish political thought and discourse. The tradition to connect 'law' with 'liberty' went back to the times of Gustav Vasa and the mediaeval provincial law of Uppland.[47] Gustav III was also to build his political propaganda principally on this theme.[48] During the Age of Liberty, the fundamental laws of the realm and their irrevocability and unassailability were seen as the foundations on which Swedish freedom reposed. The fundamental laws were sacred, as they were supposed to follow the "law of nature".[49] Constantly referring to them can be interpreted as typical expressions of a constitutionalism that did not lack republican features.[50]

The law should protect liberty at the same time as it marked its limits, and liberty was thus bound by the law. Definitions of liberty as bound by the laws can be found in Hobbe's, Locke's and Montesquieu's as well as in

---

44 Malmström, *Sveriges politiska historia från K. Carl XII:s död till statshvälfningen 1772*, vol. 6, p. 144. See also *Sveriges ridderskaps och adels riksdagsprotokoll från och med år 1719*, tjugosjunde delen 1769–1770, I, 22 april–24 oktober 1769.
45 See Carlsson, *Olof von Dalin och den politiska propagandan inför "lilla ofreden"*, pp. 222–223, according to which the Caps used the conceptual couple 'law' vs. 'slavery' as a counterweight to the Hat's 'liberty' and 'licence'.
46 See, for instance, Clas Julius Ekeblad's diary 1766–1770, KB, Engeströmska samlingen, vol. I e 14.
47 "*land skall med lag byggas*", 1296. See, for instance, Lagerroth, *Frihetstidens författning*.
48 Alm, *Kungsord i elfte timmen*, pp. 136–137.
49 Fahlbeck, "Studier öfver frihetstidens politiska idéer", *Statsvetenskaplig Tidskrift*, vol. 19 (1916), p. 35.
50 Lagerroth, *Frihetstidens författning*, p. 144.

Swedish eighteenth-century works. According to Montesquieu, "a free people is not the one that has this or that form of government: it is the one that enjoys the form of government established by Law".[51] Montesquieu, whose works contributed to familiarising the Francophone Swedish elite with English political theory (above all Locke) and played a role in the drafting of the Gustavian constitution, also meant that liberty is the ability to do everything permitted by the laws.[52] A rather similar definition can be found in Schönberg's declaration from 1769:

> The liberty of the Swedish people consists in the security that everyone should enjoy in the law, so that one citizen needs not to fear for the other; otherwise it will lead to constraint, party rule and oppression, where the weaker part of those who have the power in their hand will be crushed.[53]

If Montesquieu may have been at hand, Schönberg's explanation also corresponds, to some amount, to the English, "neo-Roman" perception of liberty in the sense that liberty was the absence of fear of constraint, but it differs from it by its emphasis on the common laws and rules of society which prevent a person from abusing his freedom to the prejudice of others and the public.[54] The older idea that liberty needed limits in order not to harm other people is present in Petter Forsskåhl's *Tankar om borgerliga friheten* from 1759.[55]

'Liberty' and the 'Age of Liberty' were of course also the opposites of sovereignty, autocracy and arbitrary oppression. All the more remarkable are the paradoxical terms in which liberty was sometimes paid tribute to. In the most positive way, law-bound liberty was interpreted as a rule of the law, a "sovereignty of the law" as Fersen put it, which was an indirect way

---

51 "A free people is not one that has this or that form of government: it is one that enjoys the form of government established by Law. [...] As, in a corrupted monarchy, the passions of the Prince may become fatal for private persons, in a corrupted republic the faction that dominates can be as furious as an angry prince, and one can read about this in the beautiful passage by Thucydides on the state of diverse republics in Greece." The original goes: "*Un peuple libre n'est pas celui qui a une telle ou une telle forme de gouvernement : c'est celui qui jouit de la forme de gouvernement établie par la Loi [...]. Comme, dans une monarchie corrompue, les passions du Prince peuvent devenir funestes aux particuliers, dans une république corrompue, la faction qui domine peut être aussi furieuse qu'un prince en colère, et on peut voir là-dessus le beau passage de Thucydide sur l'état de diverses républiques de Grèce.*" Montesquieu, "De la liberté politique", *Mes pensées* (631/884, vol. 2, f. 6), éd. Roger Challois, vol. 1, Paris, 1949, pp. 1152–1153. On Montesquieu and Locke in Sweden, cf. Fahlbeck, "Studier öfver frihetstidens politiska idéer", *Statsvetenskaplig Tidskrift*, vol. 19 (1916), p. 121–122.

52 "*La liberté est de faire tout ce que les lois permettent [...].*" Montesquieu, *De l'esprit des lois*, XI, 4.

53 "*Svenska folckets frihet består uti den säkerhet, en hvar uti lagen niuta bör, så at den ene medborgaren ej behöfver frugta för den andre; annars leder det til tvång, partievälde och förtryck, där den svagare delen af dem, som hafva magten i händerne, förkrossas.*" *Sveriges ridderskaps och adels riksdagsprotokoll från och med år 1719*, tjugosjunde delen 1769–1770, I, 22 april–24 oktober 1769, p. 107. On Schönberg and the influence of Montesquieu, see Kjellin, *Rikshistoriografen Anders Schönberg*, pp. 114–123.

54 Cf. Quentin Skinner, *Liberty before Liberalism*, Cambridge, 1998, pp. 59–99.

55 Summarised in Lindberg, *Den antika skevheten*, p. 187.

of stressing the legislative power of the Estates.[56] In other words, power should be based on the law, and the rulers always keep the fundamental laws as their guide. This was, according to Fersen, the condition of a happy, safe, well-organised and equitable society:

> When the King bases his power and the Estates their liberty on law, then the body of the realm gains its right strength and comfort, then the seeds bloom, which have been sowed for the general happiness, and eventually bear for the authorities and the subjects the most delicious fruits, produced on the one hand by justice and fealty, and by obedience and love on the other; then each one enjoys his own right to happiness and security, then concord and mutual confidence are secured, and truth and unity destroy the designs that envy and anger meanly prepare to their own shame and ignominy. [...] May [the Lord of all Kings] make this palace remain, for eternal times, the happy encounter of a mild and just King and subjects free by the law, in immortal memory of a law-bound and blissful rule.[57]

For Fersen, the laws constituted barriers to the arbitrariness of the monarch. For the royalists, they were barriers to the power exercised by the aristocratic Hats or Caps in the Senate. The law could therefore be used as an argument in, for instance, the struggle between the king and the Senate during the first half of the 1750s, when Adolph Frederick argued that he had to follow his conscience and therefore could not ratify the decisions that he disliked.[58] The Senate then claimed that the realm could not be ruled according to the king's conscience, but should be governed according to the law.[59] That the

56 A similar, positive use of the term *envälde* can be found in a speech by Count Eric Gustaf Oxenstierna from the end of the Diet of 1766: "*Om wi här församlade ege alle thet inwärtes witnesbörd, at, under thenne nu til ända skredne Riksdag, endast hafwa arbetat, för Kongl. Maj:ts Lagliga Hög- och Myndighet, Ständers uti dyrt beswurne Grundlagar utstakade Fri- och Rättigheter och hwarje med-undersåtes uti Lagarne utlåfwade beskydd, som jemte förtroende til Lagarne och kärlek för thess rättwise handhafware, bör skapa thet rätta Enwälde öfwer Swenske Män: Om wi alle, säger jag, therpå arbetat, böre wi ock tro, at Allmagten ej tager sin hand ifrån sådane författningar som et för sitt Fosterland wälsinnat folk widtagit.*" [Eric Gustaf Oxenstierna], *TAL, hållit af Grefwelige Brahe-Ättens Fullmäktig, Friherre ERIC GUSTAF OXENSTIERNA til Eka, tå S. T. Herr Landt-Marskalken Stafwen återlemnade. Then 15 Octob. 1766*, Stockholm, s.d. [1766].
57 "*När Konungen grundar dess magt, och Ständerne deras frihet på lag, då vinner rikskroppen dess rätta styrka och trefnad, då blomstra de frön, som till allmän sällhet utsådda blifvit, och bära omsider för öfverhet och undersåtare de härliga frukter, som rättvisa och huldhet å den ena sidan, samt lydnad och kärlek å den andra framalstra; då nyttjar hvar och en dess tillständiga rätt med glädje och trygghet, då befästas samdrägt och inbördes förtroende, och sanning och enighet förstöra de anslag, som afvund och arghet sig sjelf gemenligen til skam och nesa bereda. [...] [Alla Konungars Herre] låte detta palats till evärdeliga tider blifva en mild och rättvis Konungs, och, genom lagen, frie undersåtares glada möte till odödeligt minne af en lagbunden och lycksalig regering.*" [Axel von Fersen], *Landtmarskalk grefve Axel von Fersens tal på rikssalen den 21 Oktober 1756*, in *Sveriges Ridderskaps och Adels riksdags-protokoll från och med år 1719*, nittonde delen 1755–1756, I, 17 Oktober–20 November 1755, Stockholm, 1923, pp. 13–16.
58 Malmström, *Sveriges politiska historia från K. Carl XII:s död till statshvälfningen 1772*, vol. 4, pp. 84–266.
59 This was an anti-absolutist and anti-theocratic view, while older theocratic doctrines underlined that the king's conscience and responsibility in front of God would prevent him

king followed the law and not only his conscience and that he freely had renounced the arbitrary exercise of power was an argument that Gustav III would use to prove that his rule was not autocratic, although the fact that the king himself had dictated the law made this legalism somewhat relative. The same argument – that the law stood before the conscience and that the king could not override the law – was presented by Fersen during the Diets of 1772, 1786 and 1789, but these times he referred to the Gustavian constitution of 1772.[60]

A far-reaching philosophical consequence of this principle was expressed by the periodical *Ärlig Swensk* in February 1755. It subtly claimed that the Estates could not renounce their liberty without violating the consitution of 1720 and by the same revoke their own power, which would invalidate the decision. Neither should the king have overly extensive powers to appoint officials; otherwise he would soon own his subjects' liberty.[61] From this perspective, the Estates were absolutely bound by the constitution, since all steps towards a reinforcement of monarchic prerogative would lead to anarchy, that is, it would do away with all laws and legalty and thus erode the foundations of the Swedish political community. It was a categorical but efficient way of expressing the immobility of the fundamental laws.

When the monarchy tried to hold its own with the Estates and the Senate, the aristocratic speakers of the Diet could disarm it rhetorically and ideologically and grant the Estates a minimum of power by repeating formulas such as "king of a free people" and "king of a free nation". Baron Claes Rålamb spoke at the opening of the Diet of 1765 about "the free and unforced respect of a free People for a mild and caring Dear King, who does not ask us for any constrained submission but a cheerful and willing obedience" and also used the expression "a law-bound care for liberty", which underlined that not ony liberty had been secured by law, but it was also the legal duty of the Dietmen to defend it.[62] In his speech to King Adolph Frederick at the beginning of the Diet in Norrköping 1769, the Marshal of the Diet Count Fersen stated, once more:

> Autocratic Lords must often lack solutions to the most urgent needs, for the will, heart and powerlessness of an oppressed People make the means for the first ones adventurous, and impossible for the latter ones; but a King of a Free Nation, on the contrary, finds his treasure in the Property

from becoming a tyrant. On contemporary theocratic alternatives, see, for instance, Michel Antoine, *Le conseil du roi sous le règne de Louis XV*, Genève, 1970, pp. 6–9.

60 [Axel von Fersen], *Riksrådet och fältmarskalken mm. grefve Fredrik Axel von Fersens historiska skrifter*, utg. R. M. Klinckowström, del I, andra upplagan, Stockholm, 1869, pp. XXI–XXXIV.

61 Malmström, *Sveriges politiska historia från k. Carl XII:s död till statshvälfningen 1772*, vol. 4, p. 111.

62 "*Et fritt Folks fria och okrafde wördnad, för en mild och wårdande Dyr Konung, som ej någon twungen undergifwenhet utan en glad och willig lydna af oss begär*"; "*En lagbunden omsorg om friheten*"; [Claes Rålamb], *TAL, Hållit til Höglofl. Ridderskapet och Adelen, Samt wid Landt-Marskalks Stafwens aflemnande, Af Présidenten och Commendeuren af Kongl. Nordstierne-Orden, Högwälborne Herr Baron CLAES RÅLAMB, Wid Riksdagens början i Stockholm Then 21. Januarii 1765*, Stockholm, s.d. [1765].

of His subjects, they share it of their free will, often beyond their capacity, to serve a Fatherland to which they believe they owe everything, and the rise and improvement of which brings their own [prosperity] in double measures.[63]

A greater glory than to have extended powers was, according to this ideology, to govern a free people. It can here be observed that Fersen talks about "an oppressed People" but "a Free Nation". The "Nation" is here associated with political liberty and honour, while the "powerlessness" of the oppressed people becomes a rhetorical antipode, not to say an antonym for the nation, where the subjects have a will of their own. If the "Nation" here refers to the Diet, we have a double contrast: where the people are oppressed, there is no nation, all the less as there is no Diet, while the liberty of the Swedish Estates makes the Swedish subjects something more than a people, that is, a free nation with a free political will. In Fersen's speech, the nation seems to have a greater conceptual plenitude than only 'people', which is not an explicit synonym for the nation, although Fersen uses terms like "Free Peoples" (*Fria Folckslag*) and "As a Free People they have a Fatherland" earlier in the same speech. Anyway, we have here a rather early and interesting association between the concept of 'nation' and liberty.[64] The idea – which is not without a Christian dimension – that the liberty of the people gave greater honour to the ruler than the glory of extended power was repeated by the Chancellery President, Count Clas Ekeblad, who at the closing of the same Diet in January 1770 spoke, according to the already well-established tradition of the Age of Liberty, on behalf of the monarch: "in the Royal Majesty's mind no honour equals the one of ruling over a free people".[65]

If the law was interpreted by constitutionalist advocates of the liberty of the Estates as a surety for liberty and a barrier against monarchistic claims,

63 "*Enwålds Herrar måste ofta sakna utwägar til de nödigaste behof, ty wilja, hjerta och wanmagt hos et undertrykt Folk, gjör medlen för de förra äfwentyrliga, och för de sednare omöjeliga; men deremot finner en Konung öfwer en Fri Nation, sin skattkammare uti Sine undersåtares Ägendom, de dela den af fri wilja, ofta öfwer sin förmåga, för et Fäderleslands tjänst, åt hwilcket de tro sig alt wara skyldige, och hwars upkomst och förkofran, medförer i fördubblad måtn deras egen.*" [Axel von Fersen], *Til Kongl. Maj:t, Landt-Marskalkens, Generalens, Riddarens och Commendeurens af Kongl. Maj:ts Orden, Högwälborne Grefwe Herr AXEL FERSENS Hållne Underdånige TAL, På Riks-Salen i Norrköping Den 22. April 1769*, Norrköping, 1769.

64 The appearance of the nation as a political subject in a free society does not necessarily mean that the nation is identical with the people or that the entire political community identifies itself with the nation and, like in nationalism, depends on its survival. On 'people' and 'nation' and the political meanings of these concepts, see Lindberg, *Den antika skevheten*, pp. 124–170. For contradictory views consequent to the ethnosymbolist Anthony D. Smith's polemic against Benedict Anderson's classical *Imagined Communities: Reflections on the Origin and Spread of Nationalism*, see, for instance, Jonas Nordin, "I broderlig samdräkt? Förhållandet Sverige–Finland under 1700-talet och Anthony D. Smiths *ethnie*-begrepp", *Scandia* 64 (1998: 2), pp. 195–223; Nordin, *Ett fattigt men fritt folk*, pp. 21–34, and Ihalainen, *Protestant Nations Redefined*, particularly pp. 1–18, which do not refute Smith's principles, and Jussi Pakkasvirta & Pasi Saukkonen (toim.), *Nationalismit*, Helsinki, 2005, which also present more critical views.

65 "*uti Kongl. Maj:ts sinne ingen ära är jämlik emot den, at regera öfwer et fritt folk*"; [Clas Ekeblad], *På Kongl. Maj:ts Wägnar, Herr Riks-Rådets, Cantzelie-Presidentens, Öfwerste*

the concept 'law-bound liberty' could also be interpreted as a liberty *bound* by the law, in fact as a limitation of an excessive freedom that was running the danger of corrupting into licence. This was the royalist view. According to them, liberty should be bound by law so that licence could be restricted.[66] The Gustavian view, partly inherited from the last years of the Age of Liberty, was that the freedom of the Age of Liberty had degenerated into licence and anarchy. Gustav III therefore would claim to have "saved" the "true liberty" and re-established a law-bound liberty in the same way as he presented himself as the "law-bound but sovereign" (*lagbundne men maktägande*) monarch of a "free but law-abiding" people.[67] In the expression "law-bound but potent" (*lagbunden men maktägande*) it becomes obvious how "law-bound" has received the sense of "bound", not "granted": power should be exercised within the pale of the law.

Legalism could in other words become, and became, a means of moderation and control. While liberty, according to a radical reading, was to do everything that was not forbidden by law, under Gustav III gradually everything became forbidden that was not explicitly authorised by law.[68] The possibility of this redescription of liberty had something to do with the obvious change in the purpose of the laws: while the fundamental laws of the Age of Liberty had been dressed as a shield from autocratic oppression, the Gustavian constitution was intended as a safeguard against what was perceived as excessive liberty and unbearable licence. This change in what was considered a political threat also made it possible to construct new conceptual compounds that at first sight may seem absurd or paradoxical, such as the "right liberty" or "liberty and obedience", which all were redescriptions of liberty that contributed to the rooting of an authoritarian ideology.

Marskalkens och Åbo Academiae-Cantzlerens, samt Cantzlerens, Riddarens och Commen-deurens af Kongl. Maj:ts Orden, Högwälborne Grefwe, CLAS EKEBLADS Håldne Tal, Til Riksens Ständer, då Riksdagen slutades, den 30. Januarii 1770, Stockholm, 1770.

66 See, for instance, Brahe's speech to the nobility, where he explains the importance of a law-bound liberty and of the majesty of the authorities in the prevention of excessive liberty: "*En Riddersman må wist wara nögd, tå han, enligit sin Riksdagsmanna rättighet, fått oförkränk upgifwa och framföra, hwad han, til thet allmännas uprätthållande, finner lämpeligast. // Therigenom giöres et rent Samwete tilfyllest, therigenom warnas Efter-kommande, samt upmuntras til en från sielfswåld luttrad frihets rätta förswarande. // Ja, thet är för them säkraste bewis, at Ridderskapets och Adelens ögnamerke warit Rikets uprätthållande, Öfwerhetens tilständiga Höghet, samt frihetens och rättigheters owanskeliga stadfästande, så at magt och myndighet, af Lagbunden frihet understödde, må öka Fäder-neslandets anseende, samt kunna befrämja, så allmän, som enskild wältrefnad.*" [Eric Brahe], *Öfwerste-Lieutenantens Högwälborne Grefwe ERIC BRAHES TAL, Hållit på Riks-Salen I Stockholm, När Riksdagen slöts then 4. Junii, 1752*, Stockholm, 1752.

67 Hallberg, *Ages of Liberty*, pp. 249–250, 258.

68 Nordin, "Frihetstidens radikalism", p. 67.

The right and liberty of the Estates, the liberties and rights of the nation

Let us return to prescribed liberty. "Law-bound liberty" can also be read as liberties granted by the law, which may also imply a certain notion of 'rights'. The shorter Swedish word for "right", *rätt*, could stand for "law" or "legal right", but it could also mean, like the derived form *rättighet*, right in the sense of civil rights or liberties. From the "right and liberty" of the Estates as stated in the constitution of 1720, the idea of certain rights that derived from the state of freedom was gradually extended to a larger political community than the Estates alone.

An example of the use of the term "liberties and rights" can be found in a speech by the Chancellery President of the Cap government, Count Carl Gustaf Löwenhielm, on behalf of King Adolph Frederick at the end of the Diet in 1766:

> [...] as they [the Estates] in all times have given convincing proofs of their respect for the King, their love for the Fatherland, and their affection for the Laws of the Realm, upon which the unaltered persistence of their Liberties and Rights is based.[69]

What did the fundamental laws say about the *citizens'* rights and liberties? By the middle of the eighteenth century, it was by no means particulary revolutionary that the fundamental laws, in the case a state had some, granted the subject certain liberties, privileges or rights. On the contrary, natural law – known in Sweden through the works of Pufendorf – had reinforced the notion of civic liberty and rights.[70] This notion was gradually conceptualised in one of the most conservative and consensualistic media of Swedish political discourse in the Age of Liberty – the ceremonial speeches at the beginning and the end of each Diet. During this process, the concept of 'rights' was extended from having primarily concerned the Estates to include the subjects, in a similar way as 'citizen' would designate other subjects than the Dietmen themselves.

As we have seen in the previous chapter, the concepts 'right' and 'liberty' used in Swedish political discourse could refer both to the privileges of the Estates and to the rights of the subject more generally, thus concerning both the Diet and the realm and its inhabitants as a whole.[71] The refutation of the *principalatsläran* – a theory according to which the Dietmen only received a limited mandate from their electors – signified that the Estates, not the

---

69 "[...] *som the i alla tider gifwit öfwertygande prof af sin wördnad för Konungen, sin kärlek för Fäderneslandet, och sin ömhet om Rikets Lagar, hwarpå theras Fri- och Rättigheters orubbade bestånd är grundadt.*" [Carl Gustaf Löwenhielm], *På Kongl. Maj:ts Wägnar, Herr Riks-Rådets, Cancellie-Présidentens, Academiae-Cantzlerens, Riddarens och Commendeurens, samt Cantzleres af alla Kongl. Maj:ts Orden, Högwälborne Grefwe CARL GUSTAF LÖWENHIELMS Hålldne TAL, Til Riksens Ständer, tå Riksdagen slutades then 15. Octob. 1766*, Stockholm, 1766.

70 See Lindberg, *Den antika skevheten*, pp. 183–184.

71 Lagerroth, *Frihetstidens författning*, pp. 93–94.

people designating them, detained the sovereign political power and thus "were to be considered", as Scheffer put it, "the nation itself".[72]

Many times, the continuously celebrated liberty also seems to have belonged, at least in the minds of the politicians, above all to the Dietmen rather than to any subject of the realm, and further, at the House of Nobility, liberty was mentioned in terms that underlined the liberties of the noble estate.[73] In the meantime, the common formula "rights and liberties of the Estates of the Realm" was expanding to signify the rights of the nation.[74] This was the case in the *Riksakt* of 21 August 1756, where any abolition was described as a "reduction of the liberty and security of the nation":

> The neglect, real or invented, of [certain] persons in [their] offices, has been depicted as the fault of the regime, the legal authority of the Senate has been regarded as an aristocratic authority, leading like autocracy to the oppression of liberty, and the simple-minded have been deluded into considering as an improvement of the Constitution what would only serve the enlargement of the king's power with the loss of the rights of the Estates and consequently a reduction of the liberty and security of the nation.[75]

The *Riksakt* thus implied that a stronger monarchy would not threaten only the Estates but also the "nation". What was at stake, according to the Senate and the sympathising Estates, was the constitution itself and thereby the freedom of the Estates, their rights and the liberty of the country. The liberty and security of the nation was, in other words, presented as the utmost purpose of the Estate rule and of Swedish politics. We have seen what Scheffer understood by "nation": the Estates as the sovereign and inviolable representatives of society. Although this Swedish nation was not explicitly sovereign and there were no equal signs between 'nation' and 'people' as later in, for instance, the case of the first French national assembly, there was the notion of an inviolable nation with certain rights. The concept of 'nation' is many times all the more unclear as it often, as is likely here, referred to the realm, the sovereignty of which was much easier to conceptualise than that of the people.[76]

---

72 "[…] *i Swerige Riksens Ständer äro att anse såsom nationen sjelf*", Lagerroth, "En frihetstida lärobok i gällande statsrätt", pp. 188–189.

73 Diet speeches and minutes abound with this kind of pride.

74 The formula "*Riksens Ständers fri- och rättigheter*" can be found in, for instance, Höpken's speech *På Kongl. Maj:ts Wägnar, Herr Riks-Rådets, Cancellie Praesidentens, samt Riddare och Commendeurens af Kongl. Maj:ts Orden, Högwälborne Friherre ANDERS JOHAN VON HÖPKENS TAL, Hållit uppå Riks-Salen wid Riksdagens början then 21 Octobr. 1755*, Stockholm, *s.d.* [1755].

75 "*Personers förseelser uti ämbeten, grundade eller uppspundne, hafva blifvit afmålade såsom regeringssättets fel, rådets laglige myndighet ansedd för en aristocratisk myndighet, lika ländande till frihetens förtryck som enväldet, och den enfaldigare förledd att räkna för en förbättring af RF., hvad som tjente att öka konungens makt med förlust af ständers rättigheter och följakteligen med minskning af nationens fri- och säkerhet.*" Quoted in Brusewitz, *Frihetstidens grundlagar och konstitutionella stadgar*, pp. 185–186.

76 As an example of this use of the concept 'nation', the dictionary of the Swedish Academy gives the seventeenth-century formula "*Wår Swenske nation, den der altijdh är wahn att regeras af en Konung*" (1650). "Nation", *Svenska Akademiens ordbok* (SAOB), http://g3.spraakdata.gu.se/saob/.

In any case, ideas, although vague, of an inviolable 'right' and 'rights' existed. As the rights or liberties were expanded from the Estates to the nation – particularly if this "nation" was preceded by the adjective "entire" or, as in Scheffer's explanation, was used as an alternative word for 'society' – the notion of civic rights was not distant. At the same time, the concept of 'subject' was giving more and more room to that of 'citizen' in the political language.[77] In 1742 the Chancellery President Count Carl Gyllenborg talked about the liberties and rights of the *subjects* ("to maintain His faithful subjects in their liberties and rights").[78] Ten years later, in front of the Senate, his successor Count Tessin spoke about his affection for his "fellow Citizens' liberty" and the "liberty of Swedish Men".[79]

As in the case of 'nation', we may suppose that by the phrase "[fellow] citizen", the speakers primarily referred to their direct listeners, who were politically active themselves, that is the nobility assembled at the House of Nobility and the other members of the Diet. The people of the realm were not excluded from these concepts, neither were they attributed any active role as citizens in these speeches, but rather treated as a subordinated *familia* of the Estates and the Dietmen.

The task of the Dietman was to ensure that the laws were abided by and the security of the inhabitants of the realm thereby was granted. In this context, in 1762, the Marshal of the Diet, Count Fersen, spoke to King Adolph Frederick about the "protection of the rights of free citizens", using both the concept of 'citizen' and the term "protection", previously generally used with reference to the weaker 'subjects' (cf. the mediaeval concept of *miserabilis personae*) and undefined "people" (*folk*), together:

> The Knighthood and Nobility have for their part, after the best conscience and utmost capability herein tried to do the duty that incumbs to them as Dietmen. The objects of their aims have been the glory of the Name of GOD, the *Gloire* of Your Royal Majesty, the advantage of the Fatherland, the sanctity of the Laws and the protection of the rights of free citizens.[80]

77 Nordin, "Frihetstidens radikalism", p. 65.

78 *"at bibehålla Des trogna undersåtare wid deras Fri- och Rättigheter"*; [Carl Gyllenborg], *På Kongl. Maj:ts Wägnar, Herr Riks-Rådets och Praesidentens i Kongl. Maj:ts och Riksens Cancellie-Collegio, Högwälborne Grefwe CARL GYLLENBORGS Hålne Tal Til Riksens Ständer på Riks-Salen då Riksdagen begyntes den 25. Augusti 1742*, Stockholm, 1742.

79 *"min owanskeliga tro och och nit för min Öfwerhet, samt min med them förknippade ömhet för mine Medborgares frihet"*; *"Ett fritt och nögt Folks wälsignelse ware Eders Kongl. Maj:ts Wård!"*; *"Swenske Mäns frihet"*; [Carl Gustaf Tessin], *Underdånigst Tal Til Hans Kongl. Maj:t, Hållit uti Råds-Salen Then 30. Martii 1752. Af Hans Excellence Herr Riks-Rådet, Cancellie-Praesidenten, Hennes Kongl. Maj:ts Öfwerste-Marskalk, Hans Kongl. Höghets Cron-Printsens Gouverneur, Academiae-Cantzleren, Riddaren, Commendeuren och Cantzleren af Kong. Maj:ts Orden, samt Riddaren af Swarta Örn, Högwälborne Grefwe CARL GUSTAF TESSIN, Tå Hans Excellence af-lade Cancellie-Praesidentskapet*, Stockholm, s.d. [1752].

80 *"Ridderskapet och Adelen hafwa för sin del, efter bästa samwete och yttersta förmåga häruti sökt fullgjöra then them åliggande Riksdagsmanna plikt. Theras upsåt har haft til föremål GUDs Namns ähra, Eders Konl. Maj:ts Gloire, Fäderneslandets båtnad, Lagarnes helgd och fria medborgares rättigheters beskydd."* [Axel von Fersen], *TAL, Til Theras Kongl. Majestäter Och Hans Kong. Höghet Cron-Printsen, Hållne af Landt-Marskalken,*

In addition to equalling 'citizen' with '[free] subject', Fersen's speech has another dimension. To believe it, rights and liberty were the fundaments of a state governed by law, a modern view close to John Locke's rule of law. This view recurs in Fersen's later dialogues with Gustav III, whose politics he opposed.[81] Like many other Swedish politicians of the time, Fersen had studied law, more precisely in Lund in the 1730s, when David Nehrman-Ehrenstråle, Sweden's most important jurist of the time and a dedicated advocator of natural law, worked as a professor there. Natural law, with its contractual theories, had by then conquered the Swedish universities, and Pufendorf was read almost everywhere during the eighteenth century.[82]

We shall return to the Swedish concept of 'citizen' in the next chapter. As for the development of the notion of 'rights', Annabel S. Bratt argues that the idea of civic rights originated in two mediaeval conceptions of rights. According to the first, rights were moral faculties deriving from the existence and prescriptions of the laws. According to the other, rights were to be understood as original liberties, remnants of the original state of liberty that had preceded the social contracts and then been limited by the laws.[83] If the origin of the law is to be considered as a part of the social contract, it was consequently natural that man, by the law, recovered a part of this original freedom in the form of rights. Among the speeches of the Marshals of the Diet, the expression "natural and legal rights" occurs for the first time in a speech by Thure Gustaf Rudbeck at the opening of the Diet in 1765:

> [...] we have the as natural as legal right to, without fearing any principles of persecution, unfeignedly reveal all our shortcomings [...]. Times and people change, but Virtue, Magnanimity and Justice last from Generation to Generation; it is on these supports that the Liberty and Security of Society repose; it is also from these qualities that a Free People takes such advice that makes their Memory immortal to posterity.[84]

The theories of natural law and social contracts also made it possible to conceptualise the rights of both the nation and the people. At the Diet of 1769 both concepts, 'people' and 'nation', were already used in parallel and

General-Lieutenanten och Commendeures af Kongl. Maj:ts Swärds-Ordem, Högwälborne Herr Grefwe AXEL FERSEN Tå Riksdagen slutades i Stockholm then 21 Junii 1762. Såsom ock Tal, hållne wid Landt-Marskalks Stafwens aflemnande, Stockholm, s.d. [1762].

81 See [Axel von Fersen], *Riksrådet och fältmarskalken mm. grefve Fredrik Axel von Fersens historiska skrifter*, utg. R. M. Klinckowström, del I, pp. XXI–XXXIV.

82 See Lindroth, *Svensk lärdomshistoria. Frihetstiden*, pp. 530–542; see also Ingemar Carlsson, *Parti – partiväsen – partipolitiker 1731–43. Kring uppkomsten av våra första politiska partier*, Stockholm, 1981, p. 32.

83 Bratt, "The development of the idea of citizens' rights", p. 100.

84 "[...] *wi äge then så naturliga som lagliga rättigheten, at utan farhoga för persecutions principier, oskrymtadt få uptäcka alla wåra brister* [...]. *Tider och menniskior äro ombytelige, men Dygd, Ädelmod och Rättwisa, warar ifrån Släkte til Släkte; Thet är på thesse grundpelare som Samhällets Fri- och Säkerhet hwilar; Thet är ock af thesse egenskaper som et Fritt Folk hämtar sådane rådslag, som skola göra theras Äreminne odödeligit hos efterwerlden.*" [Thure Gustaf Rudbeck], *Landt-Marskalkens, Öfwerstens och Commendeurens af Kongl. Swärds-Orden, Wälborne Herr THURE GUST. RUDBECKS Håldne TAL, Wid Landt-Marskalks Stafwens emottagande, Then 21 Januarii 1765*, Stockholm, 1765.

almost as synonyms. Olof von Nackreij could thus talk about "a free people, caring for its rights and its laws", while his colleague Lorentz Creutz spoke of "the liberties and rights of the nation, based upon the law" and Carl Magnus Sparrschiöld in the same breath managed to mention both "the right and liberty of the people" and "the liberties and rights of the nation".[85] Thus the concepts of liberty and rights had been explicitly connected to the people as a political actor: the "right and liberty of the Estates" were finally the right and liberty of the Swedish people, and this people a nation with political rights.

Whose liberty?

To whom did liberty finally belong? Was it the liberty of the Estates, the liberty of the free men, the noble liberty, the people's freedom, the nation's liberty or even the king's freedom to chose and rule? In the Swedish political language of the eighteenth century, the concept of 'liberty' was accompanied by a huge amount of various attributes and epithets, which is characteristic of key concepts that gradually lose their flavour and become obscure because of their almost amorphic manifoldness. It is also one of the concepts that no political faction managed to monopolise completely, despite diverse attempts.

Contrarily to many other, more negative concepts such as 'sovereignty' or 'aristocracy', and despite redescriptions and transitions of meaning, 'liberty' in itself never became an insulting word but was almost always associated with virtue and patriotism (the enemies were always those who did not defend liberty). Liberty, like the common good and the fatherland, was thus one of the most community-building concepts in eighteenth-century Sweden, and like *salus publica* it was carved as an adage into the wall of the House of Nobility, to be celebrated by legislators and politicians such as Fersen:

> The God of peace and concord, may he guide our deliberation towards impartiality, patience and mutual confidence, and may he engrave our hearts with the words that have been written above our heads in this temple of liberty: *Pro Patria et Libertate*.[86]

"Right and liberty" and the stressing of the liberty of the legislative Estates resulted in a conceptual assimilation between 'law' and 'liberty', which was

---

85 Nackreij: *"ett fritt folck, ömt om sine rättigheter och sina lagar"*; Creutz: *"nationens i lag grundade fri- och rättigheter"*; Sparrschiöld: *"både konungahögheten och nationens frij- och rättigheter ramla under herraväldet"*; *Sveriges ridderskaps och adels riksdagsprotokoll från och med år 1719*, tjugosjunde delen 1769–1770, I, 22 april–24 oktober 1769, pp. 85, 110–111, 114.

86 *"Fridsens och enighetens Gud, han styre vår överläggning till oveldughet, tolamod och inbördes förtroende och intrycke i våra hjertan de orden, som öfver våra hufvuden i detta frihetens tempel teknade äro:* Pro Patria et Libertate." Fersen at the House of Nobility, 8 November 1755, in *Sveriges Ridderskaps och Adels riksdags-protokoll från och med år 1719*, nittonde delen 1755–1756, I, 17 Oktober–20 November 1755, Stockholm, 1923, pp. 4–5.

the expression of a legalistic view. As far as liberty as a regime was concerned, it became a variety of constitutionalism where the law was used as an argument in the defence of liberty. Correspondingly, legality was used as an argument when liberty was reduced in the name of the eradiction of licence, which during the latter part of the eighteenth century appeared to be a greater danger than sovereignty. From the expression "the right and liberty of the Estates" borrowed from the old constitution of 1634, the concepts of liberty and rights expanded to concern other conceptualised political actors. Among these other, somewhat unspecified actors was the 'nation', which started to be used in new contexts from the 1760s, although there are divergent opinions among researchers on exactly what this concept signified: the realm and the Diet as sovereign bodies, or the people and their representatives.

Some examples that have been quoted here may give the twenty-first-century reader a mistaken impression of modernity or radicalism, which is increased by the presence of elements of natural law. These may contribute to a vague, metaphorical notion of popular sovereignty, which still remains far from evident in the speeches of the Marshals of the Diet or in Scheffer's explanation of the fundamental laws. The question of what is meant by 'people' and 'nation', to what extent these were assimilated concepts and to what extent only words without specific content, would require an analysis of its own.[87]

It is possible to ask whether there was a transition towards a more collective perception of liberty and the political community. At the same time as the concept of 'nation' was being used as a political subject, the citizens' liberty and rights made their appearance in the discourse. That liberties became liberty and the right became rights was a pre-requisite for further transitions. This made it possible for liberty to become the liberty of the nation, and no longer the liberties of the subjects, and for the citizens, not only the Estates, to have rights granted by the law. As liberty was seen as a state or a singular virtue, it was also possible to turn it into an abstraction and provide it with the most contradictory epithets.

---

87 See, for instance, Pasi Ihalainen, "The Sanctification and Democratisation of 'the Nation' and 'the People' in late Eighteenth-Century Northwestern Europe: Proposing a Comparative Conceptual History", *Contributions to the History of Concepts*, vol. 3 (2007:2), pp. 121–151. On 'people', see also Pasi Ihalainen, *Agents of the People*, Leiden & New York, 2009 (forthcoming).

Chapter 3: Citizens and subjects

In the Sweden of the last third of the eighteenth century, virtuous loyalty towards the political community and its values was formulated in the concepts of patriotic zeal (*patriotisk zele/nit*) and patriotism. *Patria* and "patriot", which in the seventeenth century had usually referred to the place of birth and fellow countrymen, were used as moral terms from the beginning of the eighteenth century, as well as the adjective "patriotic". The term "patriotism" (*patriotism(e)*) in its turn appeared around 1760. As a moral and political notion, patriotism was above all associated with a moral sense of duty towards the fatherland. Thus it was strongly associated with the ideal of a virtuous citizen, one that put the interests of the community before his own. During the last decades of the eighteenth century, a Swedish synonym for patriotism was developed in the concept of *medborgerlighet* ("civic spirit", from *medborgare*, "citizen", and the adjective *medborgerlig*, "civic/civil"), which was used with particular reference to the subjects' unconditional loyalty to the regime, which had by then turned monarchical.[1]

Classical patriotism and civic duty were central elements in the political self-image of the nobility. They were associated with virtue, service and duty. To be patriotic or *medborgerlig* was to be a virtuous citizen, in other words, not only to be a member of the political community, a political actor with certain liberties and duties, but also to feel the moral obligations of loyalty and sacrifice that derived from this relation of belonging to a community. The balance between the defence of liberty and the unselfish fulfilment of duty formed the patriotic, civic ideal.

Long before *medborgerlighet* became commonplace in Swedish political discourse, the semantic field of 'citizen' had been developing alongside with those of 'patriotism' and 'fatherland', partly in its Latin version, *civis*, used at the House of Nobility in the seventeenth century and in Swedish academic literature.[2] The concept of 'citizen' was central in the legalist,

---

1 "Patriot", *Svenska Akademiens ordbok* (SAOB), http://g3.spraakdata.gu.se/saob/; Lindberg, *Den antika skevheten*, pp. 116–121; Jakob Christensson, *Lyckoriket. Studier i svensk upplysning*, Stockholm, 1996, pp. 105–169. On the obligations of loyalty inherent to the concept of citizen, see Lindberg, *Den antika skevheten*, p. 111.

2 Lindberg, *Den antika* skevheten, pp. 109–11.

republican perception of the political community, based as it was on a familiarity with Roman authors. In the Roman conception of citizenship, the citizen was characterised by his virtue, which was the essential quality of a courageous man.[3] Morals were essential in politics, not only to prevent corruption, but more generally to permit the defence of common affairs and public interest.[4] The citizens of the ancient city-states were worthy, free men, generally not women, slaves or servants; they were born in the republic or were naturalised subjects of the empire. Provided with moral probity and social credit, they were perceived as honourable persons that could be entrusted with public offices.

In Sweden, the qualities of the citizen applied more or less to all Swedish men – for instance, servants were not formally denied civic qualities, although they were seldom offered participation – and consequently also to all the estates represented at the Diet. Nevertheless, under the influence of attitudes common to the border-crossing European aristocracy, the concept of 'honour' was particularly assimilated and easily monopolised by the nobility, which represented itself as a politically more significant estate than the others and tended to give the concept of *civis* an aristocratic colour.[5]

It was easy for the nobility to perceive and present itself as a class of citizens above others. Courage and value were traditionally put forward as virtues proper of the military order.[6] The habit of underlining noble values was easily married to the Latin tradition practised at the Swedish universities, where the eloquence curriculum aimed at forming rhetorically skilled politicians and administrators for the realm, creating an elite of brilliant political orators capable of arguing in a distinctive fashion.[7] A problem for the nobility, however, was that the neo-Roman conceptions of citizenship that had started to appear in the eighteenth century, together with conceptions of natural law, also included the members of other estates, neglecting birth as a criterion for virtue, prescribing equality in rights and privileges, and thus challenging the aristocratic paradigm in politics.[8] During the eighteenth century, the concept of 'citizen' expanded, partly *via* the concept of 'subject', to increasingly include elements of 'the people'. At the end of the Swedish Age of Liberty, as accusations of aristocratic rule were becoming frequent and commoners realised their capacity for participation, the debate on

---

3 In classical political theory as well as for Montesquieu, civic virtue was particularly characteristic of the citizens of free states or republics. On 'republic' and 'state', see Lindberg, *Den antika skevheten*, pp. 58–65.

4 On morals in politics, see Alasdair MacIntyre, *After Virtue: a Study in Moral Theory*, London, 1985 (1981).

5 On this ideology, see Mark Motley, *Becoming a French aristocrat. The education of the court nobility 1580–1715*, Princeton, 1990. For Sweden, see Englund, *Det hotade huset*. On *civis*, see Lindberg, *Den antika skevheten*, p. 110.

6 Cf. Marisa Linton, *The Politics of Virtue in Enlightenment France*, Basingstoke, 2001, pp. 31–37.

7 Lindberg, *Den antika skevheten*, p. 110; see also Lindroth, *Svensk lärdomshistoria. Frihetstiden*, pp. 572–586.

8 In ancient Rome, too, the senatorial estate was constantly under pressure, and it was not impossible for members of the plebs to ascend the social scale.

privilege gave a deeper dimension to the discussion on citizenship and citizens' rights.[9]

In this chapter, the aim is to examine the nobility's perceptions of citizenship with particular emphasis on the duties derived from bounds of loyalty. Who were the citizens, and what was the extent of their field of action? Which were the qualities, virtues and duties associated with the concept of 'citizen' or the idea of civic behaviour?

The concept of 'citizen'

Aristotle defined the citizen in the strictest sense as not the citizen of a certain place, but a person that "shares in the administration of justice, and in offices". "He who has the power to take part in the deliberative or judicial administration of any state is said by us to be a citizen of that state; and, speaking generally, a state is a body of citizens sufficing for the purposes of life."[10] This definition of citizenship as an empowered, participating subject was the basis of classical republican as well as of democratic perceptions of the citizen. In ancient Rome, citizenship was as much defined by the place, the *civitas*, as by political participation, but as the republic expanded, *cives* were no longer only the inhabitants of the city, but also those of the inhabitants of the larger *patria* that had acquired Roman citizenship. It is to note, however, that this notion of Roman citizenship, despite the universalism of the Roman empire, was always defined through its Romanity. Another feature that should be noted is that the term *cives* originally meant "fellow citizens" before it acquired the primarily political sense that we have grown accustomed to.[11]

The Swedish word that would, during the second half of the eighteenth century, become the established term for 'citizen' was *medborgare*. As Bo Lindberg has shown, there were rival terms as well, which may seem less associated with the idea of active citizenship but nevertheless were long used in parallel almost as synonyms, as 'citizen' was strongly associated with free regimes and republics in particular.[12] The most important of these was *undersåte*, literally "subject" (*subditus*), which did not have a republican connotation and consequently suited the inhabitants of a monarchy.[13] The subject could also be provided with virtues (*undersåteliga dygder*) as well as with duties – although these were perhaps not exactly the same as the ones associated with the citizen – and the concept did not have the depreciative nuance that the term 'subject' would acquire at the very end of

9 Lindberg, *Den antika skevheten*, p. 114; see also Nurmiainen, "Gemensamma privilegier för ett odalstånd. Alexander Kepplerus som borgmästare och samhällstänkare", pp. 171–190.

10 Aristotle, *Politics*, III:1, translation by Benjamin Jowett, published in The Internet Classics Archive, http://classics.mit.edu/Aristotle/politics.html (read 24.1.2007).

11 See Claude Nicolet, *Le métier de citoyen dans la Rome républicaine*, p. 38; Nicolet borrows the history of the term *civis* from Émile Benveniste, *Vocabulaire des institutions indo-européennes*, Paris, 1969. See also Lindberg, *Den antika skevheten*, pp. 111, 113.

12 Lindberg, *Den antika skevheten*, pp. 100–104.

13 Lindberg, *Den antika skevheten*, p. 109.

the eighteenth century, particularly in France. Another substitute for *undersåte* was [*rikets*] *innebyggare*, "inhabitants [of the realm]", which was used to designate the non-active subjects who were not present at the Diet.[14]

An illustrating example of how *undersåte* and *medborgare* were understood as different sides of the same medal is a phrase by Elis Schröderheim in 1789, who stated: "I have always believed wicked citizens to be wicked subjects; their duties must be fulfilled together."[15] This phrase indicates a slight difference between the duties of the politically active and participating citizen and those of the passive, but loyal and deferent subject.

Like the Latin *civis*, the word *medborgare*, related to the term *borgare*, "burgher", seems to have been used in the sense "fellow burghers" before it expanded to "fellow citizens" and finally received the narrower sense of "citizen". In a speech held at the closing of the Diet on 12 September 1743, Count Alexander Matthias von Ungern-Sternberg addressed the burghers' estate as *Eder och Edra medborgare* ("you and your fellow burghers [at home]"). "Fellow citizen" is present in Chancellery President Tessin's speech to the assembled Estates on 14 December 1747, in which he talked about the welfare, growth and prosperity of the realm and the fellow citizens among the Diet members (*Rikets och sine Medborgares wälfärd, tilwäxt och förkofring*). It also appears in Tessin's speech of 30 March 1752 (*mine Medborgares frihet*, "my fellow citizens' liberty") and in Fersen's speech of 21 October 1756, where the lack of confidence between the citizens is mentioned (*misstroende bland medborgare*).[16] A synonymous expression

14 For instance, "*en fri Inbyggares sällhet*": [Clas Ekeblad], *På Kongl. Maj:ts Wägnar, Herr Riks-Rådets, Cancellie-Présidentens, Öfwerste-Marskalkens, Åbo Academiae Cantzlerens, Riddarens, Commendeurens och Cantzlerens af alle Kongl. Maj:ts Orden, Högwälborne Grefwe CLAS EKEBLADS TAL, Hållit uppå Riks-Salen i Stockholm wid Riksdagens början then 24 Januarii 1765, s.l., s.d.* [Stockholm, 1765]; "*Rikets samtelige Inbyggare, Wåre käre Medbröders förmon*": [Carl Fredrich Sebaldt], *TAL, Til Samtelige Rikets Städers Herrar Fullmägtige Hållit af Håf-Rätts-Rådet och Borgmästaren Herr CARL FREDRICH SEBALDT, Tå han, efter slutad Riksdag, afträdde thes Talesmans Embete, then 16 October 1766,* Stockholm, *s.d.* [1766].

15 "*Jag har alltid trott elaka medborgare vara elaka undersåtare, deras pligter måste gemensamt uppfyllas.*" Brev till Gustaf III från statssekreterare Schröderheim, 1789, LUB, DelaGardieska samlingen, historiska handlingar, vol. 22:2.

16 [Matthias Alexander von Ungern-Sternberg], *Landt-Marskalkens Högwälborne Baron MATTHIAS ALEXANDER Von UNGERN STERNBERGS TAL, Hållit på Riks-Salen I Stockholm, När Riksdagen slöts then 12. September 1743,* Stockholm, *s.d.* [1743]; [Carl Gustaf Tessin], *På Kongl. Maj:ts Wägnar, Herr Riks-Rådets, Praesidentens uti Kongl. Maj:ts och Riksens Cancellie Collegio, Öfwerste-Marskalkens hos Theras Kongl. Högheter, Och Åbo Academiae Cancellerens Högwälborne Grefwe CARL GUSTAV TESSINS Hållne TAL, Til Riksens Ständer, tå Riksdagen slutades then 14. December 1747,* Stockholm, *s.d.* [1747]; [Carl Gustaf Tessin], *Underdånigst Tal Til Hans Kongl. Maj:t, Hållit uti Råds-Salen Then 30. Martii 1752. Af Hans Excellence Herr Riks-Rådet, Cancellie-Praesidenten, Hennes Kongl. Maj:ts Öfwerste-Marskalk, Hans Kongl. Höghets Cron-Printsens Gouverneur, Academiae-Cantzleren, Riddaren, Commendeuren och Cantzleren af Kong. Maj:ts Orden, samt Riddaren af Swarta Örn, Högwälborne Grefwe CARL GUSTAF TESSIN, Tå Hans Excellence af-lade Cancellie-Praesidentskapet,* Stockholm, *s.d.* [1752]; [Axel von Fersen], *Landt-Marskalkens högwälborne Grefwe AXEL FERSENS TAL, Hållit Til Ridderskapet och Adelen Wid Landt-Marskalk-Stafwens afgifwande then 21 October 1756,* Stockholm, *s.d.* [1756].

for *medborgare* meaning "fellow citizens" was the fraternal *medbröder*, "fellow brothers", which was frequently used. We can find it, for instance, in another speech by Fersen on 21 October 1756 ("their fellow Brothers, the other respective Estates").[17]

Medborgare in the narrower sense of *civis*, long translated as *borgare* alone, started to appear in the 1760s, like so many other modern forms of Western European political concepts.[18] On 21 June 1762, in the closing address to the Royal Family at the end of the Diet, the Marshal of the Diet, Count Fersen, talked about the duties of each Diet member to work for "the glory of the Name of GOD, the *Gloire* of Your Royal Majesty, the advantage of the Fatherland, the sanctity of the Laws and the protection of the rights of free citizen".[19]

It is interesting to note that this new concept of the citizen as a political subject often appeared together with the concept of 'rights' (civic rights). This association, "the citizens' rights", can also be found in speeches by Fersen's rival from the Cap party, Thure Gustaf Rudbeck, a couple of years later (*Medborgarnas rättigheter*).[20] Even so, we can still find an example of the older meaning of *medborgare* as "fellow citizen" combined with the idea of civic rights. Baron Eric Gustaf Oxenstierna used the older concept *undersåte* provided with the prefix *med-* in *medborgare* when mentioning "the protection promised by the Law to each fellow subject" (*hwarje med-undersåtes uti Lagarne utlåfwade beskydd*).[21]

While the pre-eminence of the nobility over other estates and the pre-eminence of the aristocracy over other noblemen were often underlined in political documents during the first half of the seventeenth century, this had changed by the middle of the eighteenth century. At the beginning of the Age of Liberty, conflicts of precedence between the old aristocracy and the families of low or younger nobility at the House of Nobility led to the defeat of the old aristocracy, which also had lost many positions of influence to a

17 *"theras Medbröder, the öfrige Respective Stånden"*; [Axel von Fersen], *Landt-Marskalkens högwälborne Grefwe AXEL FERSENS TAL, Tå han Å Ridderskapets och Adelens wägnar, tog Afsked af the andre Respective Stånden, På Riks-Salen, Then 21 Octob. 1756*, Stockholm, *s.d.* [1756].

18 On *Borgare* and *medborgare*, see Lindberg, *Den antika skevheten*, p. 112.

19 *"Guds namns ähra, Eders Kongl. Maj:ts gloire, Fäderneslandets båtnad, Lagarnes helgd och fria medborgares rättigheters beskydd"*; [Axel von Fersen], *TAL, Til Theras Kongl. Majestäter Och Hans Kongl. Höghet Cron-Printsen, Hållne af Landt-Marskalken, General-Lieutenanten och Commendeures af Kongl. Maj:ts Swärds-Ordem, Högwälborne Herr Grefwe AXEL FERSEN Tå Riksdagen slutades i Stockholm then 21 Junii 1762. Såsom ock Tal, hållne wid Landt-Marskalks Stafwens aflemnande* (Stockholm *s.d.* [1762]).

20 [Thure Gustaf Rudbeck], *Landt-Marskalkens, Öfwerstens och Commendeurens af Kongl. Swärds-Orden, Wälborne Herr THURE GUST. RUDBECKS Håldne TAL, Wid Landt-Marskalks Stafwens emottagande, Then 21 Januarii 1765*, Stockholm, 1765; [Thure Gustaf Rudbeck], *TAL, til Ridderskapet och Adelen, af Landt-Marskalken General-Majoren och Commendeuren af Kongl. Maj:ts Swärds-Orden, Wälborne Herr THURE GUSTAF RUD-BECK, wid Landt-Marskalks Stafwens nedläggande, then 15. Octob. 1766, s.l., s.d.* [Stockholm, 1766].

21 [Eric Gustaf Oxenstierna], *TAL, hållit af Grefwelige Brahe-Ättens Fullmäktig, Friherre ERIC GUSTAF OXENSTIERNA til Eka, tå S. T. Herr Landt-Marskalken Stafwen åter-lemnade. Then 15 Octob. 1766*, Stockholm, *s.d.* [1766].

new aristocracy of capable administrators during the period of Caroline absolutism. As virtue or merit finally, by the beginning of the 1740s, had won over birth, the idea of virtue and merit was gradually integrated into noble self-perception. Above all, the Estates' desire to avoid a return to the strong aristocratic influence in the politics of the middle of the seventeenth century had made anti-aristocratism a consensual feature of Swedish political discourse.[22]

As a consequence of these anti-aristocratic tendencies, by the second half of the eighteenth century the concept of *medborgare*, at least in the sense of "fellow subject" and "fellow citizen", could be used for members of any estate. Nevertheless, this apparent equality between the estates did not exclude that some citizens could be perceived as citizens in a deeper sense than others. The ways the concept of *medborgare* was used in Diet speeches to underline the value and cohesion of the Estates seem to suggest that the civic virtues inherent in the concept were particularly characteristic of the Estates and their representatives at the Diet, which stood above the other subjects and the common people of the realm.[23]

It was also possible to put forward one active citizen and suggest that he stood, by his virtues, above all of the members of the Diet as the foremost citizen of the fatherland. In October 1761, C. F. Meijerfeldt congratulated Fersen on his nomination to the office of Marshal of the Diet, stating that he would now "become the first Citizen of his fatherland".[24] This concept of the first citizen of the state went back to the Roman honour *princeps senatus*, the first member by precedence of the Roman senate, who was chosen among the patrician senators of consular rank. The *princeps senatus* should have an impeccable political record. Having the right to speak first, he eventually received the prerogatives of a presiding magistrate. In the Sweden of the Age of Liberty, the parallel between the presidency over the Swedish Diet and the presidency of the Roman senate was rather obvious. It was a typical classical reference amidst the politicians of the Age of Liberty, who had studied the classics and were imbibed with republicanism (cf. the translation of the old Council of the Realm into *Senate*, described in chapter one).

This idea of a *primus inter pares* was also repeated by the monarchs, such as the honour *princeps* that with the end of the Republic was transferred to the emperor (*princeps senatus*, *princeps civitatis*, and shortly, *princeps*, from which has derived the word "prince"). Subordinating the power of the *princeps* to the reason of state, King Frederick II of Prussia called himself "the first servant" (*premier domestique*) of the state in his *Antimachiavel* of

22 Valentin, *Frihetstidens riddarhus*, pp. 1–96; Englund, *Det hotade huset*, p. 29–30. The anti-aristocratic tendency at the House of Nobility was called *riddarhusdemokrati* by Valentin. On virtue and noble self-perception, see Motley, *Becoming a French Aristocrat*. On the necessity of virtue, see also Matti Klinge, "Télémaques budskap i Sverige", *Det roliga börjar hela tiden. Bokförläggare Kjell Peterson 60 år den 20 december 1996*, Stockholm, 1996, pp. 149–151.

23 See previous chapter and Charlotta Wolff, "Pro Patria et Libertate. Frihetsbegreppet i 1700-talets svenska politiska språk", *Historisk Tidskrift för Finland*, vol. 92 (2007:1), pp. 34–62.

24 "*Je vous felicite de grand cœur seigneur de l'honneur & du bonheur que vous allés avoire aujourd'hui à devenir Le premier Citoyen dans vôtre patrie.*" Carl Fredrik Meijerfeldt to Fersen, 6 October 1761, RA, Stafsundsarkivet, Axel von Fersen d.ä.:s arkiv, vol. 7.

1740, a critical treaty on Machiavelli's *Il principe*.[25] Gustav III of Sweden called himself "the first citizen" of a free people in his speech at the opening of the Diet on 25 June 1771 and again, on the morning of the royal revolution of 19 August 1772, when making a formal disavowal of "the abominable royal absolutism or the so-called Sovereignty, which would deprive me of my utmost honour to be the first citizen of a righteous free people".[26]

In other words, although the use of the concept of 'citizen' was enlarged in the second half of the eighteenth century to include members of the political community other than those who actually were involved in state-level politics, this did not necessarily imply an egalitarian understanding of the concept as in the modern democratic notion of citizenship as membership in a nation. On the contrary, in the eighteenth century as in earlier times, significant hierarchic, honorific and functional distinctions were made between citizens, some of which were elevated above and before the others. Neither did the concepts of citizen and citizenship contain any particularly democratic premises; even princes called themselves (the first) citizens. The terms sprang from classical republican conceptions of a civic ideal, but it would be a mistake to interpret these ideals as applicable to democratic – or aristocratic – republics only.

Civic virtues and the duties of the citizen

As demonstrated above, the concept of *medborgare* in the sense of an active political citizen was not used in public speech acts by the Swedish nobility until the mid-1760s. This does not mean, however, that the notion of civic behaviour and of the citizen as an active subject had not existed before the concept was used in this sense (in addition, there was always the Latin term *civis*, which filled this conceptual gap for the elite). In Diet speeches of the second half of the Age of Liberty, Swedish politicians described the ideal citizen through the virtues and duties attached to worthy or honest and free (*redelige och frie*) Swedish men and Diet members, following a model established by Cicero's *De officiis*. These descriptions of the qualities attached to 'citizen' complete the semantics of a term in itself yet unstable and slightly unspecific.

On one hand, the political duties and virtues expected from the active citizens derived from their responsibilities in common affairs and public

---

25 Theodor Schieder, *Friedrich der Grosse. Ein Königtum der Widersprüche*, München, 1983, p. 106.

26 *"Född och upfödd ibland Eder, har jag alt ifrån de spädaste åren lärt, at älska mit Fäder-nesland, at anse för den största lycka, at wara Swensk, och den största Ära, at wara den förste Medborgaren ibland et Fritt Folk."* [Gustav III], *Hans Kongl. Maj:ts Tal, Til Riksens Ständer Uppå Riks-Salen Wid Riksdagens början Den 25 Junii 1771*, Stockholm, 1771; *"Jag afsäger mig nu, som Jag redan thet giordt, thet förhateliga Konungsliga Enwäldet, eller then så kallade Souverainiteten, anseende nu som förr, för Min största ära, at wara then förste Medborgaren ibland et rättskaffens fritt Folk: Så sant Mig Gud hielper til Lif och Själ."* [Gustav III], *Kongl. Maj:ts Nådiga Försäkran, Til Thes Lif-Garde, Artillerie och samteliga trogne undersåtare här i Residence-Staden Stockholm, Gifwen Then 19. Augusti 1772, s.l., s.d.* [Stockholm, 1772].

offices. In this sense, particularly the Dietman was perceived as a citizen who should be of utmost moral quality. It was the citizen's duty to oversee the fulfilment of and respect for the law. Particularly, it was the task of every Dietman to supervise how the fundamental laws were followed as well as the doings of the Senate, if necessary through a legal commission.[27] Reading the complaints of the subjects was part of these obligations. Of course, there were also writings on the duties of the Dietmen.[28]

On the other hand, civic virtues and duties were precisely a moral matter. Which desirable virtues and ideals were associated with the idea of the politically active citizen? Diet speakers rather rarely made direct political use of the term for virtue, *dygd*, but the words used to express the moral qualities of a person in charge of political matters were all the more frequent. Tessin, in 1747, expressed the wish "may virtue be a common cause",[29] and Fersen, in October 1760, talked about "knightly virtues".[30] In addition to the notion of political virtue, the Swedish term *dygd* contained, above all, a strong connotation of (sexual) morality and self-constraint.[31]

A frequent political synonym for "virtuous" was *redelig*, "honest" with nuances of "worthy", "capable" and "honourable". This was one of the most frequent terms in solemn speeches. For instance, in 1743, the Marshal of the Diet Ungern-Sternberg used the expression "honest Diet member".[32] "To be an honest Swedish man" was the most important quality of decision-makers, and *redelige Swenske män* the most common metaphor for virtuous citizen.[33]

27 RO 1723, art. 13, in Brusewitz, *Frihetstidens grundlagar och konstitutionella stadgar*, pp. 240–241.

28 See e.g. *En Ärlig Riksdags-Mans Syldigheter* [sic], Uppsala 1769, and *Tankar Huru en Riksdags-Man Bör Utöva Sina Öma Pligter Emot Medborgare och Fädernesland*, Stockholm, 1769.

29 "*Dygden må wara allmän sak, och blifwe allmänt hägnad!*"; [Carl Gustaf Tessin], *TAL, Til Samtelige Riksens Högloflige Ständer, Af Herr Riks-Rådet, Cantzli-Rådet, Öfwerste-Marskalken och Academiae Cancelleren, Högwälborne Grefwe CARL GUSTAV TESSIN, Tå Riksens Ständer in Pleno Plenorum uppå Stora Riddarhus Salen woro församlade, then 31. Martii 1747*, Stockholm, 1747.

30 "*Ridderliga dygder*"; [Axel von Fersen], *Landt-Marskalkens, General-Lieutenantens och Commendeurens af Kongl. Swärds-Orden, Högwälborne Herr Grefwe AXEL FERSENS Håldne TAL, Wid Landt-Marskalk Stafwens emottagande, Then 20 October 1760*, Stockholm, s.d. [1760].

31 This too, however, could be a political virtue. Chancellery President Clas Ekeblad, in 1762, mentioned "pure manners" (*rena seder*) among the qualities of the assembled Swedish political community. [Clas Ekeblad], *På Kongl. Maj:ts Wägnar, Herr Riks-Rådets, Cancellie-Présidentens, Öfwerste-Marskalkens och Åbo Academiae Cantzlerens, samt Cantzlerens, Riddarens och Commendeurens af Kongl. Maj:ts Orden, Högwälborne Grefwe CLAS EKEBLADS Håldne TAL, Til Riksens Ständer, tå Riksdagen slutades then 21. Junii 1762*, s.l., s.d. [Stockholm, 1762].

32 "*ärlig Riksdagsman*"; [Matthias Alexander von Ungern-Sternberg], *Landt-Marskalkens Högwälborne Baron MATTHIAS ALEXANDER Von UNGERN STERNBERGS Tal, Hållit wid slutet af 1743 års Rikdsdag Tå Riksens Ständer togo afsked af hwar annan på Riks Salen*, Stockholm, s.d. [1743].

33 E.g. Tessin: "*at wara en redelig Swensk man*"; [Carl Gustaf Tessin], *TAL, Til Samtelige Riksens Högloflige Ständer, Af Herr Riks-Rådet, Cantzli-Rådet, Öfwerste-Marskalken och Academiae Cancelleren, Högwälborne Grefwe CARL GUSTAV TESSIN, Tå Riksens Ständer in Pleno Plenorum uppå Stora Riddarhus Salen woro församlade, then 31. Martii 1747*, Stockholm, 1747. On the concept of *dygd*, see, for instance, Leif Runefelt, *Dygden som välståndets grund. Dygd, nytta och egennytta i frihetstidens ekonomiska tänkande*, Stockholm, 2005, pp. 25–27.

The noun *redlighet* and its adjective *redelig* contained the idea of integrity, which could also be expressed by terms like "probity" (*rättrådighet*), "impartiality" (*oväldughet*), "justice" (*rättwisa*), "honesty" (*ärlighet*) and "truth" (*sanning*). In a political culture that traditionally valued concord and unity, parties and factions – although a part of everyday political life – were seen as negative phenomena that signalled moral decay.[34] It is probably not a coincidence that impartiality seems to have been particularly stressed during the period of the harshest party struggles in the 1760s, as, for example, in speeches by Chancellery President Count Clas Ekeblad and Baron Eric Gustaf Oxenstierna.[35] To advocate impartiality, honesty and truth was a way of exorcising the fatal "party spirit".

Among the personal qualities required for the exercise of this kind of virtue were prudence (*försiktighet*), wisdom (*wishet*), discernment (*insigt*), intelligence (*urskillning*) and knowledge (*witterhet*). These qualities were often enumerated in an admonishing way. Ungern-Sternberg, in 1743, listed probity, knowledge and bravery among the qualities of Swedish Dietmen.[36] Tessin, in a long list of positive qualities of the Dietmen of 1752, mentioned "truth and honesty", "a pure conscience, zeal, faith, honesty, intelligence, wisdom, prudence, constancy, justice, gentleness, concord, capacity and efficiency".[37] According to Fersen in 1760, political virtues, particularly of the noble estate, were discernment, constancy and love for "the Common" (*thet Allmänna*), which could be translated as "the public interest" or "the common good".[38]

---

34 Cf. Ihalainen, "Lutherska drag i den svenska politiska kulturen i slutet av frihetstiden. En begreppsanalytisk undersökning av fyra riksdagspredikningar", pp. 73–89; see also Pasi Ihalainen, *The Discourse on Political Pluralism in Early Eighteenth-Century England. A Conceptual Study with Special Reference to Terminology of Religious Origin*, Helsinki, 1999, pp. 159–228.

35 "*owäldughet och inbördes kärlek*"; [Clas Ekeblad], *På Kongl. Maj:ts Wägnar, Herr Riks-Rådets, Cancellie-Présidentens, Öfwerste-Marskalkens och Åbo Academiae Cantzlerens, samt Cantzlerens, Riddarens och Commendeurens af Kongl. Maj:ts Orden, Högwälborne Grefwe CLAS EKEBLADS Håldne TAL, Til Riksens Ständer, tå Riksdagen slutades then 21. Junii 1762, s.l., s.d.* [Stockholm, 1762]. "*Enighet, Owäldughet, agtning för Lagarne och afsikt på Allmänna bästa*"; [Eric Gustaf Oxenstierna], *TAL, hållit af Grefwelige Brahe-Ättens Fullmäktig, Friherre ERIC GUSTAF OXENSTIERNA til Eka, tå S. T. Herr Landt-Marskalken Stafwen återlemnade. Then 15 Octob. 1766*, Stockholm, s.d. [1766].

36 "*Rättrådighet, witterhet och tapperhet*"; [Matthias Alexander von Ungern-Sternberg], *Landt-Marskalkens Högwälborne Baron MATTHIAS ALEXANDER Von UNGERN STERNBERGS Tal, Hållit för Ridderskapet och Adeln Wid Landt-Marskalks-Stafwens afgifwander Then 12. September 1743*, Stockholm, s.d. [1743].

37 "*sanning och redlighet*","*et godt Samwete, Nit, Tro, Redlighet, Urskillning, Wishet, För-sicktighet, Ståndacktighet, Rättwisa, Warkunsamhet, Enighet, Drift och Wärkställighet*"; [Carl Gustaf Tessin], *Underdånigst Tal Til Hans Kongl. Maj:t, Hållit uti Råds-Salen Then 30. Martii 1752. Af Hans Excellence Herr Riks-Rådet, Cancellie-Praesidenten, Hennes Kongl. Maj:ts Öfwerste-Marskalk, Hans Kongl. Höghets Cron-Printsens Gouverneur, Academiae-Cantzlaren, Riddaren, Commendeuren och Cantzleren af Kong. Maj:ts Orden, samt Riddaren af Swarta Örn, Högwälborne Grefwe CARL GUSTAF TESSIN, Tå Hans Excellence af-lade Cancellie-Praesidentskapet*, Stockholm, s.d. [1752].

38 "*Insigt, ståndaktighet, och kärlek för thet Allmänna*"; [Axel von Fersen], *Landt-Marskalkens, General-Lieutenantens och Commendeurens af Kongl. Swärds-Orden, Högwälborne Herr Grefwe AXEL FERSENS Håldne TAL, Wid Landt-Marskalk Stafwens emottagande, Then 20 October 1760*, Stockholm, s.d. [1760]. On the concept of *Allmänna*, see Hallberg, *Ages of Liberty*, and Nurmiainen, *Edistys ja yhteinen hyvä vapaudenajan ruotsalaisessa poliittisessa kielessä*.

78

Some virtues that were often mentioned in Swedish political texts appear more timeless, remaining important throughout the Age of Liberty despite the ideological radicalisation perceptible in other concepts. These were the fear of God, the subject's respect for his rulers and pure manners. A very traditional way to express attachment to the crown and the community was to pray for the authorities or for the rulers and the motherland. Such manifestations of loyalty through prayer or praise were mentioned at the beginning or end of so many speeches that they seem to have been carried on, as commonplaces, by tradition without being particularly digressed upon. They rather tended to be less and less emphasised towards the second half of the Age of Liberty, and their formal role was more and more taken over by the institutionalised divine services at the beginning and end of each Diet.[39]

Less religious and more rationalised eighteenth-century terms for the citizen's loyalty and commitment to the political community were faith (*tro*), constancy (*ståndacktighet*), abidance by the laws (*laglydighet*) and zeal (*nit*). Faith, obedience and zeal were closely related concepts, associated with being law-abiding and fulfilling the duties of a virtuous subject towards his rulers or the political community.

Obedience and zeal for the authorities was not seen as incompatible with the Swedish ideal of liberty, quite the contrary. As honesty and integrity of mind should characterise a good citizen, submission to common ideals and loyalty towards the formal institutions of the regime were also part of civic virtue. As Tessin stated in 1752, "a faithful subject who quietly does his duty and sings the deserved praise of his King, contributes in his way to common happiness".[40] Another speaker, the Marshal of the Diet Thure Gustaf Rudbeck of the Cap party, stated in 1765 that "willing obedience" was always "the distinctive feature of good citizens".[41]

This zeal to obey and execute was understood positively as a fervent desire to construct or defend something, in political discourse generally a common ideal, which in the middle of the eighteenth century often was liberty. From the middle of the century, the term was more and more often used in the expression "patriotic zeal" (*patriotisk nit*) or the perhaps more established version "zeal for the Fatherland" (*nit för Fäderneslandet*).[42]

39 The Diet sermons analysed by Pasi Ihalainen are other examples of a category of sources full of commonplaces, the function of which was to reassure the listeners of the speaker's sincerity. Cf. Ihalainen, *Protestant Nations Redefined*.
40 "*En trogen undersåte, som sin plickt, i stillhet upfyller, och sin Konungs förtienta låf utbreder, bidrager, efter sitt mått, til allmän sällhet.*" [Carl Gustaf Tessin], *Underdånigst Tal Til Hans Kongl. Maj:t, Hållit uti Råds-Salen Then 30. Martii 1752. Af Hans Excellence Herr Riks-Rådet, Cancellie-Praesidenten, Hennes Kongl. Maj:ts Öfwerste-Marskalk, Hans Kongl. Höghets Cron-Printsens Gouverneur, Academiae-Cantzleren, Riddaren, Commendeuren och Cantzleren af Kong. Maj:ts Orden, samt Riddaren af Swarta Örn, Högwälborne Grefwe CARL GUSTAF TESSIN, Tå Hans Excellence af-lade Cancellie-Praesidentskapet*, Stockholm, *s.d.* [1752].
41 "*then williga lydnad, som alltid är goda medborgares kännemärke*"; [Thure Gustaf Rudbeck], *Landt-Marskalkens, Öfwerstens och Commendeurens af Kongl. Swärds-Orden, Wälborne Herr THURE GUST. RUDBECKS Håldne TAL, Wid Landt-Marskalks Stafwens emottagande, Then 21 Januarii 1765*, Stockholm, 1765.
42 Cf. Fersen's statement from 1756, concerning liberty and its natural limits: "The inestimable benefit of being free thrives badly on abuse, and it is abused when the Law of Conscience

79

To be zealous necessitated, and in the case of the nobility supposed, qualities such as courage, bravery and manliness (*tapperhet, mandom*). Other words for the desirable zeal to advance common interests were diligence (*flit*), ardour (*drift*), assiduity and effectiveness (*wärkställighet*).[43]

Ungern-Sternberg, in 1743, talked about the "faithful zeal" of Diet members.[44] He also mentioned abidance by the law, concord, mutual confidence between citizens and inclination towards general prosperity.[45] Good intentions and personal reasons for promoting certain matters should not be a reason for citizens to forget that these matters should be of public interest. Almost every more extensive Diet speech contained references to the common good, general prosperity or "the Common" (*det Allmänna*). Persons speaking from a position of authority also paternally exhorted the members of the Diet to mutual confidence, love, affection, gentleness, friendship, concord and unity. Oxenstierna mentioned concord, impartiality,

---

does not confirm the application of the Laws of the Realm, and when love and reference for God and the Authorities as well as an unfeigned *Patriotic* zeal do not guide the Deliberations and consolidate the Decisions." – "*Den oskattbara förmån at wara fri, wantrifs i missbruk, och då missbrukas den, när intet Samwets-Lagen styrcker Riks-Lagarnas tillämpning, och när intet kärlek och wördnad för Gud och Öfwerheten och en oförfalskad* Patriotisk *nit leda Rådslagen och fästa Besluten.*" [Axel von Fersen], *Landt-Marskalken, Generalens, Riddarens och Commendeurens af Kongl. Maj:ts Orden, Högwälborne Grefwe Herr AXEL FERSENS Hållne TAL Wid Landt-Marskalks Stafwens Emottagande Den 22. April 1769*, Norrköping, 1769.

43 "*mandom och tapperhet*": [Thure Gustaf Rudbeck], *TAL, til Ridderskapet och Adelen, af Landt-Marskalken General-Majoren och Commendeuren af Kongl. Maj:ts Swärds-Orden, Wälborne Herr THURE GUSTAF RUDBECK, wid Landt-Marskalks Stafwens nedläggande, then 15. Octob. 1766, s.l., s.d.* [Stockholm, 1766]; "*tapperhet emot Rikets fiender*", "*flit och oförtrutenhet*": [Clas Ekeblad], *På Kongl. Maj:ts Wägnar, Herr Riks-Rådets, Cancellie-Présidentens, Öfwerste-Marskalkens och Åbo Academiae Cantzlerens, samt Cantzlerens, Riddarens och Commendeurens af Kongl. Maj:ts Orden, Högwälborne Grefwe CLAS EKEBLADS Håldne TAL, Til Riksens Ständer, tå Riksdagen slutades then 21. Junii 1762, s.l., s.d.* [Stockholm, 1762]; "*then nitfulla drift och the utmärkte böjelser för frihet, för mandom, dygd och wett, som befästa et utmattadt Fädernesland och äro Swenske-Ridders Mäns yppersta Sköldemärken*": [Axel von Fersen], *TAL, Til Theras Kongl. Majestäter Och Hans Kongl. Höghet Cron-Printsen, Hållne af Landt-Marskalken, General-Lieutenanten och Commendeures af Kongl. Maj:ts Swärds-Ordem, Högwälborne Herr Grefwe AXEL FERSEN Tå Riksdagen slutades i Stockholm then 21 Junii 1762. Såsom ock Tal, hållne wid Landt-Marskalks Stafwens aflemnande,* Stockholm, s.d. [1762]; "*Drift och Wärkställighet*": [Carl Gustaf Tessin], *Underdånigst Tal Til Hans Kongl. Maj:t, Hållit uti Råds-Salen Then 30. Martii 1752. Af Hans Excellence Herr Riks-Rådet, Cancellie-Praesidenten, Hennes Kongl. Maj:ts Öfwerste-Marskalk, Hans Kongl. Höghets Cron-Printsens Gouverneur, Academiae-Cantzleren, Riddaren, Commendeuren och Cantzleren af Kong. Maj:ts Orden, samt Riddaren af Swarta Örn, Högwälborne Grefwe CARL GUSTAF TESSIN, Tå Hans Excellence af-lade Cancellie-Praesidentskapet,* Stockholm, s.d. [1752].

44 "*trogen nit*"; [Matthias Alexander von Ungern-Sternberg], *Landt-Marskalkens Högwälborne Baron MATTHIAS ALEXANDER Von UNGERN STERNBERGS Tal, Hållit wid slutet af 1743 års Rikdsdag Tå Riksens Ständer togo afsked af hwar annan på Riks Salen,* Stockholm, s.d. [1743].

45 "*Rättrådighet, witterhet och tapperhet*", "*Laglydnad, enighet, inbördes förtrolighet*", "*almän wälgång*"; [Matthias Alexander von Ungern-Sternberg], *Landt-Marskalkens Högwälborne Baron MATTHIAS ALEXANDER Von UNGERN STERNBERGS Tal, Hållit för Ridderskapet och Adeln Wid Landt-Marskalks-Stafwens afgifwande Then 12. September 1743,* Stockholm, s.d. [1743].

respect for the laws and inclination towards the common good,[46] while his party comrade Rålamb talked about unity, wisdom and prudence.[47] Count Fersen interestingly associated unity and concord not only with a rational constitution, but also with the degree to which the community had been instructed about it: "Unity and concord, the soul of good constitutions and their successful application, should not lack amidst an enlightened people."[48]

In a similar way, when enumerating his own political virtues, Tessin quoted his reverence and love as a subject, his faithfulness and zeal for the authorities, his care for fellow citizen's liberty, and the prayers of an honest man for the authorities and the "motherland" – here Tessin used *fosterjord*, the country of upbringing, which had a slightly more subjective or emotional dimension than the Swedish term for *patria, fäderneslandet*.[49]

Another way of defining civic virtues was to enumerate the vices that a good citizen should avoid. This was done by Count Tessin in his speech from April 1739, which gives us an idea of what was acceptable and what was not in the political culture of the Age of Liberty, although we have to remember that the speech has its rhetorical figures, including hyperboles and antiphrases, through which Tessin evaded the insinuations of his political enemies. When returning the marshal's baton, he enumerated all the offences that he had not committed. Among these were mentioned arranged voting, bribed meetings, convincing someone to speak in one's favour and advancing someone's particular interest.[50] In a similar speech eight years later, he added a cold heart for the fatherland, accepting bribes, laying traps for one's enemies, efforts to persuade someone in an illegal way, discrediting someone for money, "dark acts" (*mörka gärningar*), doing harm to the realm and persecuting its inhabitants.[51]

46 *"Enighet, Owäldughet, agtning för Lagarne och afsikt på Allmänna bästa"*; [Eric Gustaf Oxenstierna], *TAL, hållit af Grefwelige Brahe-Ättens Fullmäktig, Friherre ERIC GUSTAF OXENSTIERNA til Eka, tå S. T. Herr Landt-Marskalken Stafwen återlemnade. Then 15 Octob. 1766*, Stockholm, *s.d.* [1766].

47 *"enighet"*, *"wishet"*, *"saktmod"*; [Claes Rålamb], *TAL, Hållit til Höglofl. Ridderskapet och Adelen, Samt wid Landt-Marskalks Stafwens aflemnande, Af Présidenten och Commendeuren af Kongl. Nordstierne-Orden, Högwälborne Herr Baron CLAES RÅLAMB, Wid Riksdagens början i Stockholm Then 21. Januarii 1765*, Stockholm, *s.d.* [1765].

48 *"Enighet och samdräkt, Själen af alla goda Författningar, och deras lyckeliga utförande, bör icke fela hos et uplyst folck"*; [Axel von Fersen], *Til Kongl. Maj:t, Landt-Marskalkens, Generalens, Riddarens och Commendeurens af Kongl. Maj:ts Orden, Högwälborne Grefwe Herr AXEL FERSENS Hållne Underdånige TAL, På Riks-Salen i Norrköping Den 22. April 1769*, Norrköping, 1769.

49 *"Undersåtelig wördnad och kärlek"*, *"tro och nit för min Öfwerhet"*, *"ömhet för mine Med-borgares frihet"*, *"en redlig Mans böner för Öfwerhet och Fosterjord"*; [Carl Gustaf Tessin], *Underdånigst Tal Til Hans Kongl. Maj:t, Hållit uti Råds-Salen Then 30. Martii 1752. Af Hans Excellence Herr Riks-Rådet, Cancellie-Praesidenten, Hennes Kongl. Maj:ts Öfwerste-Marskalk, Hans Kongl. Höghets Cron-Printsens Gouverneur, Academiae-Cantzleren, Riddaren, Commendeuren och Cantzleren af Kong. Maj:ts Orden, samt Riddaren af Swarta Örn, Högwälborne Grefwe CARL GUSTAF TESSIN, Tå Hans Excellence af-lade Cancellie-Praesidentskapet*, Stockholm, *s.d.* [1752].

50 [Carl Gustaf Tessin], *Landt-Marskalkens Högwälborne Grefwe CARL GUSTAF TESSINS Tal, Hållit för Ridderskapet och Adeln Wid Landt-Marskalks Stafwens afgifwande Den 19. Aprill 1739*, Stockholm, *s.d.* [1739].

51 [Carl Gustaf Tessin], *TAL, Til Samtelige Riksens Högloflige Ständer, Af Herr Riks-Rådet, Cantzli-Rådet, Öfwerste-Marskalken och Academiae Cancelleren, Högwälborne Grefwe*

To sum up the political virtues characterising the Swedish Estates was more common in the speeches held to all the estates by the Chancellery President. Unlike the Marshals of the Diet, the Chancellery President, although always an aristocrat himself, did not speak on behalf of the noble estate, but on behalf of the king, and his speech was addressed to all the assembled estates. Consequently, they were more likely to draw on consensual topics than on particular or innovative views. The respected Count Ekeblad, a moderate representative of the Hat party and known for his amiability and piety, summed up the features that characterised the subjects and citizens of the realm and particularly the Dietmen. He mentioned the true fear of God, pure manners, abidance by the laws, defence of Liberty, abhorrence of licence and self-interest, courage against the enemies of the Realm and friendship with fellow citizens, impartiality and mutual love, diligence and assiduity in the attendance of offices, posts and tasks, enlightened and zealous subjects, and love and affection for each other and the Realm.[52]

If these were very general features of the virtuous citizen, regardless of his estate, were there any particularly noble virtues that were not necessarily shared by other estates? As Swedish political discourse after the death of Charles XII tended to be both anti-autocratic and anti-aristocratic and as the political elite had been renewed with younger families at the end of the Caroline rule, politicians of the Age of Liberty might have been cautious of any explicit declarations on the superiority of the nobility over other estates. Clear distinctions were, however, maintained in the adjectives used to characterise the different estates: the representatives of the nobility were "highly well-born" and "well-born", the clergy "reverend", "highly learned" and "venerable", the burghers "honourably born", "wise" and "well-esteemed", and the peasants "honourable" and "worthy".[53]

It can also be noted that while 'virtue' was a rather rare term in political speeches generally, as has been mentioned above, the term was used when speakers addressed themselves to the nobility only and in particular. According to Peter Englund, until the second half of the seventeenth century, 'virtue' had been used as an argument opposed to 'birth' when promoting legitimacy built on merit instead of pedigree in politics and administration. The nobility, however, particularly after it had been partially renewed by families that had merited themselves in the Caroline administration, integrated the rhetoric of virtue at the end of the seventeenth century. The

---

CARL GUSTAV TESSIN, *Tå Riksens Ständer in Pleno Plenorum uppå Stora Riddarhus Salen woro församlade, then 31. Martii 1747*, Stockholm, 1747.

52 "*Sann GUDsfruktan*", "*rena seder*", "*lydnad för lagen*", "*Frihetens försvar*", "*afsky för sielfswåld och egennytta*", "*tapperhet emot Rikets fiender och wänskap för medborgare*", "*owäldughet och inbördes kärlek*", "*flit och oförtrutenhet at sköta theras ämbeten, sysslor och handteringar*", "*uplyste och nitiske undersåtar*", "*kärlek och ömhet för Sig och Riket*"; [Clas Ekeblad], *På Kongl. Maj:ts Wägnar, Herr Riks-Rådets, Cancellie-Présidentens, Öfwerste-Marskalkens och Åbo Academiae Cantzlerens, samt Cantzlerens, Riddarens och Commendeurens af Kongl. Maj:ts Orden, Högwälborne Grefwe CLAS EKEBLADS Håldne TAL, Til Riksens Ständer, tå Riksdagen slutades then 21. Junii 1762, s.l., s.d.* [Stockholm, 1762].

53 See, for instance, the speeches addressed by the Chancellery President to the Estates in the name of the king.

nobility that based its rise on the needs of the Caroline state thus presented itself as both well-born and virtuous, in other words, as a "meritocratic aristocracy".[54] By the middle of the eighteenth century, virtue reconciled with birth had become one of the key concepts of noble self-understanding.

When the Marshal of the Diet returned the marshal's baton to the dean of the nobility at the end of the Diet, he would make a short speech in which he effaced himself before the line of glorious Swedish noblemen having held the baton to conduct public affairs and contribute to the happiness of the fatherland. In his speech of 21 June 1762, Count Fersen chose to point out the nobility's natural dispositions to the political virtue that was required in a free regime by mentioning "the Noble mind, the zealous ardour, and the eminent inclinations for liberty, for manliness, virtue and wit, which consolidate an exhausted fatherland and are the utmost armorial bearings of Swedish men of honour".[55] The Marshal of the next Diet, Rudbeck, in his turn, evocated manliness and courage, justice and reason as timeless characteristics of the noble estate, and stated that "it is on the path of Virtue that Swedish noblemen have walked to Glory", but he did not make the connection between virtue and liberty that was so typical of Fersen's speeches.[56]

Besides the very concept of 'virtue', the other central topic in noble self-reflection was 'honour'. Both concepts contained the idea of integrity, manliness and courage central to noble identity. The Swedish language had two concepts for honour, *heder* and *ära*, which were not quite the same. While *heder* was associated with inner qualities such as honesty and integrity (including physical integrity), *ära* referred to outer marks of honour, to reputation and glory.[57] In political texts, honour was often mentioned as an aside, such as in the phrase *heder- och ärewördige ständer*, but in the eighteenth century it was more seldom digressed upon. It went without saying that a Dietman should be honourable (*redelig*) and honest (*hederlig*). *Ära* in the sense of "glory" was achieved by devotion to the fatherland, but it was dealt with as something rather external, a mark or a consequence of honourable conduct. *Heder* in the sense of personal reputation was one of the most important political qualities. In plenary speeches it was present mainly in

54 Englund, *Det hotade huset*, pp. 153 ff., 181–182.
55 "*thet Ädla sinnelag, then nitfulla drift, och the utmärkte böjelser för frihet, för mandom, dygd och wett, som befästa et utmattadt Fädernesland och äro Swenske Ridders Mäns yppersta Skiöldemärken*"; [Axel von Fersen], *TAL, Til Theras Kongl. Majestäter Och Hans Kongl. Höghet Cron-Printsen, Hållne af Landt-Marskalken, General-Lieutenanten och Commendeures af Kongl. Maj:ts Swärds-Orden, Högwälborne Herr Grefwe AXEL FERSEN Tå Riksdagen slutades i Stockholm then 21 Junii 1762. Såsom ock Tal, hållne wid Landt-Marskalks Stafwens aflemnande*, Stockholm, s.d. [1762].
56 "*Mandom och Tapperhet, Rättwisa och Förstånd*" […], "*Thet är på Dygdenes wäg, som Swenske Riddersmän wandrat til Ära*"; [Thure Gustaf Rudbeck], *TAL, til Ridderskapet och Adelen, af Landt-Marskalken General-Majoren och Commendeuren af Kongl. Maj:ts Swärds-Orden, Wälborne Herr THURE GUSTAF RUDBECK, wid Landt-Marskalks Stafwens nedläggande, then 15. Octob. 1766, s.l., s.d.* [Stockholm, 1766]. The "path of virtue" may be an allusion to Cicero, *De officiis*, 1, XXXII (118).
57 Cf. Ville Sarkamo, "Karolinernas akillesval. Krigaräran inom den karolinska armén under stora nordiska kriget (1700–1721)", *Historisk Tidskrift för Finland*, vol. 90 (2005:4), pp. 413–438.

the frequent allusions to the value of particular estates. More often it appeared in non-public documents such as correspondence and diaries under terms such as *renommée*. Personal honour was also of course alluded to in commemorative speeches for deceased persons. In the plenary speeches, a quite rare occurrence of the term can be found in Tessin's speech to the assembled Estates in March 1747, in which he declared that his time, property and life belonged to his fatherland, and that the only thing he entirely possessed was his honour (*ära*).[58]

The moral quality behind honour in politics was mostly translatable as "integrity". An irreproachable conduct to the benefit of the community was a moral duty, which was all the heavier since it derived from political responsibilities. Virtue, honour, *redelighet* and a citizen's zeal for the fatherland were not only empty words used on solemn occasions. Their frequent appearance in private correspondence and diaries seems to indicate that the nobility also reflected on their sense and tried to adopt a way of thought, if not a conduct, that was in line with civic ideals. To put it in French as did Carl Adlermarck in a letter to Count Fersen in 1761, they tried to "[*penser*] *en vrai citoyen*".[59]

The ideal of good citizenship, *medborgerlighet*, implied a morally irreproachable conduct in politics, but also a strong attachment to values shared by the community. In the Sweden of the Age of Liberty, such values were liberty, the constitution or the fundamental laws of the realm, and the common good. More vague objects of attachment or loyalty that the feelings of devotion or patriotic zeal would target could be larger, abstract objects such as the ruler, the crown or the state one served, the country or community of fellow countrymen one served together with, or even a way of life. These shared values or objects of devotion constituted the political fatherland, which was, as an abstraction, conceived, articulated and conceptualised through the terms of 'citizen', 'patriotic zeal' and 'patriot'.[60] The terms used to articulate the virtuous participation of the ideal citizen in public affairs were at the same time periphrases for the love of fatherland. As Count Fersen stated, according to this view, a citizen was one that had a fatherland, in other words, a person worthy and able to belong to the political community and who would act accordingly: "As a Free People they have a Fatherland", he stated in his speech to the king when talking about the Estates assembled in front of him in April 1769.[61]

---

58 *"Min Tid, min Egendom, mit Lif, bör jag ej längre räkna mig tilhörige, än in til thess mit Fädernesland them påkallar: Thet enda jag fullkomligen äger, och ingen i werlden mig frånta kan, är min ära [...]"*; [Carl Gustaf Tessin], TAL, Til Samtelige Riksens Högloflige Ständer, Af Herr Riks-Rådet, Cantzli-Rådet, Öfwerste-Marskalken och Academiae Cancelleren, Högwälborne Grefwe CARL GUSTAV TESSIN, Tå Riksens Ständer in Pleno Plenorum uppå Stora Riddarhus Salen woro församlade, then 31. Martii 1747, Stockholm, 1747.

59 *"J'ai toujours pensé en vrai Citoyen"*; Carl Adlermarck to Fersen, 7 November 1761, RA, Stafsundsarkivet, Axel von Fersen d.ä.:s arkiv, vol. 7.

60 See Wolff, *Vänskap och makt*, chapters 10–12.

61 *"Såsom Fritt Folck hafwa de et Fädernesland"*; [Axel von Fersen], *Til Kongl. Maj:t, Landt-Marskalkens, Generalens, Riddarens och Commendeurens af Kongl. Maj:ts Orden, Hög-wälborne Grefwe Herr AXEL FERSENS Hållne Underdånige TAL, På Riks-Salen i Norrköping Den 22. April 1769*, Norrköping, 1769.

Patriotic duties and state reason

The development of natural law and the modern concept of 'citizen' generally brought with it the idea of civil rights and liberties, as is shown elsewhere in this book. At least as important as the notion of rights or liberties was the idea that the citizen, in exchange for his liberty and the protection granted by the state, had the duty to serve the community according to his personal capacities. It may also be supposed that it was through this sense of duty towards the crown, the state or the realm that loyalties and strong feelings of belonging were developed and articulated in terms such as 'patriotism', 'zeal' or 'national sprit'.

For the nobility, there were several ways of serving the fatherland, one of which, the political one, has already been mentioned. Above all, the idea and ideals of service were associated with the exercise of offices in the military and civil administration. Service to the Crown was, to a high degree, seen as the duty and privilege of the nobility and was traditionally given as the reason for the nobility's various tax exemptions and other immunities. The duty of public service was, as Peter Englund has stated, the "vital principle" of the noble estate.[62] The Swedish constitution of 1720 stated that appointments to public offices should be made on the basis of talent and capacity, but the privilege chart of 1723 reserved the highest offices for the nobility. In practice, all senators, governors and commissioned army officers were noblemen, and 'merit', which seems to have become just another word for birth and titles, often prevailed on the ideals of capacity.[63]

Generally, the development of an ideal of service, duty and meritocracy is often associated with the birth of the Prussian state. During the second half of the eighteenth century, at the same time as concepts such as 'patriot', 'fatherland' and 'nation' were becoming more frequent from the middle of the century onwards, Prussian office holders developed a strong attachment to the crown.[64] Similar tendencies can be observed in most parts of Europe. In Austria, Russia and France, schools for civil and military officers were established to educate and indoctrinate loyal servants of the state. An increasing amount of French treatises not only criticised the administration in place, but also reflected on what the ideal civil servant should be like.[65]

In Sweden, while the commoners' estates conquered parts of the political citizenship, the offices and the duties attached to them remained central to the nobility's identity as an administrative and military elite. The old

62 Englund, *Det hotade huset*, p. 29.
63 RF 1720, art. 40; Ridderskapets och adelns privilegier den 16 oktober 1723, art. 2–3; in Brusewitz, *Frihetstidens grundlagar och konstitutionella stadgar*, pp. 39–40, 108; see also Ingvar Elmroth, *Nyrekryteringen till de högre ämbetena 1720–1809. En socialhistorisk studie*, Lund, 1962; Carlsson, *Ståndssamhälle och ståndspersoner 1700–1865*. Cf. Englund's concept of 'aristocratic meritocracy'; Englund, *Det hotade huset*, p. 182.
64 See Robert M. Berdahl, *The Politics of the Prussian Nobility. The Development of a Conservative Ideology 1770–1848*, Princeton, 1988, pp. 95–97; see also Hans Rosenberg, *Bureaucracy, Aristocracy, and Autocracy: The Prussian Experience, 1660–1815*, Cambridge, Mass., 1958.
65 See, for instance, Smith, *Nobility Reimagined*, pp. 104–142.

conception according to which a nobleman should deserve his status by serving the fatherland was particularly stressed in the debates on nobility during the second half of the eighteenth century and onwards, including the harsh Swedish public debate of 1766–1771.[66]

As the value of service was becoming easier to legitimate than status by birth only, the value of good civil servants (*ämbetsmän*) was stressed by the nobility, to the point that the *ämbetsman* tended to outrank the simple *adelsman* (nobleman). Already Count Tessin, in the middle of the century, had stressed the esteem and consideration that was gained by heavy responsibilities in public administration.[67] Only some decades later, the Swedish debate of the early 1770s on commoners' privileges and rights made it more difficult for the nobility to claim precedence. The debate marked larger transformations in how citizenship, civic and political rights, and social equality were conceived, transformations that the noble estate would have to face and which affected noble identity. In 1789, at the eve of the French revolution, the elderly Count Fersen, who was writing his memoirs, expressed his concern for the future social legitimacy of a nobility that was no longer interested in public offices:

> When the nobility abandons the employments and offices of the Realm, it gives up its influence in government; it will then be replaced by commoners. The honour and happiness which accompany the service and the positions of honour of the Realm and which in all times have maintained the nobility, disappear, and with them the reputation and fundament of the nobility. The commoners' estates consider noblemen as wasting members of society, and they become such when they cease to serve the fatherland by wits or by arms.[68]

In other words, for this representative of the nobility and of the political elite of the former Age of Liberty, the definition of the citizen as the servant of the community remained crucial. It was a neutral one and did not imply a bias against the country, the ruler or even the nature of the regime. If the nobility wished to maintain its status, it could not afford to neglect political participation and public service.

---

66 On this debate, see Hallberg, *Ages of Liberty*, pp. 205–231.
67 *"Ju drygare answaret är, som af en Ämbetsman äskas, ju fullkomligare synes theremot förtroendet til thes förwaltning böra wara."* [Carl Gustaf Tessin], *TAL, Til Samtelige Riksens Högloflige Ständer, Af Herr Riks-Rådet, Cantzli-Rådet, Öfwerste-Marskalken och Academiae Cancelleren, Högwälborne Grefwe CARL GUSTAV TESSIN, Tå Riksens Ständer in Pleno Plenorum uppå Stora Riddarhus Salen woro församlade, then 31. Martii 1747,* Stockholm, 1747.
68 *"När adeln öfverger Rikets sysslor och tjenster, öfverlemnar den influencen i styrelsen; den skall då ersättas af ofrälse män. Den heder och lycka, som Rikets tjenst och hedersställen åtföljer och som i alla tider upprätthållit adeln, försvinner, samt adelns anseende och grundfäste med dem. De ofrälse stånden anse adelsmän som tärande medlemmar uti samhället, och de blifva det, när de upphöra att med vett eller vapen tjena fosterlandet."* [Axel von Fersen], *Riksrådet och fältmarskalken m.m. grefve Fredrik Axel von Fersens historiska skrifter,* utg. af R. M. Klinckowström, vol. 7, Stockholm, 1872, pp. 118–119 (1789).

If we look at how the experiences of these transformations have been studied, it appears that modern Swedish research on the transformation of identities during the breaking up of estate society sometimes has preferred to analyse historical development in terms of modern categories such as 'class', 'gender' or 'ethnicity', rather than examine how the processes were experienced and articulated by individual members of formerly important but now vanished groups.[69] Also, research on the civil or military administration of early modern Sweden has often been primarily concerned with the relationship between the authorities and local society, often from a perspective of struggle or polarisation. Rather than how members of the ruling elite perceived themselves and their mission, popular perceptions of the administrators have been studied.[70] Ideas and terms used to express feelings of loyalty, duty or even the self-perceptions of higher office holders themselves have more rarely been the object of study, perhaps because they are less obvious sources of inspiration for a more or less teleological "proto-history" of nineteenth- and twentieth-century democratic developments. This has left a blank in what we know on eighteenth-century perceptions of citizenship, while the processes of the enlargement of the concept are better known.[71] Respectively, many theories have been written on identification, but there are still many eighteenth-century personal documents that have been only rarely used for this purpose. Personal correspondence and diaries, often written in French, are obvious sources of information on how events were experienced and feelings articulated.

One testimony of what the administrative elite may have thought about its duties and obligations towards the state and society is the correspondence between Count Fersen and Count Ekeblad from the years 1757–1760, the time of the Seven Years' War, which Sweden fought on the French side against Prussia, mainly in Pomerania.[72] The Seven Years' War has often been pointed to as an important stage in the transformations that affected European self-perceptions and minds in the eighteenth century.[73]

The unsuccessful progress of the war, which had been badly prepared for, deeply upset the nearly forty-year-old Fersen, who himself had previously been one of the keenest advocators of the war. Fersen served as a major general in the Swedish troops in Pomerania and had an impressive military record including service in the French army during the war of Austrian succession. In his letters to his brother-in-law, the senator and *rikskansliråd*

---

69 A recent example of this tendency is the textbook series by Thomas Lindkvist & Maria Sjöberg, Susanna Hedenborg & Lars Kvarnström, *Det svenska samhället*, Lund, 2006 (2 vols).

70 Cf., for instance, Maria Cavallin, *I kungens och folkets tjänst. Synen på den svenske ämbetsmannen 1750–1780*, Göteborg, 2003.

71 On this enlargement, see Wolff, "Pro Patria et Libertate. Frihetsbegreppet i 1700-talets svenska politiska språk"; Åsa Karlsson-Sjögren, *Männen, kvinnorna och rösträtten. Medborgarskap och representation 1723–1866*, Stockholm, 2006; Nordin, "Frihetstidens radikalism".

72 KB, Engeströmska samlingen, B VII 2.1; RA, Stafsundsarkivet, Axel von Fersen d.ä.:s arkiv, vol. 7.

73 Blitz, *Aus Liebe zum Vaterland*; David A. Bell, *The Cult of the Nation in France. Inventing Nationalism 1680–1800*, Cambridge, Mass., 2001; Ihalainen, *Protestant Nations Redefined*.

(Chancellery Councillor of the Realm) Count Ekeblad, Fersen complained about his health problems, about the general lack of food, money and equipment, and above all, about the insubordination and poor direction of the army. The highest command was first held by Fersen's political rival Count Ungern-Sternberg, of the Cap party, but at an early stage, in December 1757, the Senate replaced him with Count Gustaf Fredrik von Rosen, who left his post after only six months. His successor Lieutenant General Gustaf David Hamilton lost the battle of Fehrbellin against the Prussians on 28 September and resigned in November 1758. It then took several months for the Senate to agree on the choice of his successor.[74]

Under these circumstances Ekeblad seems to have tested Fersen's disposition to accept the command, but Fersen rejected all half-disguised offers, formally because he feared the task was too risky. Finally, the Senate appointed Fersen's other brother-in-law Johann Jacob Lantingshausen. By then Fersen and Ekeblad's exchange had developed into a more philosophical discussion on the extent of a citizen's duty to accept public offices.

For Fersen, it was self-evident that a citizen should serve his fatherland, particularly under the circumstances of war. At an early stage of his war correspondence with Ekeblad, he stated that "my fatherland needs to be served" (1757), and a couple of years later mentioned "a citizen's duties towards his Fatherland" (1759) respectively "the duties of patriotism" (1760).[75]

Like many European noblemen of the time, Fersen considered the duties towards the fatherland as imperative and greater than individual lives, but he did not have any illusions of Sweden as a morally greater country than any other. On the contrary, he stated coolly that his generation was not that of Charles XII and that the efforts made to change "the nation's genius, taste and customs" had "made a military people quite unsuitable to its profession".[76] Furthermore, he even wrote that "both the interest and the glory of the state are compromised; it is vain for the Nation to believe itself invincible and stronger than all the other nations".[77] Although he seems to have had a certain idea of what Sweden ideally should have been like and of what would have been more dignifying for his country, he felt that the misery of the army was shameful for Sweden – "the real state of our affairs degrades the nation and is ignominious to Sweden" – to the point that he wished to be

74 See, for instance, Patrick Bruun (utg.), *Vardagsslit och sjuårskrig. Upplevt och beskrivet av den nyländske dragonen Carl Johan Aminoff*, Helsingfors, 1994, pp. 398–409. Fehrbellin was a bad omen since the troops of the Margrave of Brandenburg had won one of his greatest victories over the Swedes there in 1675.

75 *"ma patrie a besoin d'etre servie"* (25 October 1757); *"les devoirs d'un cijtoyen a sa Patrie"* (29 December 1759); *"les devoirs du patriotisme"* (8 March 1760), KB, Engeströmska samlingen, B VII 2.1.

76 *"Notre generation nest pas celle de Charles XII et les soins que lon sest donné a faire changer le genie, le gout, et les usages de la Nation ont fait un peuple militaire bien impropre au metier quil doit faire."* (15 July 1758), KB, Engeströmska samlingen, B VII 2.1.

77 *"et l'interrerrest et la gloire de Letat sont compromise, La Nation est vaine, se croire invincible, et formée dune trampe superieure a touttes les autres nations"* (9 October 1759), KB, Engeströmska samlingen, B VII 2.1.

able to change state and fatherland, which, it went without saying, was not possible, at least not in his situation and under the circumstances of war.[78]

The cause of the fatherland was above all a question of morals and honour, and for this reason it could not be neglected by a gentleman or a man of honour. Serving it was, with Fersen's words, what constituted "the very glory and zeal of a citizen".[79] The same idea is present in an autobiographical note by Gustaf Stenbock from 1789:

> I have neglected no occasion to learn and make me worthy to serve the State. That was my motive for trying the Navy. That was the motive that made me take part in the deliberations of the Estates, to know the duties of a good citizen, a faithful subject.[80]

More important than the name of the sovereign, the community or the country that was being served was the moral principle of rewarding with gratitude and service the community that had nourished and protected the citizen. This duty compelled putting the interest of the state or the community before one's own. The opposite of this unselfish patriotic spirit was personal ambition, the forming of factions and the use of intrigue to promote a particular interest.

As a part of this patriotic rhetoric, Fersen strongly rejected rumours according to which he had taken steps to assure his re-election as Marshal of the following Diet (to be summoned in 1760). How could anyone believe that he would abuse his credit to raise himself "above my rank and my fellow citizens", and why would he be so conceited that he would wish to govern an ungovernable state? His argument continues:

> Here I am at my duty; nothing can draw me away from it. I will see my fatherland again only at the return of the Army. Here I shall share the good and the bad luck of my fellow countrymen, and if my career comes to an end it will be without rumours. My fatherland has nothing that I regret and I have lived enough to have seen its misfortunes and its miseries.[81]

---

78 "*le vrai etat de nos affaires degrade la nation et avilit la Suede*" (29 December 1759), "*Que ne puisje changer d'etat et de Patrie.*" (8 March 1760), KB, Engeströmska samlingen, B VII 2.1.

79 "*la veritable gloire et le zele d'un citoyen*" (5 April 1760), KB, Engeströmska samlingen, B VII 2.1.

80 "*[…] j'ai négligé aucune occasion pour m'instruire et me rendre digne de servir L'état. C'etois ce motif, qui me fit faire un essay d'apprentissage dans la Marine. C'etois ce motif, qui m'engageoit à prendre part aux délibérations des Etats, Pour connoître les devoires d'un bon Citoyen, d'un sujet fidele.*" Greve G. Stenbocks brev till Gustaf III, 1789, LUB, DelaGardieska samlingen, historiska handlingar, vol. 22:2.

81 "*Comment est il possible que lon se meprenne jusqu'a ce point sur mes sentimens; pour former des factions il faut avoir des vues ? et quelles pourroient etre les miennes, m'aton vu courir apres la dignité dont j'ai été revetu la derniere Diette m'at'on vu mettre a profit le credit que j'avois alors pour m'elever hors de mon Rang au dessus de mes compatriotes, me suije servi des conjunctures pour server mon interest particulier, la chimerique vanité de vouloir gouverner un etat, qui nest pas gouvernable, mauroit elle saisi dans ce moment? [...] Ici je suis a mon devoir, rien ne pourra m'en tirer, mes yeux ne reverront ma patrie qu'au retour de l'Armée, ici je partagerez la bonne et la mauvaise fortune de mes compatriotes et*

On a moral level, Fersen thought that a citizen owed everything to the state and would be ready to sacrifice everything for it, except his honour.[82] Here, his view was exactly the same as Tessin's, mentioned above: honour was the only thing a nobleman should never sacrifice; it was better to die than to lose one's honour, be it even for the fatherland. It is interesting to note that Fersen, like Tessin and Stenbock, here used the word *l'État*, the state. The Swedish term *staten*, formerly used above all in a budgetary sense, was still only acquiring its modern significations, while the French word had already the established meaning of a political body.[83] To write in French had many advantages; among these, it offered the possibility to clearly and quickly express, and consequently assimilate, notions that were only in the process of being conceptualised in Swedish.

The way in which Fersen and Tessin mentioned their readiness to sacrifice themselves for the state also seems to suggest that they shared a notion of state reason, the idea of an eternal state that should endure, while regimes, rulers, persons and systems were transient and perishable. The idea of state reason, which had been developing since the Renaissance, reinforced the classical idea of patriotism that could be resumed under the motto *non sibi, sed patriae natus*. This line, often used by Cicero, remained a principle of noble upbringing all over Europe and was recurrent in reflections on how noblemen should be educated and on what attitude they should adopt towards the state and the Crown.

On the other side of the enemy lines in Pomerania, the family von Podewils served the Prussian state. Frederick II's minister Count Heinrich von Podewils, born 1695, had written his autobiography around the years 1751–1752, which he hoped would be useful to his children for their instruction.[84] Paraphrasing the Roman theme on patriotic abnegation and virtue, he wrote:

> I hope and wish that they will become decent people, which should always be their principal merit, as I have tried to make it my own, and by which I have made my way in the world, rather than in any other way; may they never deviate from the path of honour and probity, may they serve their sovereign and their fatherland with an unbreakable fidelity, and with all imaginable zeal, may they in that follow the example of their forefathers, of which not one has made himself unworthy of his birth, may they not

si jy trouve la fin de ma carriere ce sera sans murmures, ma patrie n'a rien que je regrette et j'ai assez vecue pour voir ses malheurs et ses misères." (27 October 1758), KB, Engeströmska samlingen, B VII 2.1.

82 "*Au reste nous devons tout a l'etat et nous sommes pret a lui tout sacrifier excepté notre honneur.*" (4 September 1758), KB, Engeströmska samlingen, B VII 2.1. In the same letter, Fersen mentions zeal for the common good or public interest, "*zele pour le bien public*". This patriotic argument is accompanied, in Fersen's letters, by doubt of the comfort of a high position in a nation characterised above all by its "jealousy": "*tout ce qui a l'air de faveur est odieux dans cette nation jalouse, envieuse, et ou chacun se croit un egalle portion de merite et egallement authorisé a pretendre*" (10 March 1759); "[…] *sentiment de jalousie dont toutte la nation est obsedée, et qui de tout tems la caracterise*" (11 March 1760), KB, Engeströmska samlingen, B VII 2.1.

83 Lindberg, *Den antika skevheten*, pp. 79–87.

84 Mémoire des principales circonstances de ma vie pour l'Instruction de mes Enfants, GStA Berlin, VI Hauptabteilung, Nachlaß Heinrich von Podewils, Nr 1.

bury themselves in a shameful idleness, and may they know that they were not born for themselves, but to serve well their sovereign and their fatherland [...].[85]

State reason and patriotic abnegation, however, had their reasonable limits. It was the duty of a good citizen to serve the fatherland, but according to Fersen and Ekeblad's letters, this duty was not a slavish one, and it did not exclude the use of discernment and conscience. Neither was patriotic duty a reason to compel a citizen to give up his honour, not was it particularly dignifying to serve half-heartedly. Fersen wrote:

> I agree that it is a duty to serve the fatherland, but I don't believe that this obligation extends to the loss of prudence, and as far as the commandment of the Army is concerned, not to be tempted by it is enough to make one unsuitable for it.[86]

"The zeal for the public interest demands much, but prudence has its rights", Fersen wrote to Ekeblad in May 1759.[87] In December 1759, still fearing that he would risk his head if he took up the highest command unless the circumstances of the war would not soon take a happier turn, he continued on this theme: "A citizen is made to give his blood for his fatherland, but that is not on a scaffold."[88] This had been the fate of General Charles Emil Lewenhaupt, who in 1743, after the unsuccessful war against Russia, had been trialled and beheaded for his failures in the conduct of the war. Besides a pragmatic attitude, Fersen's refusal to submit himself to this kind of state

85 *"J'espere et souhaite qu'ils deviennent des honnettes Gens, ce qui doit etre leur principal merite, ainsi que j'ai toujours taché d'en faire le mien, et par lequel je me suis poussé dans le Monde, que par toutes les autres voyes ; qu'ils ne s'ecartent jamais du Chemin de l'honneur et de la Probité, qu'ils servent leur souverain et leur Patrie avec une fidelite a toute Epreuve, et avec tout le Zele imaginable, qu'ils tachent a faire en cela les Exemples de leurs ancetres, dont pas un s'est rendu indigne de sa Naissance, qu'ils ne s'ensevelissent point dans une Oisivete honteuse, et qu'ils sachent qu'ils ne sont pas nés pour eux memes, mais pour bien servir leur souverain et leur Patrie, qu'ils ne soient pas Dissipateurs, mais que par une sage Oeconomie et sans Lesine, ils conservent au moins le peu de bien que je leur laisse, et dont Dieu mercy il n'y a pas un sous de mal acquis ; qu'ils fuyent le jeu, les gonselles, et les debauches de toutes sortes, aussi bien que les mauvaises compagnies, qu'ils tachent de frequenter toujours preferablement et plutot les personnes elevées au dessus d'eux, que leurs Egaux, mais qu'ils n'en adoptent pas les defauts, qu'ils ayent de la Religion, sans etre bigote, et qu'ils rendent toujours à l'Etre supreme le Culte raisonnable que nous lui devons ; qu'ils soient persuadés, que la vertu ne reste jamais sans Recompense, et qu'un homme de Probité a toujours et à la longue un avantage infini sur celui qui n'en a point, et dont souvent la Fortune la plus brillante finit par des Catastrophes et les disgraces les plus terrible."* Mémoire des principales circonstances de ma vie pour l'Instruction de mes Enfants, GStA Berlin, VI Hauptabteilung, Nachlaß Heinrich von Podewils, Nr 1.

86 *"Je conviens qu'il est du devoir de servir la patrie, mais je ne crois pas que cette obligation s'etende jusqu'au prejudice de la prudence, et quand au commandement des Armées, il suffit, de n'en pas etre tenté, pour n'y pas etre propre."* (29 December 1759), KB, Engeströmska samlingen, B VII 2.1.

87 *"Le zele pour le bien public exige beaucoup mais la prudence a ses droits."* (12 May 1759), KB, Engeströmska samlingen, B VII 2.1.

88 *"un cijtoyen est fait pour verser son sang pour sa patrie mais ce nest pas sur un echaffaut"* (9 October 1759), KB, Engeströmska samlingen, B VII 2.1.

violence and violation of honour and life may also have reflected the influence of natural law, which he had studied during his years at Lund University. According to natural law contract theories, the citizens should serve the state, which in return owed its citizens protection. Persecution of or depriving citizens of their lives was not part of the contract.

It seems, however, to have been clear to Fersen that public opinion and the government's credibility were the central problems of the war and the government that was conducting it. Fersen made a clear distinction between the interests of the state and the demands of public opinion, this mobile force that could influence hesitant decision-makers and called for the immolation of scapegoats. Warfare required a strong commitment and a serene administration, otherwise it became necessary to "defend the welfare of the state against the fury of the public".[89] In other words, what was needed was "a government and a national spirit constituted for the war".[90] This use of the concepts of 'nation' and 'national', with clear reference to the coherence of the community and not only to its characteristic features, appeared in Fersen's letters to Ekeblad for the first time in June 1759. In the spring and summer of 1760, he used terms such as "the vows of the nation" and "the novelty of a national party".[91] Fersen's uses of 'nation' in 1759–1760 seem to point at a rapid assimilation of a new way to conceptualise the political community. The chronology also matches observations made in other countries concerning the appearance of, for instance, "national spirit" as an expression.[92]

The appearance of the word "nation" in this new sense, should, however, not be over-interpreted with regard to its presumed role in possible early forms of nationalism. Fersen himself took a very suspicious attitude towards all forms of fanaticism, demagoguism and too strong emotions, and stated, in May of 1760:

> I do not believe in the reunion of the true patriots; I know many of them who are systematically out of their mind. All virtues, when pushed to the sublime, are close to madness; the love of fatherland and of liberty is susceptible, like the love of God, of schism and pietism.[93]

On the whole, Fersen himself could not decide on what attitude to adopt regarding the offers that he was made – the final one, in 1760, was no longer

---

89 *"defendre le bien de letat de la fureur publique"* (9 October 1759), KB, Engeströmska samlingen, B VII 2.1.

90 *"un gouvernement et un esprit national constitué pour la guerre"* (12 June 1759), KB, Engeströmska samlingen, B VII 2.1.

91 *"les voeux de la nation"* (5 April 1760); *"la nouveauté dun parti national"* (19 July 1760), KB, Engeströmska samlingen, B VII 2.1.

92 See, for instance, Ihalainen, *Protestant Nations Redefined*, pp. 409–410, where the appearance of the expression in British parliamentary sermons is dated to the Seven Years' War and, more precisely, the spring of 1758.

93 *"Je ne crois pas a la reunion des vrais patriotes, jen connois plusieurs a qui la téte tourne sistematiquement, touttes les vertus, poussez au sublime tiennent a la follie, l'amour de la Patrie, et de la liberté est susceptible, ainsi que lamour de Dieu, dun chisme, et de pietisterie."* (5 May 1760), KB, Engeströmska samlingen, B VII 2.1.

the command of the army, but a candidature for the role as Marshal of the Diet: "Despite repeating to myself everything that the spirit of Patriotism, the zeal of a citizen and the duty of a subject require, and despite hearing it repeated by Mr Lantingshausen, I can't make up my mind."[94]

In one of his longer answers to his brother-in-law during the war, Count Ekeblad had balanced the arguments and summed up the reasons for which a citizen should, in general, not refuse to take up important offices even though they sometimes presented considerable risks. He described the commitment to serve the state as a "veritable vocation", using terms such as honour, duty, reputation, gratitude and posterity.[95] He underlined the moral implications of a public career, which should be a free and reflected choice, and compared its obligations to those of matrimony:

> First, I admit that no matter how much one owes to one's reputation and one's fatherland, this obligation does not extend to having one's head cut off, when as the only fruit of one's zeal and sorrows, one sees the scaffold at the end of the commission that one has taken charge of; but at the same time I think that one must stand at least at the edge of the precipice and even have one foot over it, before the need to save ourselves makes us renounce the rules that ambition has established generally and the duties that the fatherland may require, and still one is perhaps badly justified in the eyes of the public and posterity. I have the idea that once one has done as much as devote oneself to a career, one has to run all the risks of it, and this for three reasons [...]: The first one: because one has been the master of one's choice. The second: because one is, consequently, supposed to have anticipated, weighed and examined everything glorious that it offers, on the one hand, and everything disagreeable, on the other. The third one: because there is justice in supporting the inconveniences of a profession if one wants to enjoy its advantages. It is a contract, or rather a marriage with the state. One should share with it the good luck and the bad luck. I would strongly blame someone that would go to a battle because he had a physical certainty of getting his head shot off by a cannon ball, but I would blame even more the one who would not go there because there is a possibility of being killed. What becomes of the gratitude that we owe to the fatherland that nourishes and protects us, if, because we may lose ourselves, we refuse it our services at the moment when they are the most needed? And how many important charges would be filled, if one only took into account the trouble, the criticism and the risks that accompany it and if one paid too much attention to regarding as inseparable from it the loss of one's honour and one's life?[96]

94 "*J'ai beau me dire tout ce qu'exigent l'esprit de Patriotisme, le zele de cijtoyen, et le devoir de sujet, j'au beau l'entendre repeter par Mr de Lantingshausen, je n'en suis pas moins indécis.*" (5 April 1760), KB, Engeströmska samlingen, B VII 2.1.

95 "*C'est une veritable vocation*" (Ekeblad to Fersen, 19 October 1759), RA, Stafsundsarkivet, Axel von Fersen d.ä.:s arkiv, vol. 7.

96 "*Je conviens d'abord, que quioiqu'on doive à sa reputation et à sa patrie, l'obligation ne va point jusqu'à se faire coupper la tete sur un echaffaut, quand pour tout fruit de son zele et de ses peines, on le voit infailliblement au bout de la commission, dont on se charge; mais je crois en même tems, qu'il faut se trouver pour le moins sur le bord du precipice et avoir même deja un pied dedans, avant que le soin de se sauver nous fasse renoncer aux regles que l'ambition a etablies generalement, et aux devoirs que la patrie peut exiger, et encore*

At some stage of their war correspondence, Ekeblad decided to quote a letter from the Chancellery President Baron Anders Johan von Höpken to one of his complaining friends in the war, in order to urge his brother-in-law to put aside his doubts for the moment. In this letter there is a strong ambience of crisis and a dramatic tone. The fatherland is in danger, and there is no time for personal animosities; on the contrary, the impending threat to the state requires that private matters be temporarily set aside for the fulfilment of public duties:

> As for the rest of it, I implore you by your conscience, by your patriotic sentiments and by everything that is holy and sacred, do not join the blamers. Think of it: remember that you are face to face not with the enemy of the Senate but with the enemy of the state and of your fatherland. The Senator's faults and the faults of the Senate should not be revenged on Sweden at the cost of its glory and its consideration. Think of this, and help others to do so, too. Now serve your dear fatherland, and when this time is over, revenge yourself as much as you like on the Senator, on the Senate and on me, if you find us guilty.[97]

Ekeblad's and Höpken's appeal to their friend to put private animosities or feelings of wounded honour aside when the fatherland was in danger appears as an example of classical, Machiavellian *raison d'État*. In this case, it seems to have worked at least partly: the government of the Hat party, although it would receive strong criticism at the following Diet and was forced to dismiss a couple of its senators, survived and was not overthrown until 1765.

---

est on peutetre mal justifié aux yeux du public et de la posterité. J'ai l'idée que dès qu'on a tant fait, que de se voüer à une carriere, il en faut courir tous les risques; et cela par trois raisons, comme dit Mr Pincé dans le tambour nocturne. La premiere, parce qu'on a eté le maitre de la choisir. La seconde, parce qu'on est par consequent censé d'avoir prevu, pesé et examiné tout ce qu'elle offre de glorieux d'un coté, et de desagreable de l'autre; la troisieme, parce qu'il y a de la justice à supporter les inconvenients d'un metier, si on pretend en jouir des avantages. C'est un contract, ou plutot un mariage avec l'etat. Il faut partager avec lui la bonne et la mauvaise fortune. Je blamerois fort quelqu'un qui se trouveroit à une bataille s'il avoit une certitude physique d'avoir la tete emportée par un boulet de canon, mais je blamerois encore davantage celui qui n'y iroit pas, parce que la possibilité d'etre tué, y est. Que devient la reconnaissance que nous devons à la patrie qui nous nourrit et nous protege, si, parce que nous pouvons nous y perdre nous mêmes, nous lui refusons nos services dans le moment ou ils lui sont le plus necessaires ? et combien de charges importantes seroient remplies, si on ne consideroit que le chagrin, la critique et les risques qui les accompagnent et qu'on s'attachât trop à en regarder comme inseparable la perte de son honneur et de sa vie ?" (Ekeblad to Fersen, 19 October 1759), RA, Stafsundsarkivet, Axel von Fersen d.ä.:s arkiv, vol. 7.

97 *"Au reste je vous conjure par votre conscience, par vos sentiments patriotiques et par tout ce qui est saint et sacré, ne paroissés point au nombre des clabaudeurs. Songés y, songés que vous etès vis à vis, non de l'ennemi du Senateur ni de celui du Senat, mais vis à vis de l'ennemi de l'etat et de votre patrie. Les fautes du Senateur et les fautes du Senat ne doivent point etre vengés sur la Suede et aux depens de sa gloire et de sa consideration. Faitès ces reflexions, aidés à les faire faire à d'autres. Servés à present votre chere patrie, et quand cette epoque, sera finie, vengés vous tant qu'il vous plaira sur le Senateur, Sur le Senat et Sur moi, Si vous nous trouvés en faute."* (Ekeblad to Fersen, 30 May, year unknown), RA, Stafsundsarkivet, Axel von Fersen d.ä.:s arkiv, vol. 7.

But what if the nature and moral principles of government changed to such a degree that the subject would consider the original covenant or social contract to have been broken by the state and consequently no longer would feel bound by his duties as a citizen? For the Swedish nobility of the late eighteenth century, there were two such moments where liberty was threatened by the growing aspirations of authority of the monarchic state. The first was the royal revolution of 1772, and the second the war against Russia of 1788–1790 and the political and moral crisis that accompanied it. It is now time to look at how the nobility reacted to these.

Chapter 4: Fealty, corrupted virtue and the right to rebellion

For the European old-regime nobility, the relationship to the monarch was always a particular and sometimes strained one, particularly when sovereigns started to expand their prerogatives. Traditional noble identity had been built on the idea of service and mutual favours, the nobleman receiving recognition of his position by his liege lord and king, who would grant him privileges, revenues and protection, in exchange for which the nobleman would faithfully serve the crown. In conformity with a chivalric ideal, many noblemen also usually expected the king to take advice from his loyal servants. This was the primitive conception of a parliament or a council, an assembly of free landowners, which equilibrated the regal power. The nobility's political self-representation was to a large extent based on this idea of recognition. The ideal form of government of the nobility, both European and Swedish, was thus a mixed one, where the power of the monarch was balanced by an assembly representing the privileged estates or the free men enjoying political and civil liberties.[1]

In this respect, the Swedish constitution of 1720, with its concessions to the claims of the aristocracy, was fairly representative of a noble conception of politics. It retained the principle of monarchy by tradition and as the image of divine order, but extended the prerogatives of the Estates. With regard to the radicalisation of the political discourse of the late Age of Liberty, it may seem somewhat surprising that the nobility ended up by throwing itself at the feet of the sovereign, who put an end to this regime by strengthening royal prerogative. In these transitions from one regime to another, the nobility played a key role. Without the passive support of the nobility, the royal revolution would hardly have succeeded so completely.

How should the gradual transition back to royal absolutism from 1772 onwards be explained and interpreted? What was the attitude of the nobility once this transition had taken place? A study of the attitudes adopted towards the monarchy could explain royalist thought between 1720 and 1772, and the amazing success of Gustav III's *coup d'État* and royal propaganda. Above

---

1 See Jouanna, *Le devoir de révolte*; Smith, *Nobility reimagined*, pp. 26–103; Lagerroth, *Frihetstidens författning*.

all, the conclusions of such an investigation also give keys to understanding the eventual rejection of the king.

The reasons for the end of the Age of Liberty and the revolution of 1772 have been thoroughly debated in Swedish and Finnish history writing over two centuries, but they have not very often been examined from the perspective of the history of political ideas and concepts.[2] Recently, the social factors behind the nobility's choice have convincingly been put forward.[3] By the end of the 1760s, the nobility's position as a leading estate had become less self-evident than ever before. The nobility needed the monarchy and the king to balance the increasing political weight of the commoners' estates, which were becoming conscious of their position and were making claims for enlarged privileges. The nobility, however, did not expect to see its own political role cut down so markedly, as soon became apparent. A look at the political concepts and ideals frequent in the nobility's political writings helps to understand the logic of the process of transition as it was perceived by contemporaries in the light of classical political theory. Not only do we find descriptions of the failings of a free regime and of the moral reasons for accepting a reinforced monarchy, but at the same time it becomes clear why the monarchical reign would also be rejected. If we were to look only at the ideas and concepts and how they were presented, it could be possible to argue that the same ideals both legitimated Gustav III and murdered him; only the concepts used to articulate them were put in a slightly different order.

In *Le devoir de révolte* (1989), Arlette Jouanna describes the political ideals of the nobility in sixteenth- and seventeenth-century France and the conflict between these ideals and the development of royal absolutism. For the unsatisfied nobility (*les malcontents*) described by Jouanna, the ideal regime was a mixed government where the king shared his power with an assembly of free landowners, the noblemen, who would defend conceded liberties and traditional legislation. The ideal also comprised a notion of a primitive social contract sealed by mutual oaths, the coronation oath sworn by the king and the oath of fealty sworn by the subjects. Furthermore, the common good of the community, or, to put it in classical terms familiar to seventeenth-century educated elites, public welfare (*bien public*), was seen as the primary goal of politics.[4]

For the French nobility, the manifestations of absolutism were perceived as violating the juridical and administrative traditions of the country.[5] The ideal of a mixed government and the urge to defend the fundamental laws and the liberties of the nobility and, gradually, the French nation were equally

---

2   A recent exception is Hallberg's *Ages of Liberty*. Pasi Ihalainen has also touched on this issue to some extent in *Protestant Nations Redefined*, although it is not the primary subject of the book.

3   See Skuncke & Tandefelt, *Riksdag, kaffehus och predikstol*, particularly Nurmiainen, "Gemensamma privilegier för ett odalstånd. Alexander Kepplerus som borgmästare och samhällstänkare", pp. 171–190, and Skuncke, "Medier, mutor och nätverk", pp. 255–286.

4   Jouanna, *Le devoir de révolte*.

5   Jouanna, *Le devoir de révolte*, p. 9.

present in the remonstrances and other texts later produced by the French *parlements* during their struggle with the centralised monarchy throughout the eighteenth century, although their position, according to Jouanna, was more ambiguous as they were officers of the crown.[6] Jouanna suggests that these ideas, elaborated during the civil wars of the sixteenth and early seventeenth century, were significant for the mental developments that led to the participation of enlightened aristocrats at the beginning of the French revolution.[7]

A central idea in these political representations was that if the king broke the contract with his subject by breaking his oath or the fundamental laws of the realm, violence became a legitimate means of defending political liberties. Were the king to become a tyrant, he should be deposed and could even be assassinated. This latter argument was developed by the so-called *monarchomaques*, the "king killers" among the French political theorists of the sixteenth and early seventeenth century. For sixteenth- and seventeenth-century French noblemen acting as a collective, armed rebellion and violence were ways to make the voice of the subjects heard if the representative bodies did not fill this function properly.[8] According to the notion of "the king's two bodies", rebellion against the weakness of the king or the incompetence of his councillors and administrators could be seen as a rebellion on behalf of the king, and such a rebellion was always presented as patriotic.[9]

If we speak in the terms of the political theory used by French noble thinkers, or the classical political thought familiar to many of the politically active members of the Swedish nobility, it is possible to state that Gustavian Sweden experienced both an armed rebellion (the Anjala League) and a tyrannicide (1792). It might be particularly interesting to look at these phenomena from a conceptual point of view. As will be shown below, the contemporaries themselves experienced that they were living a period when concepts were given new meanings. What was happening? How did it affect the way noble loyalties were articulated?

"Faithful subjects"

A rhetorical, commonplace formula in documents where contemporaries were to express their relation to the sovereign was "faithful subjects" (*trogna undersåtare*). As we have seen in the previous chapter, faithfulness and respect for the authorities of the state were seen as civic virtues in the solemn discourse of Swedish eighteenth-century politics. Here, the relationship

6 Jouanna, *Le devoir de révolte*, pp. 11–12.
7 Jouanna, *Le devoir de révolte*, pp. 396–399; see also Smith, *Nobility Reimagined*, pp. 222–279.
8 Jouanna, *Le devoir de révolte*, p. 10; Quentin Skinner, *The Foundations of Modern Political Thought. Volume 2: The Age of Reformation*, Cambridge, 1978, pp. 302–348.
9 Jouanna, *Le devoir de révolte*, pp. 282–290. The theory is fully exposed in Ernst H. Kantorowicz, *The King's Two Bodies. A Study in Mediaeval Political Theology*, Princeton, 1957.

between the subject and his ruler was expressed in terms such as "faith and love", "loving respect", "reverence and love", "faith and zeal", "honest love for our Gracious King" or "faithfulness to God, King and Fatherland".[10] It was described as a relationship of love and faith, not unlike the one between children and their father, or the one that united Christian believers and God. The same terminology of faith and allegiance can also be found in almost any letter addressed to the Royal Majesty by constituted bodies, institutions or individual subjects. Respectively, in speeches made on behalf of the Royal Majesty as well as in the king's coronation oath, the king's attitude towards his subjects was depicted in reverse, that of a father's love and care for his children.

Following the mediaeval European tradition, the bond between the subjects and their ruler was formalised by mutual oaths. Oaths of allegiance and fealty (in Swedish *tro- och huldhetsed*, cf. German *Huldigung*) were taken every time a new ruler was installed, when Swedish rule was extended to conquered provinces and when the fundamental laws were changed or there were other changes in the status of a constituted body. In addition, officials swore a personal oath of fealty upon their installation. When a new king was coronated, the Diet convened. In front of the assembled Estates, the king first forswore unlimited royal autocracy and promised, among other things, to keep the realm in the Lutheran faith, to preserve the Estates with their privileges, not to rule without or against the Senate, not to interfere with the elections to the Diet, not to depose anyone from office without due trial, and to pass no law and start no war without the consent of the Estates. Finally he declared that were he to break his oath, the Estates would be freed from theirs. After this the senators, the representatives of the nobility, the commanders of the army, the clergymen, the burghers' estate and, finally, the peasants took the oath in their turn. When taken by the Estates, the oath

---

10 *"ständig trohet och undersåtelig kärlek"*: [Carl Gustaf Tessin], *Til Hennes Kongl. Maj:t Wår Allernådigsta Drottning Landt-Marskalkens GREF CARL GUSTAF TESSINS Underdåniga Tal, Då hos Hennes Kongl. Maj:t Ridderskapets och Adelens Deputerade, efter sluten Riks-Dag, togo underdånigt afskied den 19 April 1739*, Stockholm, *s.d.* [1739]; *"den undersåteliga och kärleksfulla wördnad"*: [Matthias Alexander von Ungern-Sternberg], *Til Hans Kongl. Maj:t, Landt-Marskalkens Högwälborne Baron MATTHIAS ALEXANDER Von UNGERN STERNBERGS Underdånige TAL Å samtel. Riksens Ständers wägnar, Då De igenom sina Deputerade i underdånighet gofwo Hans Kongl. Maj:t tilkänna, Hans Durchl. Hertigens af Holstein Gottorp förklarnade til Successor på den Kongl. Swenska Thronen. Hållit den 28 Octobris 1742*, Stockholm, *s.d.* [1742]; *"undersåteliga wördnad och kärlek"*, *"min owanskeliga tro och nit för min Öfwerhet"*: [Carl Gustaf Tessin], *Underdånigst Tal Til Hans Kongl. Maj:t, Hållit uti Råds-Salen Then 30. Martii 1752. Af Hans Excellence Herr Riks-Rådet, Cancellie-Praesidenten, Hennes Kongl. Maj:ts Öfwerste-Marskalk, Hans Kongl. Höghets Cron-Printsens Gouverneur, Academiae-Cantzleren, Riddaren, Commendeuren och Cantzleren af Kongl. Maj:ts Orden, samt Riddaren af Swarta Örn, Högwälborne Grefwe CARL GUSTAF TESSIN, Tå Hans Excellence af-lade Cancellie-Praesidentskapet*, Stockholm, *s.d.* [1752]; *"rättskaffens kärlek för wår Nådige Konung"*: [Eric Brahe], *Grefwe BRAHES TAL, Hållit til Ridderskapet och Adelen, Wid Theras första sammanträde på Riddarhuset, Wid Riksdagen then 17 Octobris 1755*, Stockholm, *s.d.* [1755]; *"Trohet emot Gud, Konung och Fädernesland"*: [Samuel Troilius], *Til Hans Kongl. Maj:t, Ärkie-Biskopens D. SAMUEL TROILII TAL, Hållit på Präste-Ståndets wägnar Uppå Riks-Salen i Stockholm, Wid Riksdagens början Then 25 Octobris 1760*, Stockholm, *s.d.* [1760].

was considered to commit all the inhabitants of the realm, were they personally present or not. The writing of the oath slightly varied according to each estate; for the nobility, it contained a promise to be a faithful subject to the Royal Majesty and to sacrifice, if necessary, one's life and possessions for this loyalty. The nobility also promised to provide military services to the crown.[11]

The procedure was renewed and the oaths modified to a certain amount when the constitution was changed on 21 August 1772. In the new oath, the subjects swore to keep Gustav III and his descendants as their legitimate ruler and to promote the highness of the Royal Majesty and the liberty of the Estates as had been prescribed by the new constitution. Both the king and the subjects forswore all inclinations towards autocracy.[12]

How were these oaths and the ties they created experienced? As a formality or as an imperative of loyalty, or even both? Were they only remnants of feudal logics in the sense that the contractors no longer necessarily reflected on their original meanings? In practice, how faithful were the subjects and particularly the nobility? Did the expected, flattering rhetoric of feudal allegiance have any practical importance, and above all, what significance did it have for the ways in which loyalties were felt and experienced?

It seems rather obvious that even at the end of the eighteenth century, regardless of their historical origins, the oaths of fealty were still felt as very binding. This is reflected by the fact that the violation of such oaths was followed by sanctions that could be rather severe. For instance, Adolph Frederick's unwillingness to cooperate with the Senate in the 1750s led to investigations and speculations on whether the king had broken his oath and what consequences should be incurred from this eventuality. Similarly, when officers having served in the Prussian military forces returned to the Swedish army at the outbreak of the Seven Years' War, there was retaliation against them on the Prussian side – and vice versa. As late as the early 1790s, when the French legislative assembly obliged all office holders in France to swear loyalty not only to the king, but also to the constitution and the national assembly, the majority of foreign officers under the flags preferred to resign rather than swear an oath that was not compatible with their other political loyalties or with their political ideals.[13] Oaths and personal ties of fidelity remained essential parts of noble self-image, even and in particular at the dawn of the *ancien régime* (when they could be strong markers of political positioning).

In a conflict of loyalty where a subject had to choose between two different lords, for instance in a war between his natural ruler and the one he temporarily served, feudal allegiances became a practical problem which could be resolved only through a violation of the contractors of the covenant

11 Nordin, *Ett fattigt men fritt folk*, pp. 115–117. The coronation oaths of the eighteenth century have been published in Brusewitz, *Frihetstidens grundlagar och konstitutionella stadgar*.

12 [Gustav III], *Kongl. Maj:ts Nådige Försäkran Gifwen Thess trogne undersåtare Samtelige Riksens Ständer på Riks-Salen Then 21 augusti 1772*, Stockholm, 1772. Contains also: "Tro- och Huldhets-Ed" and "Eds-Formulaire" for the members of the Estates and the administration.

13 Wolff, *Vänskap och makt*, pp. 322–328.

or by most inextricable juridical arguments.[14] On the other hand, as oaths of fealty were seen as mutually binding, a violation of them by one of the contracting parts would automatically free the other part from his engagement. For instance, as we shall see, the citizen's duty to love the fatherland and promote common good could, at the end of the eighteenth century, appear to be stronger than the faith and fealty sworn to the king, which were "also" committing, in particular if the king had violated his own promise.[15] In that case, a rebellion against the king could become a rebellion on behalf of the King (the state, the Crown or the realm).

Reinventing liberty: the Gustavian moment

The Age of Liberty and the rule of the Diet, from 1738 to 1765 dominated by the Francophile Hat party, had its structural and moral fragilities, despite the development of early forms of parliamentarianism. The competition between rival parties, subsidised by foreign governments, and the tensions between the different estates as well as between the Senate and the king, provoked a semi-accepted corruption and threw a doubt on the political virtue that was supposed to be the fundament of free regimes. The moral crisis was doubled by suspicions on the very nature of the regime. As the Senate was dominated by the aristocracy and the nobility remained the most influential estate of the Diet, the general fear of all forms of concentrated power made accusations of oligarchy, ministerial despotism and aristocratic arbitrariness easy weapons for discrediting political enemies, but unfortunately also stained the image of the constitution itself.[16]

The long rule of the aristocratic and republican Hat party came to an end at the beginning of the Diet in 1765, when the Cap party won the majority at the Diet. This led to a shift in the party balance of the Diet, with the formerly adamantly republican Hats now approaching the court. Meanwhile, the new Senate dominated by the younger Caps, more radical than their prudent, traditionalist fathers of the 1730s and 1740s, proceeded to implement drastic economic measures and Sweden's first, fairly permissive law on the liberty of the press in 1766. The intention may have been to encourage the printing and distribution of pamphlets criticising the former Hat administration, but the new public debate soon eluded all control and eventually developed into a channel for not only party political, but also social criticism, where the legitimacy of privilege itself was questioned. By the end of the 1760s, the nobility's position as a leading estate had become less self-evident than ever before.

The Hats and the court now found themselves before a mutual enemy. New plans for a revolution and for a modification of the constitution were

14 Wolff, *Vänskap och makt*, p. 319.
15 "Also": see the Anjala declaration (quoted below), LUB, DelaGardieska samlingen, historiska handlingar, vol. 23:1, N. 1.
16 See, for instance, Wolff, "Pro Patria et Libertate. Frihetsbegreppet i 1700-talets svenska politiska språk"; pp. 34–62; Charlotta Wolff, "Aristocratic republicanism and the hate of sovereignty in 18-century Sweden", *Scandinavian Journal of History*, vol. 32 (2007:4), pp. 358–375.

made at the court, this time with the support of the French ambassador and the consent of the Hat opposition, which hoped only to regain power at the next Diet. Particularly the Prince Royal, Gustaf, acted as an important intermediary in these preparations and negotiations.[17] The revolution, however, did not take place, despite the success of Adolph Frederick's temporary abdication in December 1768 and the final summoning of the Estates. The Diet that opened in 1769 saw a comeback of the Hats and the dismissal of the Cap Senate that had tried to prevent the summoning of the Estates, but the constitution was not yet changed. As the following Diet convened in 1771 as a consequence of the death of Adolph Frederick, the Hats were once again losing power, and the Estates were torn apart in debates concerning a possible extension of privileges to the commoners' estates and the terms of the new king's coronation oath.

On 19, 20 and 21 August 1772, the twenty-four-year-old king Gustav III, who had finally been coronated in May, put an end to the unruly Diet by arresting the senators, making the central administration swear loyalty to the new regime and imposing on the Estates a new constitution that brought Sweden back to a strong monarchy. In this transition from one regime to another, the larger part of the nobility chose the king's side, some after a certain hesitation, with the perils of 1756 in mind.[18] The nobility needed the monarchy and the king to equilibrate the increasing demands for consideration of the commoners' estates, which were becoming conscious of their position and were claiming enlarged privileges and political recognition.[19]

In the new constitution approved by the Estates – closely guarded by three battalions of the guard, loaded cannons and 100 grenadiers – on 21 August 1772, a larger portion of both the legislative and the executive power was given to the king. The Senate became a royal privy council responsible only to the monarch and no longer to the Estates. The Estates shared legislative power with the king. Nothing was said about how often they should convene, only that they should be assembled at the time and place indicated by the king. Further, the duration of the Diet was limited to three months only.[20]

With the new constitution, the Age of Liberty had come to an end, but in the discourse legitimating the new regime, key concepts were lavishly borrowed from the ideological arsenal of the former regime. However, as political power shifted, these key concepts were rapidly reformulated and given new dimensions. With new realities, new meanings appeared. The main conceptual change, of course, was to concern liberty, as this had been the ideological core of the precedent regime. It is possible that Gustav III originally and sincerely understood the liberty of his subjects as a positive

17 Erik Lönnroth, *Den stora rollen. Kung Gustaf III spelad av honom själv*, Stockholm, 1986, pp. 19–21.

18 For a complete account of the events, see Malmström, *Sveriges politiska historia från K. Carl XII:s död till statshvälfningen 1772*, vol. 6, pp. 234–457.

19 See Nurmiainen, "Gemensamma privilegier för ett odalstånd. Alexander Kepplerus som borgmästare och samhällstänkare", pp. 171–190; Nordin, *Ett fattigt men fritt folk*, pp. 390–418.

20 *Kongl. Maj:ts Och Riksens Ständers Fastställte Regerings-FORM, Dat. STOCKHOLM then 21 Augusti 1772*, Stockholm, s.d. [1772].

and necessary element against despotism. At least, this seems to have been the case in the draft for a new constitution that he approved in 1769.[21] The concept of 'liberty' is also central in the new constitution of 1772. As a matter of fact, the king hardly had any choice but to use the conceptual apparatus of the Age of Liberty, if he wished to present the change of regime as legitimate and inevitable. As Peter Hallberg has shown, the king made skilful use of concepts, the meanings of which were gradually changed.[22] This probably eventually also changed the king's own perception of their order of importance.

A first example of this is the king's solemn declaration to his guard right on the morning of 19 August 1772:

> I hereby declare that my only intention is to restore peace in My Dear Fatherland through the oppression of licence, the abolition of Aristocratic power and the revival of the ancient Swedish Liberty, and the restoration of Sweden's old Laws as they were before 1680.[23]

The intention to "restore peace" and revive liberty sounds like an echo of Marsilius of Padua, whose *Defensor pacis* belonged, like Machiavelli's *Il principe*, to the old political library of European rulers. Concretely, it was an allusion to the up to then dramatically growing tensions between not only the parties but also the Estates. In terms such as "oppression of licence", "abolition of aristocratic power" and "revival of the ancient Swedish liberty", the king outlined his thesis, which would long survive in historiography, on the corruption of liberty into licence during the so-called Age of Liberty and the king's personal role as the defender of civil peace and popular sovereignty.[24] In fact, this thesis was only a reflection of the classical theory on the danger of corruption of free regimes in the case that power was concentrated into the hands of an oligarchic aristocracy, as we have seen in previous chapters. More significant was perhaps after all the promotion of an "ancient", purer Swedish liberty. Indeed, Gustav III's revolution was explicitly a restoration, and the king's deeds would consequently, throughout his reign, be presented as a return to or at least a revival of a glorious past.[25] "Before 1680" referred to the times before Caroline absolutism, which during the Age of Liberty had been seen as the root of all evil. This perception was

---

21 Lönnroth, *Den stora rollen*, pp. 21–23.

22 Hallberg, *Ages of Liberty*, pp. 232–278.

23 "*Jag försäkrar härmed, at Mitt enda upsåt är, at åter sätta lugnet i Mitt Kära Fädernesland igienom sielfswåldets förtryckande, Aristocratiske magtens afskaffande och then urgamla Swenska Frihetens uplifwande, samt Sweriges gamla Lagars återställande, som the före 1680 warit.*" [Gustav III], *Kongl. Maj:ts Nådiga Försäkran, Til Thess Lif-Garde, Artillerie och samtelige trogne undersåtare här i Residence-Staden Stockholm, Gifwen then 19. Augusti 1772*, Stockholm, 1772. See Alm, *Kungsord i elfte timmen*, pp. 130–153.

24 On Marsilius and the *defensor pacis* see, for instance, Skinner, *The Foundations of Modern Political Thought. Volume 1: The Renaissance*, p. 65.

25 On this matter, see above all Henrika Tandefelt, *Konsten att härska. Gustaf III inför sina undersåtar*, Helsingfors, 2008; see also Alm, *Kungsord i elfte timmen*; Sven Delblanc, *Ära och minne. Studier kring ett motivkomplex i 1700-talets litteratur*, Stockholm, 1965, particularly pp. 136–186.

skilfully exploited by the king, who thus presented the aristocratic Age of Liberty as only the logical last part of a process of decadence that had begun with the despotic rule of the Carolines.[26] More acceptable were the fundamental laws of Gustav II Adolph, whom Gustav III would put forward as his predecessor in a chain of "Gustavs".[27] The constitution of 1634 was perhaps a balanced one – a *monarchia mixta* – in its full sense, reserving a real amount of power for the king, and indeed a founding piece of Swedish constitutional law. In the context of the 1770s, however, it was already very behind the times. By definition, the royal revolution of 1772 was anti-despotic and reactionary.

The king's declaration of 19 August 1772 to the inhabitants of Stockholm says more about the spirit of reaction, presented as necessary, which initially characterised this revolution. In it the king urged the inhabitants of the capital "to await with respect and silence the measures and steps that now have to be taken for general security, for the independence and the preservation of the right liberty of the Realm" and explained that "the king has needed to use his power to save himself and the realm from the Aristocratic rule".[28]

Gustav III, unlike his father and Frederick I, addressed the Diet himself. In the speeches held during plenary Diet sessions immediately after the revolution had taken place, liberty was again a central concept, which was hardly surprising in this institution previously celebrated for its freedom. In his speech to the Estates on 21 August 1772, when arguing for the necessity of the new constitution, Gustav III repeated the thesis of corruption: "[…] thus Liberty, the noblest of human rights, has been transformed into an unbearable Aristocratic despotism in the hands of the ruling Party". Interestingly, the king judged it necessary to counter any suspicions about his intentions concerning his people's freedom. "You are much mistaken, if you think that we are searching for something else than Liberty and Law", he began, then proceeded to give a long explanation that "far from touching Liberty, it is only Licence that I want to abolish, and the arbitrariness with which the Realm has been ruled". The only thing he desired was to "establish a right kind of Liberty that only can make you, my dear subjects, happy". This would be done legally and by law.[29]

26 Hallberg, *Ages of Liberty*, pp. 249–252. Cf. the king's formal disavow of "the abominable royal absolutism or the so-called Sovereignty, which would deprive me of my utmost honour to be the first citizen of a righteous free people": *"Jag afsäger mig nu, som Jag redan thet giordt, thet förhateliga Konungsliga Enwäldet, eller then så kallade Souverainiteten, anseende nu som förr, för Min största ära, at wara then förste Medborgaren ibland et rättskaffens fritt Folk: Så sant Mig Gud hielper til Lif och Själ."* [Gustav III], *Kongl. Maj:ts Nådiga Försäkran, Til Thes Lif-Garde, Artillerie och samteliga trogne undersåtare här i Residence-Staden Stockholm, Gifwen Then 19. Augusti 1772.*

27 Tandefelt, *Konsten att härska*, pp. 312–313, 317.

28 "[…] *at afwakta med wördnad och stillhet the mått och steg, som för then allmänna säkerheten, för Rikets sielfständighet och thes rätta frihets bibehållande nu tagas måste; emedan Kongl. Maj:t blifwit nödsakad at bruka then magt Honom öfrig war, för at frälsa Sig och Riket från thet Aristocratiska wäldet* […]"; [Gustav III], *Kongl. Maj:ts Nådige Kundgörelse Til Thess trogne undersåtare I Residence-Staden Stockholm*, Stockholm, 1772.

29 "*Således har Friheten, den ädlaste af mensklighetens rättigheter, blifwit förwandlad, uti en olidelig Aristocratisk despotisme i det rådande Partiets händer*", "*I misstagen Eder mycket, om I tron, at här sökes annat än Frihet och Lag.*" "*Långt ifrån at widröra Friheten, är det*

The speech made by the Marshal of the Diet, Axel Gabriel Leijonhufvud, on 26 August 1772 returned to the theme of a liberty not removed, but surrounded with fences (*omgärdad*) preventing it from being abused. As we have seen, already in the middle of the Age of Liberty, the idea of a liberty balanced by law and legalism had been strongly present. In this sense, it was possible for contemporaries to believe that the key concepts and the ideological basis of the Swedish state and political community remained unchanged, although the balance of power had shifted, and with it, the order of priority of these concepts. However, in the Gustavian discourse, although freedom was not forgotten, the emphasis was now slightly more on law and obedience. The "fences" surrounding liberty, as Leijonhufvud put it, suggest a very static conception of liberty as a cherished value but no longer an active force that made the nation progress and become a model of virtue and prosperity for other free people, as in Tessin's speech of 1747.[30]

The Estates and with them the formerly mighty House of Nobility, in which the antique hierarchic divisions into classes were now reintroduced, had thus consented to reduce their own power. It had happened under armed threat and constraint, with a part of the members of the Diet imprisoned, but formally, it happened by consent and without bloodshed. For this reason, the revolution of Gustav III was presented to the world, and to a credulous posterity, as a "liberation".[31] To the critical reader, these heroic claims of the royalist cause may seem rather preposterous and propagandistic. More relevant in our context, however, than to present arguments for or against the sincerity of the discourse of freedom used by the king is to try to understand how and why it was possible for the Estates, and above all the nobility, which in this study has been presented as fairly republican and anti-absolutist, to accept the change.

Several reasons could be invoked, the first of which would be the sudden lack of security of the privileged estate and of the former political elite. The nobility may have seen in the reduction of the power of the Estates a way to disarm the political and social demands of the commoners and "put an end to the tyranny of the lower estates" at a time when the nobility was under pressure both at the Diet and in the press.[32] The former Hat party, in its turn, had found in the monarchy and above all the heir to the throne – whose education had been supervised by former members of the Hat elite such as Tessin and Carl Fredrik Scheffer – an ally against the Cap party. In addition, we should not underestimate the power of a developing royalism, which had always been present to some extent, particularly in military circles, and

endast Sielfswåldet, Jag wil afskaffa, och den Godtycko, med hwilken Riket blifwit styrdt", "at stadga en rätt Frihet, som endast kan göra Eder, Mine käre Undersåtare, lyckelige"; [Gustav III], *Kongl. Maj:ts TAL Til Riksens Ständer, Församlade uppå Riks-Salen i Stockholm, Den 21 augusti 1772*, Stockholm, 1772.

30 Cf. chapter 3.

31 Hallberg, *Ages of Liberty*, pp. 232–278; Alm, *Kungsord i elfte timmen*, pp. 130–153; Tandefelt, *Konsten att härska*, pp. 37–39.

32 Quote in Malmström, *Sveriges politiska historia från K. Carl XII:s död till statshvälfningen 1772*, vol. 6, p. 446.

which in the late 1760s was favoured among younger officers because of the personal charisma of Prince Gustaf and his younger brother Carl.[33]

Royalism as a new conception for unity and political concord may also have benefited from the spread and banalisation of new political notions such as 'nation', 'fatherland' or 'Swede'. As key concepts of politics were seldom explicitly defined, but rather used with an underlying assumption of consensus, many of them were vague, polysemic and easily instrumentalised for political purposes by the rhetorically most skilful speakers, to which Gustav III incontestably belonged. For a nobility accustomed to and having often served in the armies of absolutist rulers in France or Prussia, monarchy could also be experienced as greatness in a situation in which Sweden of the Age of Liberty had been weak compared to other states.[34]

Broken covenant and rebellion

When Gustav III had declared his intentions to his guard on the morning of 19 August 1772 and asked for its loyalty, the guard answered by one mouth: "We venture our life and blood at the service of Your Royal Majesty."[35] Sixteen years later, a large part of the officers' corps in Finland put their arms down, refusing to continue the war that the king had declared on Russia in the summer of 1788 as it had not been approved by the Diet. Why did the nobility, recently converted to the cause of royalty, choose rebellion?

Gustav III's constitution of August 1772 had maintained an illusion of mixed government, with a Senate and a Diet, the convocation of which depended, however, only on the king's pleasure. The frequency of the Diet actually slowed down, and after 1772 there were only four of them (in 1778, 1786, 1789 and 1792) until the king's death in 1792. By the middle of the 1780s, the initial enthusiasm over the charismatic young ruler had faded, as the economic problems of the realm had not disappeared and the constrained pleasures and favouritism of the court no longer diverted the nobility. At the Diet of 1786, most of the bills presented by the king were dismissed by the Estates. In the noble estate, resistance was laconic, firm and organised, and led by hardened veteran politicians of the Age of Liberty, such as the now elderly, icy Count Fersen, who personified the aristocratic opposition. The king's control over the press had solidified, but the opposition spread its criticism in manuscript pamphlets.[36]

---

33 See, for instance, Clas Julius Ekeblad's diaries in KB, Engeströmska samlingen, I e 14:7; see also Gustaf Johan Ehrensvärd, *Dagboksanteckningar förda vid Gustaf III:s hof af friherre Gustaf Johan Ehrensvärd*, utg. E. V. Montan, Stockholm, 1878.

34 About monarchy as greatness, cf. Tandefelt, *Konsten att härska*, pp. 222–230, and Delblanc, *Ära och minne*, on the invention of a glorious past. About Swedish nobles serving in foreign armies and particularly *"le service du Roi [de France]"*, see Wolff, *Vänskap och makt*, pp. 146–185, 322–328.

35 *"Vi våga lif och blod til Eders Kongl. Majts tjenst"*, C. G. von Liewen in *Handlingar om 1772 års revolution*, KB, D 1019, Strödda handlingar till Gustaf III:s historia (före 1788).

36 Lönnroth, *Den stora rollen*, p. 116; Alm, *Kungsord i elfte timmen*, pp. 213–229; Elmar Nyman, *Indragningsmakt och tryckfrihet 1785–1810*, Stockholm, 1963, pp. 30–55.

In its resistance against the king, the opposition returned the *topos* of law and obedience often used by the king, in terms recalling those used at the Diets of the Age of Liberty. During the debate over the Estates' right to decide on the use of its own budget, Fersen stated:

> It is an equally necessary as estimable characteristic of a Law-abiding subject to know the Laws that he should follow. We have a Constitution that is our holy and immovable Fundamental Law, the limit of which both King and subjects have committed themselves by a sacred Oath not to trespass.[37]

To divert attention from domestic problems and to profit from the Russo-Turkish war, the king decided to start a war against Sweden's eastern neighbour. According to the constitution of 1772, the king could not make war without the explicit consent of the Estates (this was in order to prevent perilous developments similar to those that had taken place during the rule of Charles XII).[38] An incident on the Russian border at Puumala in South-Eastern Finland on 28 June 1788 provided a formal reason to attack. Historians nowadays tend to believe that the incident had been arranged at the king's request.[39] This was also the opinion of many contemporaries, at least if we give credibility to the stream of oppositional pamphlets provoked by the war.[40]

The war that had started with an unclear provocation on the border did not progress as predicted. The morale of the troops was not the best; food and clothes were scarce, and above all the officers were not convinced about the strategy chosen by the king for the attack on St. Petersburg. After an unsuccessful attempt to conquer the Russian fort at Fredrikshamn on the old border of 1721, seven Finnish-born officers of the Swedish army, among them Major General Carl Gustaf Armfelt, decided to send a letter asking for peace to the empress Catherine II.[41] The note was dated in Liikkala, at the eastern side of the border river Kymi, on 9 August 1788. When this news came to the king's ears, he required that all his officers renew their oaths of fealty to the king by swearing to follow him and fight the enemy in any place. This questioning of their loyalty was perceived as an insult by many

37 "*Det är en lika så nödvändig som wärdig egenskap hos en Laglydig undersåte att wara underrättad om de Lagar han bör åtlyda. Wi hafwa en Regeringsform som är wår heliga och oryggeliga GrundLag, hwars gränts både Konung och undersåtare genom en dyr Ed förbundit sig att ej öfwerskrida.*" Fersen i bancofrågan, RA, Ridderskapets och adelns pleniprotokoller med akter, riksdagen 1786, R 171, pp. 30–31 (12 May 1786).
38 RF 1772, art. 48: "*Ej må konungen krig och örlog göra utan riksens ständers ja och samtycke.*"
39 Tandefelt, *Konsten att härska*, p. 233; Lönnroth, *Den stora rollen*, p. 159.
40 These pamphlets were clandestine manuscript copies and circulated from hand to hand. See A. R. Cederberg, *Anjalan liiton historialliset lähteet. Lähdekriitillinen tutkielma*, Helsinki, 1931, pp. 162–200.
41 The other officers were Colonel Sebastian von Otter, Colonel Johan Henric Hästesko, Chief of Battalion Per af Enehielm, Lieutenant Colonel Otto Klingspor, ADC Carl Henrik Klick, and Gustaf von Kothen, Commander of the Cavalry. J. R. Danielson-Kalmari, *Suomen valtio- ja yhteiskuntaelämä 18:nnella ja 19:nnellä vuosisadalla. Kustavilainen aika. 2. Osa*, Porvoo, 1921, p. 282.

of the officers.[42] On 13 August, the same officers, gathered at the manor of Anjala, made a public declaration, in which they explained the moral foundation of the Liikkala note, their contradictory feelings of loyalty and the miserable state of the army, and, in guarded terms, their wish for peace and their suspicion that the war had not been legally started. The document was circulated in the troops at Anjala, Keltti and Ummeljoki, all located on the river Kymi, and was finally signed by 113 officers, two thirds of them noblemen.[43]

In St. Petersburg, the Liikkala note did not produce the expected effect, but rather underlined the bad state of the Swedish army to the enemy. Gustav III, in an effort to frighten the mutinous officers, had declared their actions treacherous and offered his pardon to all those who would ask for it, but the mutinous officers declined and, on 24 August, sent a letter to the king in which they asked for an immediate summoning of the Estates. The king renewed his offer of pardon, but again, it was rejected by the officers who did not consider that they had done anything to be forgiven for. Instead, they reiterated their claims for a summoning of the Estates and asked "all patriots" to join them in their cause, in a public statement that was sent to the other Swedish troops in Finland. There were at least eleven individual or collective answers, of which only three were negative or neutral ones.[44] It was the beginning of some months of confusion that would end with the imprisonment and trials of 125 leaguers and the public beheading of one of them in Stockholm.

42 See Allan Sandström, *Officerarna som fick nog. Anjalamännen och Gustaf III:s ryska krig 1788–1790*, Örebro, 1996, p. 114, and pp. 116–117 with a quote by General C. G. Armfelt writing to his brother Magnus Wilhelm Armfelt: "I consider that I act in the right way and that I have done both my king and my country a considerable service and have hereby followed exclusively the personal wishes of the Monarch and the pressing requests that have been made by his representatives, who I knew share his confidence, trust and grace; if therefore I have done wrong it is neither by the cause nor even formally, because it was impossible for me to find some better way without compromising the king, which he himself wanted to avoid at any price." – "*Jag anser mig handla rätt och hava gjort både min kung och mitt land en betydelsefull tjänst och har härvidlag uteslutande följt Monarchens egna önskningar och de enträgna framställningar, som blifvit gjorda af hans ombud, vilka jag väl visste äga hans förtrolighet, förtroende och ynnest; om jag alltså felat är det varken uti sak eller ens till formen, ty det var mig omöjligt att kunna hitta på något bättre sätt utan att komprometttera kungen, något som han själv ovillkorligen ville undgå.*"

43 J. R. Danielson-Kalmari, *Suomen valtio- ja yhteiskuntaelämä 18:nnella ja 19:nnellä vuosisadalla. Kustavilainen aika. 2. Osa*, pp. 307–319.

44 Originals at LUB, DelaGardiesamlingen, Historiska handlingar, vol. 23:1–3. The eight statements are signed: (1) Hastfer, Stiernecrantz, Morian and Ehrenstolpe, at Rantasalmi (neutral); (2) Curt von Stedingk, at Rantasalmi (negative); (3) Stedingk and 22 other officers at Rantasalmi (neutral); (4) Magnus Brunow and a handful of officers at Rantasalmi (positive); (5) Bergenstråle, Gripenberg, Furuhjelm and Uggla, at Högfors (positive); (6) Duncker and Sticht, at St. Michel (positive); (7) several officers at Helsingfors (positive), and (8–11) officers from various regiments, identical form (positive).

'Nation', 'rights' and plotting on behalf of and against the fatherland

The Anjala League has now and then risen to favour in Finnish and Swedish history writing. It has repeatedly been placed in the context of a hypothetically emerging Finnish national identity. It has been asked whether the league should be seen as the manifestation of an underlying Finnish separatism or only as an oppositional cabal, and arguments have been presented both in favour of and against these theses.[45] This kind of simplistic interpretation can seem very tempting since there actually were members or sympathisers of the Anjala League (such as major Johan Anders Jägerhorn or Colonel Berndt Johan Hastfehr) who were in contact with the "traitor" and former Swedish subject in the Russian camp, Göran Magnus Sprengtporten, or who had personal interests in a redefinition of the ties between Finland and the rest of Sweden.[46] The rebellion that started as concern with the contradictory duties of officers in an illegal war soon had elements of high treason and manipulation by the Finnish separatists negotiating with the enemy, who in turn spread disinformation in the form of pamphlets. The situation became so confused that even the most perspicacious contemporaries or loyal friends of the king themselves could not always distinguish between the different factions and their intentions. In a letter to the king, Colonel Curt von Stedingk wrote, on 19 August 1788, that "Sprengtporten's old idea to make Finland a republic [...] has turned the heads of all the Finns".[47]

The idea of a larger Finnish separatism in the eighteenth century is nowadays dismissed by a majority of historians, although some members of the landed elite, partially the same persons that we find among the signers of the Anjala declaration, may have nourished dreams of a more independent status under Russian protection for the eastern part of the Swedish realm. In the context of this study, the issue on whether the Anjala League was a Finnish-national movement is perhaps the wrong question. Most of the Finnish-born officers in the league had outspokenly "patriotic" motives for their choices, but generally speaking, for Finnish-born Swedish noblemen and officers of the Swedish crown, a patriotic zeal to serve the king or the fatherland was far from being the same thing as identifying this fatherland

45 For a recent overview, see, for instance, Osmo Jussila, *Suomen historian suuret myytit*, Helsinki, 2007, pp. 151–182, 264–269.

46 Sprengtporten had been one of the key figures in the revolution of 1772, securing with his elder brother the loyalty of the garrison at Sveaborg to the king's cause. Deceived in his hopes for advancement and deceived in his expectations of reforms in Finland, he turned his back against Sweden and left for Russia in 1786. Jägerhorn was the Grand Master of the patriotic order of Walhall and a friend of Sprengtporten. Hastfehr had been a fervent royalist, distributing bribes on the king's behalf at the Diet of 1786. Sandström, *Officerarna som fick nog*, pp. 45–59.

47 Letter from Stedingk to Gustav III, Olofsborg 19 August 1788, translated quote in Danielson-Kalmari, *Suomen valtio- ja yhteiskuntaelämä 18:nnella ja 19:nnellä vuosisadalla. Kusta-vilainen aika. 2. Osa*, p. 361, French original in UUB, Collectio Mss Regis Gustavi III, vol. 45 (F 519); printed in *Mémoires posthumes du feldmaréchal Comte de Stedingk ; rédigés sur des lettres, dépêches et autres pièces authentiques laissées à sa famille par le Comte de Björnstjerna*, Paris, 1844–1847.

with Finland rather than the Swedish realm, although there are strong indications that a couple of the leaguers did make this identification.[48]

While much research has been done on the Anjala League from the perspective of Finnish national identity, surprisingly little has been written on the conflicts of loyalty experienced by the army officers with regard to their political ideals and philosophical references.[49] Still, the war years of 1788–1790 saw a considerable amount of printed and manuscript declarations, pamphlets, verses and other largely spread political leaflets in which the relationships between the monarch and his subjects, ties of loyalty and patriotism were described and to some extent even redefined, from different points of view.

For instance, in *Betracktelser wid Kongl. Svenska Ministerens Declaration, gifven Helsingfors den 2. Julii 1788*, the author, after noting the restrictions made by the king on the citizens' freedom to speak and to write, analyses the terms in the Swedish declaration of war against Russia and describes a reconceptualisation of the vocabulary of political loyalty during the reign of Gustav III. He states that "Swedish ears [...] during 16 years of time [since 1772] have been used to some words having entirely other meanings than they had before".[50] This pamphlet had been written by a person close to the Russian court and spread in Sweden as part of the Russian war propaganda, but that did not prevent it from being largely spread and, probably also, largely read and known.[51] The use of terminology in the Liikkala note and the Anjala declaration also reflects the evolution of the political and philosophical references of the Swedish nobility during the latter half of the eighteenth century. This is also the case in the most vehement and significant of the oppositional pamphlets produced by the sympathisers of the officers' mutiny, *En Finsk Officerares Försvar för Arméen, emot utkomne Smädeskrifter och i synnerhet ett så kallat Bref af d: 14. September 1788 angående vissa Stämplingar* ("A Finnish officer's apology of the army, against published lampoons and in particular a so-called Letter of 14 September 1788 on certain conspiracies"), written by no other than Klick, the very author of the Liikkala note.[52]

48 On multiple loyalties and patriotism amidst the Swedish nobility, see Wolff, *Vänskap och makt*, pp. 275–328. On the issue of Finnish patriotism in the eighteenth century and how it can be interpreted, see Jouko Nurmiainen, "Frågan om 'etnisk nationalism', nationell självbild och 1700-talets Sverige", *Historisk Tidskrift för Finland*, vol. 88 (2003:3), pp. 257–275, and Jouko Nurmiainen, "Particular interest and the common good in Swedish mid-18th-century diet politics: the 'Finnish' perspective", *Scandinavian Journal of History*, vol. 32 (2007:4), pp. 388–404.

49 Rewarding in this respect, although strongly nationalistic, is paradoxically Danielson-Kalmari, *Suomen valtio- ja yhteiskuntaelämä 18:nnella ja 19:nnellä vuosisadalla. Kusta-vilainen aika. 2. Osa*. See also Sandström, *Officerarna som fick nog*; Lesch, *Jan Anders Jägerhorn*; Yrjö Blomstedt, "Den finländska självständighetstanken på 1780-talet – ideologi eller politisk spekulation", *Historisk Tidskrift för Finland*, 1965, pp. 92–102.

50 [Anon.], *Betracktelser wid Kongl. Svenska Ministerens Declaration, gifven Helsingfors den 2. Julii 1788*, KB, Schröderheim, Historisk-politiska samlingar 2 (1788).

51 Copies can be found at least at the National Library of Sweden and at the Lund University Library. The text was printed in 1821 in *Hemliga Handlingar, hörande till Sveriges Historia efter Konung GUSTAF III:s Anträde till Regeringen*, [Stockholm], 1821.

52 *En Finsk Officerares Försvar för Arméen, emot utkomne Smädeskrifter och i synnerhet ett så kallat Bref af d: 14. September 1788 angående vissa Stämplingar*, LUB, DelaGardieska

In the original documents, the Liikkala note and the Anjala declaration, the relationship between Sweden and the part of it called "Finland" is not even addressed. Only a subordinate clause in the Liikkala note implies that the Finnish part of the realm has suffered particularly from the wars and the territorial losses of 1743. To complain about particular sufferings, however, was only too common in Diet memoranda or other political pledges of the eighteenth century.[53] The central problem, and finally the origin of both documents, is in the conflict between the duty to obey the king's command and the duty to be faithful to the constitution, to which the officers also had sworn fidelity.

The Liikkala note of 9 August 1788 begins by explaining that it was only after having crossed the front line that the officers realised that "steps had been taken [which were] contrary to the rights of the nation, which we as citizens consider ourselves obliged to guard no less than we [must] do our military duties".[54] This was an allusion to the fact that the king had started the war without consulting the Estates. "This awkward position", the text continued, "has put us in the utmost embarrassment on how to find the means to fulfil our obligations as righteous patriots without violating the duty that we carry as military [officers]."[55] The way out of this situation, the officers argued, was to explain to Her Imperial Majesty "the honest desire of the entire Nation, and in particular the Finnish one, that an eternal peace and neighbourly friendship may be preserved".[56] This was not all: taking a bold chance, the officers suggested that in case Her Majesty would agree to make peace, the best guarantee for it would be that she also returned the part of the province of Kymmenegård that had been conquered by Russia in 1743. The text ended with a phrase that shows that the officers were fully conscious of the moral ambiguity of their conduct: on the empress's reply would depend

> [...] whether we may put down our weapons and return to the peace that makes the happiness of the Realm, or whether we shall carry them in a way more honourable and more dignifying for the nation, which we believe should be the destiny of righteous Swedish men, when they know for certain that it is for the Fatherland that they brave dangers and death.[57]

samlingen, historiska handlingar, vol. 23:2. Another pamphlet adopting the same tone was *En svensk patriots försvar öfver det af Arméen i Finland vidtagne steg uti kriget 1788*, KB, Schröderheim, Historisk-politiska samlingar 2 (1788).

53 For instance, the French *parlements* mentioned "the suffering of the people". On how particular Finnish interests were defended in Swedish political discourse, see Nurmiainen, "Particular interest and the common good in Swedish mid-18th-century diet politics: the 'Finnish' perspective".

54 "[...] *steg voro gjorda stridande mot nations rättigheter, hvilka vi icke mindre som medborgare anse oss böra bevaka, än uppfylla våra militäriska skylldigheter.*" All quotes from the Liikkala note follow the copy in the Russian archives of the Ministry of Foreign Affairs, reproduced in Cederberg, *Anjalan liiton historialliset lähteet*, pp. 247–248. This one is on p. 247.

55 "*Denna brydsamma ställning har försatt oss i yttersta förlägenhet, att finna medel för att uppfylla våra skylldigheter som rättskaffens patrioter, utan att bryta mot den pligt som oss som militärer åligger.*" Cederberg, *Anjalan liiton historialliset lähteet*, p. 247.

56 "[...] *hela Nations och isynnerhet den Finskas gemensamma uppricktiga önskan, att en ewig fred och gränssämja, emellan begge dessa riken måtte bibehållas [...].*" Cederberg, *Anjalan liiton historialliset lähteet*, p. 247.

57 "[...] *det allernådigste svar af Eders Kejs. Majestät som han* [J. A. Jägerhorn] *bringar skall*

The declaration made at Anjala on 13 August 1788 is almost twice as long, more explicative and more cautious in terms. Its first paragraph stated that the army had crossed the border on the Royal Majesty's orders, that the king commanded the army and that military laws did not permit officers to doubt whether they should obey or not. However, the text continued, as the Russian command had taken only defensive actions, it seemed probable that the initial aggression had been made by "the Swedish Nation" and not by Russia.[58] In the second paragraph, the officers once again underlined their double and now conflicting duties: "as citizens", they had promised to follow the constitution according to which "the Nation" should decide on any offensive wars; as officers, however, they were supposed to obey the supreme command.[59] Here too, 'the nation' was used instead of 'the Estates'.

The third paragraph declared that after the retreat from Fredrikshamn, the officers no longer considered it glorious "to fight bravely and die", since the fatherland would not benefit from it but rather needed its servants to prevent its destruction.[60] In the three following paragraphs, they referred to the general discontent of the army and its weak motivation to fight, but promised to defend the border "until the last drop of blood", although they considered it far from certain that the Russian army would not break through in Savolax.[61]

In the seventh paragraph, the officers explained that they had contacted the empress to tell her about "the way of thought of the nation".[62] (This "nation", an easy and fashionable word in 1788, remains somewhat unclear; a more truthful way of putting it would probably have been "the opposition".) Besides their love for the fatherland and concern for its welfare, which were the first of their duties, the faith and fealty they had sworn to the king had motivated this step, the aim of which was only to help the king. Finally, the declaration ended with an oath, where the signers swore "by God's holy name and our honour" to sacrifice

---

decidera om vi få nedlägga vapnen och vända tillbaka till det lugn, som gör Rikets sällhet, eller om vi skola bära dem på ett för nationen mera hedrande och värdigt sätt, hvilket vi äro öfvertygade bör vara rättskaffens svenska mäns öde, då de med visshet veta att det är för Fäderneslandet de trotsa faror och döden." Cederberg, *Anjalan liiton historialliset lähteet*, p. 248.

58 "[…] *hafwa vi fattat den till wisshet sannolika tanka, at anfallet af Swenska Nation är gjord*t." LUB, DelaGardieska samlingen, historiska handlingar, 23:1, N. 1.

59 "*Öme som Medborgare om helgden af den Regerings-form Wi beswurit, och hwilken förbehåller Nation rättighet at döma om nödwändigheten af Offensive krig. Skyldige som Militairer at lyda wår högste Chef, hafwa Wi befunnit oss uti den för Redelige män brydsamme omständighet, at se wåra skyldigheter stridande […].*" LUB, DelaGardieska samlingen, historiska handlingar, 23:1, N. 1.

60 "*At strida med tapperhet och dö, som wanligen är så ärofullt för en Militaire, hafwa Wi uphördt at så anse, då Fäderneslandet ingenting kunde Winna […].*"LUB, DelaGardieska samlingen, historiska handlingar, 23:1, N. 1.

61 "*Gräntsen, som wåra Trupper betäcker, anse wi wäl tillbörligen bevakad och wilja äfwen den samma i händelse af anfall, till sista blodsdroppan förswara.*" LUB, DelaGardieska samlingen, historiska handlingar, 23:1, N. 1.

62 "[…] *hafwa Wi tagit det beslut, at […] wända oss till Hennes Keijserliga Maj:t och försäkra henne om Nations tänkesätt.*" LUB, DelaGardieska samlingen, historiska handlingar, 23:1, N. 1.

> [...] our lives, blood and property to prevent the misfortunes that menace the fatherland, for which reason we also hereby, by the same holy oath make the firmest covenant and Comradeship between us to advise, help and assist each other in all cases related to common and particular security.[63]

They also promised that if the empress would not accept their pledge for peace, they would consider themselves personally attacked and would not put their weapons down until the fatherland was at peace and secure. This stress on personal honour is characteristic of noble self-image and thought.

It should be noticed that the officers systematically presented their cause as a moral and patriotic one. Their intention, they argued, was only to *help* the king to put a quick end to an illegal and unsuccessful war. In the Anjala declaration, they assured their loyalty to the king.[64] They thus presented themselves as faithful servants of the Crown, who wished nothing more than to defend the common good, the happiness and the security of the fatherland. Patriotism is indeed a recurrent theme in the documents of the League. The duty of the patriot to follow the law was emphasised, but at the same time, intentionally or not, this emphasis only underlined the fact that it was the king who had broken the law. This use of patriotic rhetoric is similar to that of the American and French revolutions: the "patriots" were not the monarchs, but the virtuous citizens using their right and duty to rebellion. No references to conscience were made; the discourse remained legalistic.[65]

The answers made by different officers to the appeal circulated by the League are revealing in this respect. The most positive one, Magnus Brunow's answer, expresses satisfaction with "the righteous Zeal and Patriotism proven by our fellow commanders at Anjala" and wishes that the Estates would rapidly convene, since only the Estates, together with the king, "have the right to make and end war". It also evokes "the honour and liberty of the Swedish Nation" and a "way of thought founded on our laws and the Liberty loved by all well-thinking Swedes" in a way that might suggest that the king's neglect of the constitution was contrary to this liberty.[66]

---

63 "*I betragtande af alt detta och med full lit till den Höge lefwande Guden, som ser renheten af wåra afsikter, swärja Wi undertecknade Wid Hans Heliga Namn, och Wår heder: at med upofrande af lif, blod och egendom, söka afwärja de olyckor, som hota wårt Fädernesland, hwarföre Wi äfwen härigenom med samma heliga ed oss emellan sluta det fastaste förbund och Stallbröderskap, för at råda hjelpa och bispringa hwarandra uti alla de mål, som med allmän och enskilt säkerhet har gemenskap.*" LUB, DelaGardieska samlingen, historiska handlingar, 23:1, N.1.

64 "*troheten för Wår Konung*", LUB, DelaGardieska samlingen, historiska handlingar, vol. 23:1, N. 1.

65 Sandström, *Officerarna som fick nog*, p. 116, thinks that the officers acted in good faith.

66 "*Den rättskaffens Nit och Patriotisme, som de vid Anjala Commenderade Medbröder betygat [...] kunna vi ej annat än på det högsta gilla, och med dem anse Riksens Höglåflige Ständers skyndsammaste sammankallande, vara af den yttersta nödvändighet, emedan De äro de enda hvilka samfält med vår Allernådigste Konung hafva rättighet göra och sluta krig, samt at taga de mått och steg, som äro bäst passade med Svänska Nations heder och frihet, til återvinnande af et kärt fredslugn. Detta tankesätt grundat på våra lagar, och af alle vältänkte Svänskar älskad Frihet, förbinda vij oss, samfällt med dem, att med Gods Lif och Blod försvara til vårt yttersta.*" Magnus Brunow, 28 August 1788, LUB, DelaGardieska samlingen, historiska handlingar, 23:1.

Other answers were more hesitating, or even confused, refusing to comment on a matter that concerned the fundamental laws of the realm and consequently should be decided by the Diet, and confining themselves to an approval of everything compatible with the fundamental principles of the realm and the constitution they had promised to follow, in other words,

> [...] we assure that we approve and defend with our Lives and Blood everything that is compatible with the King's highness, the Liberty and Rights of the Estates, the Independence of the Fatherland, and the Literal abiding of the Constitution of 1772, which we have approved and enforced.[67]

Colonel Stedingk, under pressure, hesitated to the point that he made not only one, but also a second declaration, after having changed his mind. The first one, drawn in ignorance of the larger significance of the rebellious movement, stated only that "we revere our king, we love our fatherland and are sincerely the friends of those who promote public welfare".[68] The second one was already more distant and prudent:

> As a soldier I consider as my first duty to obey command, and this I have done so far. As a Swedish citizen, who sincerely loves his fatherland, I consider a good and honourable peace as beneficial, but I have too little knowledge of Sweden's position both Domestically and Abroad, to express a well-founded opinion on everything that has been decided and enforced by the officers' corps at Anjala without my cognisance.[69]

Despite declaring their embarrassment to choose between two conflicting duties, the officers, by stating their unwillingness to continue a war that they considered illegally started, had taken a legalistic position against the king. Legalistic constitutionalism had been an effective weapon for the

---

67 *"Efter det änteligen begäres, at vi skola gifva våra yttrande tilkänna huru vida vi gilla eller ingå uti de mått och steg, som en del af Herrar Officerare af Finska Arméen vid Angela uti nu varande Conjunctur vid tagit; så får vi härmed den äran at Svara, det vi suspendera alt jugement deröfver; emedan fråga är om Grund-Lagarnas förstånd och efterlefnad, och intil dess vi, som Hufvud-Män och Fulmägtige för våra Familler ibland Ricksens högt[ärade] Ständer få yttra Oss, Dem vi jämte Kungl. Majst. Allena anse berättigade at ändra, förklara samt vaka öfver deras oryggelifa och bokstafl. efterfölgd. Emedlertid försäkra vi oss, gilla och försvara med Lif och Blod, Alt det som är öfverensstämmande med Konungens höghet, Ständernas Fri och Rättigheter, Fäderneslandets Sielfständighet, Samt bokstafliga efterlefnaden av 1772 Års Regerings-forme Den vi besvurit och antagit."* (F. W. Hastfer, C. Stiernecrantz, Carl A. Morian, C. Ehrenstolpe, Randasalmi 28 August 1788, LUB, DelaGardieska samlingen, historiska handlingar, 23:1.
68 *"Wi wördar vår konung, wi älskar vårt fädernesland och äro upricktigt deras wänner som befordrar almänt wäl."* C. Steding[k] and his officers, 28 August 1788, LUB, DelaGardieska samlingen, historiska handlingar, 23:1.
69 *"Som knekt anser jag för min första skyldighet att lyda befäl, och detta har jag giort hit in tills. Som svensk medborgare, som älskar upricktigt sitt fädernesland, anser jag en god och ärorik fred för gagnlig, men jag har för liten kunskap om Sweriges både In- och Utrikes ställning, för att kunna fälla ett grundad Omdöme, om allt det, som af den wid Anjela warande Officers Corpsen, utan min wetenskap, blifwit beslutit och wärckställd."* C. Steding[k], 28 August 1788, LUB, DelaGardieska samlingen, historiska handlingar, 23:1.

opposition against the king at the Diet a couple of years earlier. It seems credible that the officers not only presented legalistic arguments, but truly also felt that they were bound to guard the constitution, as members of a Diet estate and as citizens having taken an oath to abide by the constitution.

We could argue, though, that the traditional rhetorical topic of "guarding the fundamental laws" had more in common with the duties of a Dietmen of the Age of Liberty than with the ideals one would expect of officers of a nearly absolute monarch. Swedish noble officers, however, like the French *parlementaires* but unlike e.g. Prussian officers, were used to being both politicians-Dietmen and officers of the Crown, the 'Royal Majesty' meaning, during the entire Age of Liberty, no more than 'the state'. It has been suggested that the officers seem to have referred, mentally, to the constitution of 1720 rather than that of 1772, a suggestion that relies on a draft for a new constitution supposed to have been made by the mutinous officers.[70] With regard to the efficiency of the Gustavian propaganda and the massive adherence of the (Finnish) nobility to the constitution of 1772, this still seems a bit far-fetched. It is possible, however, that their conception of good politics had more in common with the traditional ideals of a mixed monarchy and with the constitutional ideals of the Age of Liberty than with the political realities of Gustav III's Sweden in the 1780s.

The terminology used in the document is also significant. For instance, "the rights of the nation" was a rather strong way to refer to the Diet's prerogative to decide on war. During the second half of the Age of Liberty, speakers at the Diet had started to replace the traditional "rights and liberties of the estate" with "the rights of the nation" in some cases.[71] Since 1772, however, the Diet and the forms of early parliamentarian political culture that it represented had been considerably weakened. When the fact that the status of the Diet was no longer as strong as in the Age of Liberty is taken into account, the urge to put forward its prerogative is striking. The phrase "rights of the nation" seems to have been deliberately preferred because of the consensus it seemed to imply in a situation in which the king had chosen not to summon the Diet and the signers represented a minority of the officers' corps. To appeal to the 'nation', an ambiguous concept increasingly used as a synonym for the politically organised community, was a way to give rhetorical legitimacy to the claims. The desire that the Estates be summoned was largely shared by the officers in Finland. Still, the words "Diet" or "Estates" were not even mentioned in the first declarations, only in the clarifying letters sent to the king and in the written statements made by other officers in favour of or against the league. These statements generally mentioned and desired the summoning of the "Estates of the realm"; some of them also pointed out that peace would bring honour to the nation.[72] By

---

70 Cederberg, *Anjalan liiton historialliset lähteet*, pp. 34–38, 266–267.

71 Wolff, "Pro Patria et Libertate. Frihetsbegreppet i 1700-talets svenska politiska språk", pp. 55–62. The same expression, "the rights of the nation", had been used by the French *parlements*; see, for instance, the *Remontrances de la Cour des Aides de Paris, du mois de Février 1771, s.l. s.d.* [Paris, 1771].

72 The terminology in these statements is rather similar to that in the Anjala declaration and resembles Swedish political terminology in general. Some examples: "a Swedish citizen

using the term 'nation' instead of 'Estates' or 'Diet', the rebellious officers took up a political role and recalled the notion of a mutual bond between the ruler and the subjects. The same cluster of concepts – citizen, liberty, rights of nations, duties of kings – is present in Klick's pamphlet from the late autumn of 1788. To the modern reader, they may sound more revolutionary than they actually were.[73]

If we look only at the arguments presented, it is possible to draw a parallel to the models of thought studied by Jouanna in the case of the French nobility. This similarity is not surprising in any way; Sweden and even Finland were far from being intellectually isolated, and the nobility even less so.[74] Researchers have also suggested that the men behind the declaration, in particular the friends of Sprengtporten, had been influenced not only by the classically republican political traditions of the Age of Liberty, but probably also by the American revolution.[75] In a way, at a certain point of the confusion that followed the appeal to all the other troops to join the movement, the mutiny may have appeared as a union of true patriots at a time when the fatherland was in danger. The oath at the end of the Anjala declaration only gives force to this impression of fatality and gravity.

The Liikkala note and the Anjala declaration are provocative texts, as if they had been deliberately written to upset the Swedish king. Reflecting the contradictory feelings from which they sprung, they imply that the war had not been fought for the fatherland, but that the desire for peace might be patriotic, although negotiating for it in this way was certainly not very glorious. Was not this a form of self-delusion? Why use arguments that seem naïve and provocative? Was it not evident that it would mean an explicit break with the king, mutiny and possibly treason, which in turn meant great personal risks for all the officers involved? According to Allan Sandström, the officers, having discussed the fateful steps they were taking, were fully aware of the risk, but decided to take it, the situation being unstable in any case. To be deliberately provocative was an act of rebellion, and rebellion a means of being heard. Some of the leaguers may even have hoped that the situation would force the king to abdicate or to change the constitution. From the rebellious officers' point of view, the king had broken the law, which had untied the bounds of fealty. The idea may have occurred to Gustav III, since he eventually decided to call for the Estates and change the law in a more absolutistic direction in the spring of 1789. By then, a handful of his officers, principally those that had been in contact with Sprengtporten before or at the early stages of the war, had already switched loyalties and fled to Russia.[76]

who honestly loves his fatherland", "righteous zeal and patriotism", "the honour and liberty of the Swedish nation", "the King's highness, the estates' liberties and rights", "the independence of the fatherland" (very common in official language), "our common Fatherland", etc.

73 *En Finsk Officerares Försvar för Arméen, emot utkomne Smädeskrifter och i synnerhet ett så kallat Bref af d: 14. September 1788 angående vissa Stämplingar*, LUB, DelaGardieska samlingen, historiska handlingar, vol. 23:2.

74 See, for instance, Lindroth, *Svensk lärdomshistoria. Frihetstiden*; Magnus Björkenheim, *Äldre fransk litteratur på herrgårdar i Finland*, Helsingfors, 1929; Wolff, *Vänskap och makt*.

75 See, for instance, Lesch, *Jan Anders Jägerhorn*, pp. 145–146.

76 This was the case of Johan Anders Jägerhorn, Lars Glansenstierna, Adolf von Essen, Carl Henrik Klick and Gustaf Ladau. Sandström, *Officerarna som fick nog*, pp. 65–68.

Other members of the league were imprisoned and trialled in Stockholm in 1789–1790.

Liberty usurped: Gustav the Tyrant

Noble political culture generally took into account the necessity of remaining formally faithful to oaths, promises and persons that one had committed oneself to through diverse bounds of loyalty. The nobility thus found its share in the political culture of court society: as Jouanna has put it, the nobility would prefer to talk about "mutual services" rather than contracts.[77] This made it possible for the nobility to slip into and adapt itself to a court regime. But it also meant that opposition, like intrigue, would take place in secret, behind the king's back, and sometimes in ritualised forms.[78]

A significant detail is that the Anjala declaration ended with an oath, with a covenant and the mention of comradeship. This is significant, since it may give a clue to the mentality behind the conjuration. Comradeship, brotherhood, clubs and secret societies were part of military and noble sociability in late eighteenth-century Sweden. One such club was the Svenska Botten, a patriotic club for poor royalist Dietmen and noble officers, formed some months before Gustav III's revolution of 1772. In the Finnish garrisons, freemasonry and other secret societies were appreciated pastimes among the nobility in the 1780s. The order of Walhall, for instance, gathered Finnish royalist "patriots" in the early 1780s. Such societies and clubs offered a space for critical discussion, in a situation where public debate had been muffled and the representative political institutions no longer functioned. Due to the secrecy and the feeling of exclusivity that such societies cultivated, their enthusiastic ideals had sometimes rather little to do with the surrounding political realities. Many of the signers of the Anjala declaration had participated in those forms of sociability at some stage of their career.[79]

Many of the signers of the declaration were also related to each other by strong ties of friendship or kinship and may therefore have felt pressure to join the movement. The Anjala conjuration can be seen as a typical "cabal": it had a political aim, though initially somewhat vague; it did not ask for the permission of the authorities, quite the contrary; and its members swore fidelity to the common cause and to each other. The "cabal" was a usual form of aristocratic opposition in court societies, particularly in absolute monarchies.[80] As such, the Anjala conjuration was dangerous for the king and could be seen as revolutionary, although the officers abandoned the idea of arresting the king at an early stage.

77 Jouanna, *Le devoir de révolte*, pp. 40–90.
78 Cf. Henrik Stenius, *Frivilligt, jämlikt, samfälligt. Föreningsväsendets utveckling i Finland fram till 1900-talets början med speciell hänsyn till massorganisationsprincipens genombrott*, Helsingfors, 1987, pp. 99–128.
79 Stenius, *Frivilligt, jämlikt, samfälligt*, pp. 106–107.
80 See Wolff, "Kabal och kärlek. Vänskapen som alternativ sociabilitet i 1700-talets hovsamhällen", pp. 85–93, with examples from the Prussian and French courts.

The nobility's plotting, however, did not end with the arrest of the plotting officers. Quite the contrary, in December 1788, Gustav III finally summoned the Diet, which convened in February 1789. At this Diet, the king passed the "Act of Union and Security" (*Förenings- och Säkerhets Acten*), which gave the king literally unlimited powers, abolished the traditionally aristocratic Senate and limited the nobility's privileges. In the meantime, aristocratic politicians known as critics of the king or suspected of becoming such were arrested and prevented from attending the Diet, among them old Count Fersen. The nobility, opposing the king's egalitarian uses of terms such as "right" and "liberty", rejected the act, but it was approved by the other estates, and thus passed.[81]

In the meantime, the revolution had started in France and was reported eagerly by the Swedish press until the king prevented it in December 1791.[82] Colonel Johan Henric Hästesko's execution as the scapegoat of the Anjala League in September 1790 aggravated the nobility's resentment against the king. In manuscript pamphlets and verses, spread in the circles of Stockholm's high society, the king was increasingly depicted as a tyrant. A verse against the king from 1789 went:

> When by a crowd of favourites
> A King (a man he is, a man can err)
> Was lured, oh God! To become a Tyrant
> To throw himself and us into a shameful discord. [...][83]

The pamphlets generally argued that the king had become a tyrant because of his weaknesses and his vicious favourites in court. The most vehement pamphlets also presented the king as unnatural and effeminate, lacking both morals and potency.[84] This theme could even be presented under the cover of a historical narrative, as in *Gustaf III:s annaler från 1771 till 1790* and *Johannes Magni, Upsala Erke Biskops Chrönica, öfwersatt på Swenska* ("Gustav III's annals from 1771 to 1790"; "Chronicle by Johannes Magnus, Archbishop of Uppsala, translated into Swedish").[85] But there was also a part of the antimonarchic pamphlets that adopted a clearly republican and Roman terminology. This was the case in *Déclaration d'un vieux rhéteur contre l'usurpation d'Auguste*, written as a dramatic monologue in French, describing how despotism was established on the ruins of liberty.[86]

The title was of course an obvious allusion to the end of the Roman republic, also known as the Roman Age of Liberty. The "old rhetor" offers

---

81 For an account, see, for instance, Lönnroth, *Den stora rollen*, pp. 194–207; see also Alm, *Kungsord i elfte timmen*, pp. 232–239.

82 Nyman, *Indragningsmakt och tryckfrihet 1785–1810*, p. 59.

83 "*Då utaf Favoriters Skara / En Kung (han menska är, en mänska fela kan) / Blev narrad Gud! At bli Tyrann, / Att störta sig och oss uti en neslig fara.* [...]" LUB, DelaGardieska samlingen, Historiska handlingar, vol. 22:12.

84 See Mattsson, "Kvinnliga tidsfördriv och manliga mätresser. Kön och sexualitet i smädandet av Gustaf III", pp. 453–476.

85 *Gustaf III:s annaler från 1771 till 1790* and *Johannes Magni, Upsala Erke Biskops Chrönica, öfwersatt på Swenska*, LUB, DelaGardieska samlingen, historiska handlingar, vol. 22:12.

86 *Déclaration d'un vieux Rhéteur contre l'usurpation d'Auguste*, LUB, DelaGardieska samlingen, historiska handlingar, vol. 22:12.

a very tempting parallel to the Swedish Diet and its former leaders, who were in a sense moral authorities for the younger members of the opposition (although persons such as Fersen limited themselves to strictly legal forms of opposition). While the Swedes are here Romans ("tremble Romans!"), Gustav III is called Augustus and Octavian, "the oppressor of my fatherland", which is an ironic move since the king much liked to depict himself as Augustus.[87] The monologue begins with a complaint on how despotism establishes itself on the ruins of liberty, something that would be easier to cope with if one were used to slavery. The tyrannical "monster" adds an insult to his outrage, as he "dares tell me that I stand while he treads on me". The text then goes on to describe "Octavian's" physical disgrace, low spirits and two-facedness. The king is presented as having no morals or virtues and is accused of provoking discord, hatred, spreading calumny and being an impostor who conspires, lies, breaks his oaths and robs the churches. Above all, and here we recognise the political resentment of the nobility, he sets the estates against each other, practises favouritism and provokes jealousy at his court. At the end of the short text, the author expresses his relief at not having committed the crime and shame of being the organ of oppression, and he begs the sovereign judge (God) to put an end to his life or to give him male constancy to suffer the tyrant and the "vulture". Finally, the perspective of tyrannicide is evoked in terms close to those in French revolutionary poetry: "*Manes de Brutus, venez les briser* [=les chaines] *et armez mon bras de ce fer...*" ("Brutus's manes, come and break my chains and arm my hand with this blade...").[88]

The lines had a prophetical tone. On 16 March 1792, the king was shot at a masked ball. The king died from his wound on 28 March, convinced that his assassins had been influenced by Jacobine ideas. It is tempting to see a link between the progress of the revolution in France and the tyrannicide in Sweden. However, as Jakob Christensson has stated, the models and ideals of Ancient Rome had become so common and strong by the 1780s that it would be too simplistic to explain the radicalising Swedish oppositional spirit and developments by the influence of the French revolution. The attack had been planned by a conjuration of noblemen, many of which had personal reasons to hate the king. One of the conspirators was Carl Fredrik Pechlin, an old veteran politician of the Age of Liberty. Among the conspirators were also the republican Adolph Ribbing and Carl Fredrik Ehrensvärd, who saw himself as a new Brutus.[89]

The conspiracy was large, including at least eighty persons and members of the highest aristocracy, and aimed at the suppression of royal autocracy and the establishment of a new regime. Stig Jägerskiöld has shown that the conjured were convinced of the right to resist and to kill tyrants.[90] The plot was revolutionary by definition, but the right to resist and the legitimacy of

---

87 Christensson, *Lyckoriket*, pp. 141–143.
88 *Déclaration d'un vieux Rhéteur contre l'usurpation d'Auguste*, LUB, DelaGardieska samlingen, historiska handlingar, vol. 23:12.
89 Christensson, *Lyckoriket*, p. 140.
90 Stig Jägerskiöld, "Tyrannmord och motståndsrätt 1792–1809. En studie kring J. J. Anckarström", *Scandia* 28 (1962), pp. 113–168. See also Alm, *Kungsord i elfte timmen*, p. 242.

tyrannicide were part of an older political ideal than the ones initiated by the revolutions of the end of the eighteenth century. These traditional ideas of resistance and noble rebellion were probably revived by influences from revolutionary France. Yet the Swedish nobility was far from generally enthusiastic about the course of the events in France, particularly after 1790.[91]

The perpetrator of the assassination was Captain Jacob Johan Anckarström, who had witnessed Hästesko's execution in 1789 and been deeply shocked by it. His motives seem to have been rather unselfish, dictated by a morally obliging conviction that things were deeply wrong. In his "confession", *Capitainen Jacob Johan Anckarströms Bekännelse om orsaken till Konunga Mordet*, which circulated after his death, one of the reasons that had convinced him of the necessity of putting an end to the king's life was that the king had become the "enemy of the realm" by breaking his own laws. "It is best", the text continued, "to give one's life for the public, for living a miserable life here 10 years more or less is nothing compared to being able to make an entire nation's happiness."[92]

---

91 See Wolff, *Vänskap och makt*, chapter 12. A thorough study on the Swedish nobility's attitudes to the French revolution and the influence of the revolution on political ideas and concepts in Sweden is missing. Because of the extensive use of slightly different sources and methods it would require, it would easily be the subject of another monograph.

92 "*rikets fiende*"; "[…] *det är bäst wåga sitt lif för det allmänna, ty at lefva här et uselt lif 10 år mer eller mindre, är intet emot at kunna gjöra en hel Nation lyckelig.*" *Capitainen Jacob Johan Anckarströms Bekännelse om orsaken till Konunga Mordet*, KB, Schröderheim, Historisk-politiska samlingar 4 (1789, 1794), D 171:4.

Conclusion

The subject of this book has been noble political identity in eighteenth-century Sweden as it was mirrored in political language and concepts. The first group of themes dealt with was the nature of the Swedish regime from 1720 to 1772, the mixed constitution and its interpretations, noble constitutionalism and legalism. The mixed monarchy, presenting elements of both monarchy and aristocracy, was generally the traditional political ideal of the European nobilities in early modern times. In the Sweden of the Age of Liberty, the mixed government, with a weak monarchy, a strong Diet and Senate, and a general denial of the concept of 'sovereignty', became a problem both for the country's international credibility – with foreign allies distrusting or trying to manipulate the activities of the Estates and the Diet parties – and domestically. The Estates tended to extend their power, while the king, particularly Adolph Frederick from the early 1750s, had problems with conceiving the limits placed on royal power, as the 'highness' of the Royal Majesty was continuously revered in official political rhetoric even though the king's prerogatives were only formal and did not imply factual royal sovereignty.

The second and perhaps most central notion in noble political ideology and language was liberty, which also gave the regime, 'the Age of Liberty' – a significant parallel to the Roman republic – its name. The defence of liberty was the pillar of Swedish political ideology and was also presented, in Diet speeches and other official documents, as an ancient tradition. The often repeated formula "a free people" referred to the tradition of a free peasantry, but it was also and above all an incontestable way of underlining the political sovereignty of the Estates, where the peasants were represented as well as the burghers. As we have seen in Scheffer's dismissal of the need for popular control of the sovereign Estates, representing and constituting the political body and even the nation, the liberty of the people was not so much a matter of popular sovereignty, a theme absent in our sources, not to speak of democracy, an idea still avoided by the nobility as an irrelevant option until the late 1760s.[1] Allusions to a "free people" are omnipresent in

---

1 Pasi Ihalainen, "I vilken mån talades det om folksuveränitet och representativ demokrati på den svenska riksdagen 1771–1772?", *Historisk Tidskrift för Finland*, vol. 93 (2008:2), pp. 125–159.

Diet discourse, and the phrase was also repeated with the greatest ease by Gustav III, for whom the pretension of being "the first citizen of a free people" only enhanced his royal legitimacy, allowing him to short-circuit the noble estate and to present himself in a line of Augustean saviours of the fatherland and defenders of peace. This move was well perceived by the opposition, who did not fail to recognise the Augustean "usurpation" of liberty.[2]

Another theme borrowed by Gustav III from the previous regime was law as the guarantee of the right kind of liberty, or the so-called "law-bound liberty". The contrast between the glorious recent past in the Caroline era and the international reputation of weakness of the Swedish monarchy in the Age of Liberty contributed to a sensation of the fragility of the free constitution of 1720. The need and "virtuous zeal" to guard the constitution, however, were also manifested in an almost paranoid stress on virtue and in concern about the possibility that liberty, particularly in the hands of aristocratic senators, would corrupt into licence. The consequence was a parallel discourse on law and authority, which should keep liberty virtuous and maintain it in its constitutional framework. The balance between liberty and the enforcement of law, however, was a potential problem of the same kind as the one recognised by Pocock as the "Machiavellian moment" of the late Roman republic. Another central problem for the free regime, one that was being recognised by the political elite, was that of citizenship and the notion of citizens' rights and equality. During the last years of the Age of Liberty, political crises were doubled with something of a social crisis, where representatives of the commoners demanded political and social recognition in the form of extended privileges.

If we go back to one of our theoretical points of departure, Pocock's "Machiavellian moment", a first question would be whether the Swedish Age of Liberty does not constitute a "Machiavellian moment" in the sense of the appearance of republican thought or the possibility of a republic of free and equal citizens. The answer is probably yes, to a certain extent: the invention of the term "Age of Liberty" by the contemporaries to describe their own era is significant in this respect. The members of the noble estate, active at the Diet, may have felt that they were participating members of a *res publica* of equals, but noble comments on equality seem to suggest that for the nobility, political participation and power were things that were best reserved for the elite and that the possible extent of political liberty and equality depended on the definition of the citizen and the nation. From the point of view of the political elite of which the nobility counted itself a member, it seems that the citizen was mainly understood as one who participated actively in the activities of the Diet and that the nation was consequently primarily made up of these active citizens.

The second question would be whether there were the other kind of "Machiavellian moments", where liberty was threatened, in particular by the increased authority of the sovereign (the king) or the political bodies retaining sovereignty (the Estates). To this question, the answer is a less

---

2 Tandefelt, *Konsten att härska*; Delblanc, *Ära och minne*.

hesitating yes, in many respects. There were indeed several such moments, during the Age of Liberty in 1756 and 1765–1769 and the crisis that put an end to the regime in 1771–1772, as well as during the Gustavian era, particularly the turbulent years of 1788–1790/1792.

In a tradition stressing the importance of morals, morality and virtue in politics, patriotism and the fulfilment of civic duties appeared as necessary remedies or solutions in moments of crisis. In the second half of the eighteenth century, the rise of a patriotic stream in political discourse was a general European tendency. It was not limited to neo-Roman, republican discourse only; patriotic themes were also used to legitimate the most reactionary measures and attitudes, both by rulers and aristocratic oppositions. Rebellions against a king or his ministers who committed errors or even crimes would be presented as patriotic, defending the interest of the fatherland, or as or rebellions on behalf of the king, the royal person here understood as the incarnation of the state.

'Patriotism' and 'virtue', however, were not a matter of formal discourse only. The crises identified correspond above all to a moment of hesitation or threat concerning the form of government, in other words, to constitutional crises where the parties involved were motivated by either a legalist defence of the fundamental law or an urge to reform the constitution. Usually, the ideal presented by both constitutionalist and reform-makers was the traditional mixed government. The king in 1772 as well as the nobility in 1788 defended that ideal. Gustav III presented his rule as a necessary return to a balanced constitution, where the reinforcement of the monarchy would save the liberty of the people from aristocratic licence. Behind the polarisation of notions such as 'virtue' and 'licence' were deeply rooted conceptions of honour vs. dishonour or morality vs. immorality in politics.

In noble political thought, the noncompliance with mutual agreements was immoral or dishonourable, and the unilateral breaking of contracts would consequently free the other contracting party from all moral obligations. The importance of honour, a large concept that would need a separate study, in the formation of early modern and particularly noble political identities can hardly be overestimated. Legalistic and constitutionalist reactions to defend the respect of written mutual agreements can also be seen as the manifestations of ancient noble political conceptions that evolved under the influence of natural law and early modern contract theories.

Can the Anjala League and the oppositional projects for a new constitution that were made at the time of Gustav III's unsuccessful war against Russia be explained by these attitudes? It would perhaps be too simple to argue that the nobility's conception of mixed government had frozen in the formulations of the constitution of 1720. More prudent would be to state that the opposition was provoked by what it perceived as noncompliance with written contracts and constitutions in general, including those of 1772. When the good prince suddenly overthrew his own laws, he became a despot, or at least a corrupted and immoral figure. The problem was not in monarchy or royalty itself – the majority of the nobility remained faithful to the king – but in the lack of respect for legal rights and constitutional liberties and in the feeling of an "usurpation" of the good monarchy by a vicious ruler, as we have seen in the pamphlets preceding the regicide of the early 1790s.

If noble political attitudes were guided by notions of honour and morality, how can we then talk about a noble republicanism? One key is that classical republicanism was also guided by notions of virtue and honour. Another key is that 'republicanism' should here be understood as the promoting of a (moderately) free and balanced constitution that granted the elite an insight into politics and respect for its achieved liberties. Generally speaking, classical republicanism could be understood as *medborgerlighet*: civic virtue, the advancement of common good and the defence of liberty and legality. This was not particularly radical and should not be confused with the form of republicanism that seeks to establish a republic without royalty, although republican discourse could be used for radical purposes. And even though many of the ingredients of "civic spirit", *medborgerlighet*, were present in the most traditional Swedish political discourse of the eighteenth century, the kind of conscious republicanism that comprised the possibility to, if not eliminate, at least disarm monarchy politically, remained an elitist phenomenon. Its ideological formulation and manifestation at the Diet was limited to some speech acts by a limited number of front figures. During the period and moments studied here, due to the political power balance at the Diet, these persons mainly represented the Hat party, but it is not certain that things would necessarily have been different if the Caps had dominated the Diet. During the last years of the Age of Liberty, it was the Cap party that appeared as the ideologically radicalised one.

Another theoretical point of departure for this study was that of conceptual change in the second half of the eighteenth century, or, in other words, the process of conceptual modernisation often referred to by Koselleck and others. In the end, it is perhaps paradoxical that the conceptual apparatus used by the political elite of the Age of Liberty and by Gustav III to a large extent remained essentially the same: the ideological framework, with its references to Roman history and classical republicanism, was loose enough to allow slight variations and transfers of meaning inside the key concepts. There were perhaps fewer new words than new meanings attached to older concepts. Previously existing notions, such as 'liberty', were reconceptualised. Other terms, such as 'citizen' or 'people', were semantically enlarged. The important changes of the late eighteenth century took place not so much in the vocabulary but in the generalisation and extension of political key concepts to new users, actors and audiences. The increased use of 'citizen' or 'people' by Gustav III is an example of this process, where monarchy gave itself a popular legitimacy in what some researchers have termed as "the democratisation of honour", a slightly inappropriate term, since democracy was still not an alternative or even imaginable form of government.[3] Even greater conceptual changes and challenges than those experienced during the Age of Liberty and the Gustavian era, when the Swedish political language and ideology remained inside the framework of classical republican thought, would arise with the French revolution, the significance of which has not been possible to estimate in this limited study.

---

3   Delblanc, *Ära och minne*, p. 114; criticism in Tandefelt, *Konsten att härska*, pp. 41, 81, 334.

The perspective of the nobility that has been chosen for this book is, of course, a biased and elitist one. Other estates and groups would have offered different forms of radicalism or patterns of political action. Nobility was not essentially radical; noble republicanism was rather conservative in the proper sense than progressive. To look at Swedish political language in the eighteenth century through this perspective may bring to light more nuances both in the claims of how radical or advanced the Swedish regime was and in the estimates of the degree of change in 1772.

Sources and references

Manuscript sources:

Archives Nationales (AN), Paris
  399 AP 55, Chartrier de Malesherbes.
Geheimes Staatsarchiv Preußischer Kulturbesitz (GStA), Berlin
  VI Hauptabteilung, Nachlaß Heinrich von Podewils.
Kungliga biblioteket (KB), Stockholm
  Engeströmska samlingen, B VII 2.1.
  Schröderheim, Historisk-politiska samlingar 1–4, D 171:1–4.
  Strödda handlingar till Gustaf III:s historia, D 1019.
Lunds universitetsbibliotek (LUB), Lund
  DelaGardiesamlingen, Historiska handlingar, vol. 22–23.
Riksarkivet (RA), Stockholm
  Ridderskapets och adelns pleniprotokoller med akter, riksdagen 1786, R 171.
  Sekreta utskottets protokoll 1755–1756 (I), R 3045.
  Stafsundsarkivet, Axel von Fersen d.ä.:s arkiv, vol. 7.
Uppsala universitetsbibliotek (UUB), Uppsala Collectio Mss Regis Gustavi III, vol. 45,
  F 519.

Printed sources:

Aristotle, *Politics*.
Bodin, Jean, *Les Six Livres de la République*, 1576.
[Brahe, Eric], *Grefwe BRAHES TAL, Hållit til Ridderskapet och Adelen, Wid Theras första sammanträde på Riddarhuset, Wid Riksdagen then 17 Octobris* 1755, Stockholm, *s.d.* [1755].
[Brahe, Eric], *Öfwerste-Lieutenantens Högwälborne Grefwe ERIC BRAHES TAL, Hållit på Riks-Salen I Stockholm, När Riksdagen slöts then 4. Junii, 1752*, Stockholm, 1752.
Brusewitz, Axel, *Frihetstidens grundlagar och konstitutionella stadgar*, Stockholm, 1916.
Cicero, *De officiis*.
Ehrensvärd, Gustaf Johan, *Dagboksanteckningar förda vid Gustaf III:s hof af friherre Gustaf Johan Ehrensvärd*, utg. E. V. Montan, Stockholm, 1878.
[Ekeblad, Clas], *På Kongl. Maj:ts Wägnar, Herr Riks-Rådets, Cancellie-Présidentens, Öfwerste-Marskalkens och Åbo Academiae Cantzlerens, samt Cantzlerens, Riddarens och Commendeurens af Kongl. Maj:ts Orden, Högwälborne Grefwe CLAS EKEBLADS Håldne TAL, Til Riksens Ständer, tå Riksdagen slutades then 21. Junii 1762, s.l., s.d.* [Stockholm, 1762].
[Ekeblad, Clas], *På Kongl. Maj:ts Wägnar, Herr Riks-Rådets, Cancellie-Présidentens, Öfwerste-Marskalkens, Åbo Academiae Cantzlerens, Riddarens, Commendeurens och*

Cantzlerens af alle Kongl. Maj:ts Orden, Högwälborne Grefwe CLAS EKEBLADS TAL, Hållit uppå Riks-Salen i Stockholm wid Riksdagens början then 24 Januarii 1765, s.l., s.d. [Stockholm, 1765].

[Ekeblad, Clas], *På Kongl. Maj:ts Wägnar, Herr Riks-Rådets, Cantzelie-Presidentens, Öfwerste Marskalkens och Åbo Academiae-Cantzlerens, samt Cantzlerens, Riddarens och Commendeurens af Kongl. Maj:ts Orden, Högwälborne Grefwe, CLAS EKE-BLADS Håldne Tal, Til Riksens Ständer, då Riksdagen slutades, den 30. Januarii 1770,* Stockholm, 1770.

En Ärlig Riksdags-Mans Syldigheter [sic], Uppsala, 1769.

[Fersen, Axel von], *Landt-Marskalken, Generalens, Riddarens och Commendeurens af Kongl. Maj:ts Orden, Högwälborne Grefwe Herr AXEL FERSENS Hållne TAL Wid Landt-Marskalks Stafwens Emottagande Den 22. April 1769,* Norrköping, 1769.

[Fersen, Axel von], *Landt-Marskalkens, General-Lieutenantens och Commendeurens af Kongl. Swärds-Orden, Högwälborne Herr Grefwe AXEL FERSENS Håldne TAL, Wid Landt-Marskalk Stafwens emottagande, Then 20 October 1760,* Stockholm, s.d. [1760].

[Fersen, Axel von], *Landt-Marskalkens högwälborne Grefwe AXEL FERSENS TAL, Hållit Til Ridderskapet och Adelen Wid Landt-Marskalk-Stafwens afgifwande then 21 October 1756,* Stockholm, 1756.

[Fersen, Axel von], *Landt-Marskalkens högwälborne Grefwe AXEL FERSENS TAL, Tå han Å Ridderskapets och Adelens wägnar, tog Afsked af the andre Respective Stånden, På Riks-Salen, Then 21 Octob. 1756,* Stockholm, s.d. [1756].

[Fersen, Axel von], *Riksrådet och fältmarskalken m.m. grefve Fredrik Axel von Fersens historiska skrifter,* utg. af R. M. Klinckowström, Stockholm, 1867–1872.

[Fersen, Axel von], *TAL, Til Theras Kongl. Majestäter Och Hans Kong. Höghet Cron-Printsen, Hållne af Landt-Marskalken, General-Lieutenanten och Commendeures af Kongl. Maj:ts Swärds-Ordem, Högwälborne Herr Grefwe AXEL FERSEN Tå Riksdagen slutades i Stockholm then 21 Junii 1762. Såsom ock Tal, hållne wid Landt-Marskalks Stafwens aflemnande,* Stockholm, s.d. [1762].

[Fersen, Axel von], *Til Hans Kongl. Maj:t, Landt-Marskalkens Högwälborne Grefwe AXEL FERSENS TAL, Tå han, med Ridderskapets och Adelens Deputerade, aflade theras underdåniga Hälsning then 18 Oct. 1755,* Stockholm, s.d. [1755].

[Fersen, Axel von], *Til Hennes Kongl. Maj:t, Landt-Marskalkens Högwälborne Grefwe AXEL FERSENS TAL, Tå han, med Ridderskapets och Adelens Deputerade, aflade theras underdåniga Hälsning then 18 Oct. 1755,* Stockholm, s.d. [1755].

[Fersen, Axel von], *Til Kongl. Maj:t, Landt-Marskalkens, Generalens, Riddarens och Commendeurens af Kongl. Maj:ts Orden, Högwälborne Grefwe Herr AXEL FERSENS Hållne Underdånige TAL, På Riks-Salen i Norrköping Den 22. April 1769,* Norrköping, 1769.

[Frederick II], *Anti-Machiavel,* La Haye, 1740.

[Gustav III], *Kongl. Maj:ts Nådiga Försäkran, Til Thess Lif-Garde, Artillerie och samtelige trogne undersåtare här i Residence-Staden Stockholm, Gifwen then 19. Augusti 1772,* Stockholm, 1772.

[Gustav III], *Kongl. Maj:ts Nådige Försäkran Gifwen Thess trogne undersåtare Samtelige Riksens Ständer på Riks-Salen Then 21 augusti 1772,* Stockholm, 1772.

[Gustav III], *Kongl. Maj:ts TAL Til Riksens Ständer, Församlade uppå Riks-Salen i Stockholm, Den 21 augusti 1772,* Stockholm, 1772.

[Gustav III], *Hans Kongl. Maj:ts Tal, Til Riksens Ständer Uppå Riks-Salen Wid Riksdagens början Den 25 Junii 1771,* Stockholm, 1771.

[Gyllenborg, Carl], *På Kongl. Maj:ts Wägnar, Herr Riks-Rådets och Praesidentens i Kongl. Maj:ts och Riksens Cancellie-Collegio, Högwälborne Grefwe CARL GYLLEN-BORGS Hålne Tal Til Riksens Ständer på Riks-Salen då Riksdagen begyntes den 25. Augusti 1742,* Stockholm, 1742.

Hemliga Handlingar, hörande till Sveriges Historia efter Konung GUSTAF III:s Anträde till Regeringen, [Stockholm], 1821.

Hobbes, Thomas, *The Leviathan,* 1651.

[Höpken, Anders Johan von], *På Kongl. Maj:ts Wägnar, Herr Riks-Rådets, Cancellie Praesidentens, samt Riddare och Commendeurens af Kongl. Maj:ts Orden, Högwälborne Friherre ANDERS JOHAN VON HÖPKENS TAL, Hållit uppå Riks-Salen wid Riksdagens början then 21 Octobr. 1755*, Stockholm, s.d. [1755].

Kongl. Maj:ts Och Riksens Ständers Faststälte Regerings-FORM, Dat. STOCKHOLM then 21 Augusti 1772, Stockholm, s.d. [1772].

[Lewenhaupt, Charles Emil], *Til Hennes Kongl. Maj:t Wår Allernådigste Drottning, Af Grefwen och LandtMarschalken Högwälborne Herr General Majoren CARL EMIL LEWENHAUPT, Uppå Samtel. Riksens Ständers wägnar håldne Tahl wid Riksdagen A. 1734*, Stockholm, 1734.

[Löwenhielm, Carl Gustaf], *På Kongl. Maj:ts Wägnar, Herr Riks-Rådets, Cancellie-Présidentens, Academiae-Cantzlerens, Riddarens och Commendeurens, samt Cantzleres af alla Kongl. Maj:ts Orden, Högwälborne Grefwe CARL GUSTAF LÖWENHIELMS Hålldne TAL, Til Riksens Ständer, tå Riksdagen slutades then 15. Octob. 1766*, Stockholm, 1766.

Montesquieu, Charles de Secondat, "De la liberté politique", *Mes pensées* (631/884, vol. II, f. 6), éd. Roger Challois, vol. 1, Paris, 1949.

Montesquieu, Charles de Secondat, *De l'esprit des lois*, Paris, 1748.

[Osander, Olof], *Christelig Böne-andakt, Såsom et förträffeligt Wälfärds Medel för alla Swea Barn, och hela Swea Rike, I anledning af Apostelens Pauli Förmaning I Tim. 2:1, 2. Under Hans Kongl. Maj:ts Och Samtelige Riksens Högloflige Ständers närwaro, Wid Riks-Dagens slut den 21 Oct. 1756, Uti En Christelig Predikan I St. Nicolai eller Stockholms Stads Stor-Kyrko, förestäls Af Olof Osander, Biskop i Wexiö*, Stockholm, 1757.

[Oxenstierna, Eric Gustaf], *TAL, hållit af Grefwelige Brahe-Ättens Fullmäktig, Friherre ERIC GUSTAF OXENSTIERNA til Eka, tå S. T. Herr Landt-Marskalken Stafwen återlemnade. Then 15 Octob. 1766*, Stockholm, s.d. [1766].

Oxenstierna, Johan Gabriel, *Caractèrer, portraiter och epigrammer*, utg. Holger Frykenstedt, Stockholm, 1956.

Remontrances de la Cour des Aides de Paris, du mois de Février 1771, s.l., s.d. [Paris, 1771].

[Rudbeck, Thure Gustaf], *Landt-Marskalkens, Öfwerstens och Commendeurens af Kongl. Swärds-Orden, Wälborne Herr THURE GUST. RUDBECKS Håldne TAL, Wid Landt-Marskalks Stafwens emottagande, Then 21 Januarii 1765*, Stockholm, 1765.

[Rudbeck, Thure Gustaf], *TAL, til Ridderskapet och Adelen, af Landt-Marskalken General-Majoren och Commendeuren af Kongl. Maj:ts Swärds-Orden, Wälborne Herr THURE GUSTAF RUDBECK, wid Landt-Marskalks Stafwens nedläggande, then 15. Octob. 1766, s.l., s.d.* [Stockholm, 1766].

[Rålamb, Claes], *TAL, Hållit til Höglofl. Ridderskapet och Adelen, Samt wid Landt-Marskalks Stafwens aflemnande, Af Présidenten och Commendeuren af Kongl. Nordstierne-Orden, Högwälborne Herr Baron CLAES RÅLAMB, Wid Riksdagens början i Stockholm Then 21. Januarii 1765*, Stockholm, s.d. [1765].

[Sebaldt, Carl Fredrich], *TAL, Til Samtelige Rikets Städers Herrar Fullmägtige Hållit af Håf-Rätts-Rådet och Borgmästaren Herr CARL FREDRICH SEBALDT, Tå han, efter slutad Riksdag, afträdde thes Talesmans Embete, then 16 October 1766*, Stockholm, s.d. [1766].

[Stedingk, Curt von], *Mémoires posthumes du feldmaréchal Comte de Stedingk ; redigés sur des lettres, dépêches et autres pièces authentiques laissées à sa famille par le Comte de Björnstjerna*, Paris, 1844–1847.

Sveriges Ridderskaps och Adels riksdags-protokoll från och med år 1719, nittonde delen 1755–1756, I, 17 Oktober–20 November 1755, Stockholm, 1923.

Sveriges ridderskaps och adels riksdagsprotokoll från och med år 1719, tjugosjunde delen 1769–1770, I, 22 april–24 oktober 1769, Stockholm, 1962.

Swea Rikes tilstånd, s.l., 1756.

Tankar Huru en Riksdags-Man Bör Utöva Sina Öma Pligter Emot Medborgare och Fädernesland. I anledning Af en utaf Trycket nyss utkommen Skrift kallad: En Ärlig

Riksdags-Mans Syldigheter [sic], på Urtima Riksdagen 1769, Stockholm, 1769.

[Tessin, Carl Gustaf], *Landt-Marskalkens Högwälborne Grefwe CARL GUSTAF TESSINS Tal, Hållit til Ridderskapet och Adeln Wid Landt-Marskalks Stafwens emottagande Den 17. Maii 1738*, Stockholm, 1738.

[Tessin, Carl Gustaf], *På Kongl. Maj:ts Wägnar, Herr Riks-Rådets, Praesidentens uti Kongl. Maj:ts och Riksens Cancellie Collegio, Öfwerste-Marskalkens hos Theras Kongl. Högheter, Och Åbo Academiae Cancellerens Högwälborne Grefwe CARL GUSTAV TESSINS Hållne TAL, Til Riksens Ständer, tå Riksdagen slutades then 14. December 1747*, Stockholm, s.d. [1747].

[Tessin, Carl Gustaf], *TAL, Til Samtelige Riksens Högloflige Ständer, Af Herr Riks-Rådet, Cantzli-Rådet, Öfwerste-Marskalken och Academiae Cancelleren, Höfwälborne Grefwe CARL GUSTAV TESSIN, Tå Riksens Ständer in Pleno Plenorum uppå Stora Riddarhus Salen woro församlade, then 31. Martii 1747*, Stockholm, 1747.

[Tessin, Carl Gustaf], *Til Hennes Kongl. Maj:t Wår Allernådigsta Drottning Landt-Marskalkens GREF CARL GUSTAF TESSINS Underdåniga Tal, Då hos Hennes Kongl. Maj:t Ridderskapets och Adelens Deputerade, efter sluten Riks-Dag, togo underdånigt afskied den 19 April 1739*, Stockholm, s.d.[1739].

[Tessin, Carl Gustaf], *Underdånigst Tal Til Hans Kongl. Maj:t, Hållit uti Råds-Salen Then 30. Martii 1752. Af Hans Excellence Herr Riks-Rådet, Cancellie-Praesidenten, Hennes Kongl. Maj:ts Öfwerste-Marskalk, Hans Kongl. Höghets Cron-Printsens Gouverneur, Academiae-Cantzleren, Riddaren, Commendeuren och Cantzleren af Kong. Maj:ts Orden, samt Riddaren af Swarta Örn, Högwälborne Grefwe CARL GUSTAF TESSIN, Tå Hans Excellence af-lade Cancellie-Praesidentskapet*, Stockholm, s.d. [1752].

[Troilius, Samuel], *Til Hans Kongl. Maj:t, Ärkie-Biskopens D. SAMUEL TROILII TAL, Hållit på Präste-Ståndets wägnar Uppå Riks-Salen i Stockholm, Wid Riksdagens början Then 25 Octobris 1760*, Stockholm, s.d. [1760].

[Ungern-Sternberg, Matthias Alexander von], *Landt-Marskalkens Högwälborne Baron MATTHIAS ALEXANDER Von UNGERN STERNBERGS Tal, Hållit för Ridderskapet och Adeln Wid Landt-Marskalks-Stafwens afgifwande Then 12. September 1743*, Stockholm s.d. [1743].

[Ungern-Sternberg, Matthias Alexander von], *Landt-Marskalkens Högwälborne Baron MATTHIAS ALEXANDER Von UNGERN STERNBERGS TAL, Hållit på Riks-Salen I Stockholm, När Riksdagen slöts then 12. September 1743*, Stockholm, s.d. [1743].

[Ungern-Sternberg, Matthias Alexander von], *Landt-Marskalkens Högwälborne Baron MATTHIAS ALEXANDER Von UNGERN STERNBERGS Tal, Hållit wid slutet af 1743 års Riksdag Tå Riksens Ständer togo afsked af hwar annan på Riks Salen*, Stockholm s.d. [1743].

[Ungern-Sternberg, Matthias Alexander von], *Til Hans Kongl. Maj:t, Landt-Marskalkens Högwälborne Baron MATTHIAS ALEXANDER Von UNGERN STERNBERGS Underdånige TAL Å samtel. Riksens Ständers wägnar, Då De igenom sina Deputerade i underdånighet gofwo Hans Kongl. Maj:t tilkänna, Hans Durchl. Hertigens af Holstein Gottorp förklarnade til Successor på den Kongl. Swenska Thronen. Hållit den 28 Octobris 1742*, Stockholm, s.d. [1742].

References:

Alm, Mikael, *Kungsord i elfte timmen. Språk & självbild i det gustavianska enväldets legitimitetskamp 1772–1809*, Stockholm, 2002.

Anderson, Benedict, *Imagined Communities. Reflections on the Origin and Spread of Nationalism*, London & New York, 1991.

Antoine, Michel, *Le conseil du roi sous le règne de Louis XV*, Genève, 1970.

Antoine, Michel, *Louis XV*, Paris, 1989.

Bell, David A., *The Cult of the Nation in France. Inventing Nationalism 1680–1800*, Cambridge, Mass., 2001.

Benveniste, Émile, *Vocabulaire des institutions indo-européennes*, Paris, 1969.

Berdahl, Robert M., *The Politics of the Prussian Nobility. The Development of a Conservative Ideology 1770–1848*, Princeton, 1988.

Björkenheim, Magnus, *Äldre fransk litteratur på herrgårdar i Finland*, Helsingfors, 1929.

Blanning, T. C. W., *The Culture of Power and the Power of Culture. Old Regime Europe 1660–1789*, Oxford, 2002.

Blitz, Hans-Martin, *Aus Liebe zum Vaterland. Die deutsche Nation im 18. Jahrhundert*, Hamburg, 2000.

Blomstedt, Yrjö, "Den finländska självständighetstanken på 1780-talet – ideologi eller politisk spekulation", *Historisk Tidskrift för Finland*, 1965.

Bratt, Annabel S., "The development of the idea of citizens' rights", in *States and Citizens. History, Theory, Prospects*, ed. by Quentin Skinner & Bo Stråth, Cambridge, 2003.

Brunner, Otto, Werner Conze & Reinhart Koselleck (Hrsg.), *Geschichtliche Grundbegriffe. Historisches Lexikon zur politisch-sozialen Sprache in Deutschland*, Stuttgart, 1972–1997.

Bruun, Patrick (utg.), *Vardagsslit och sjuårskrig. Upplevt och beskrivet av den nyländske dragonen Carl Johan Aminoff*, Helsingfors, 1994.

Carlsson, Ingemar, *Olof von Dalin och den politiska propagandan inför "lilla ofreden". Sagan Om Hästen och Wår-Wisa i samtidspolitisk belysning*, Lund, 1966.

Carlsson, Ingemar, *Parti – partiväsen – partipolitiker 1731–43. Kring uppkomsten av våra första politiska partier*, Stockholm, 1981.

Carlsson, Sten, *Ståndssamhälle och ståndspersoner 1700–1865. Studier rörande det svenska ståndssamhällets upplösning*, Lund, 1973.

Cavallin, Maria, *I kungens och folkets tjänst. Synen på den svenske ämbetsmannen 1750–1780*, Göteborg, 2003.

Cederberg, A. R., *Anjalan liiton historialliset lähteet. Lähdekriitillinen tutkielma*, Helsinki, 1931.

Christensson, Jakob, *Lyckoriket. Studier i svensk upplysning*, Stockholm, 1996.

Danielson-Kalmari, J. R., *Suomen valtio- ja yhteiskuntaelämä 18:nnella ja 19:nnellä vuosisadalla. Kustavilainen aika. 2. Osa*, Porvoo, 1921.

Darnton, Robert, "An Early Information Society: News and the Media in Eighteenth-Century Paris", *American Historical Review*, vol. 105 (2001:1).

Delblanc, Sven, *Ära och minne. Studier kring ett motivkomplex i 1700-talets litteratur*, Stockholm, 1965.

Delon, Michel, *Le savoir-vivre libertin*, Paris, 2000.

Derathé, Robert, *Jean-Jacques Rousseau et la science politique de son temps*, Paris, 1995.

Duby, Georges, *Les Trois ordres ou l'imaginaire féodal*, Paris, 1978.

Duranton, Henri, "Comment se diffuse l'information au XVIIIᵉ siècle. L'exemple des *Lettres sur les affaires du temps* de Jacques-Élie Gastelier", in *Nouvelles, gazettes, mémoires secrets (1775–1800). Actes du colloque international, Karlstad, 17–20 septembre 1994*, dir. Birgitta Berglund-Nilsson, Karlstad, 2000.

Ehrard, Jean, *L'esprit des mots. Montesquieu en lui-même et parmi les siens*, Genève, 1998.

Elmroth, Ingvar, *Nyrekryteringen till de högre ämbetena 1720–1809. En socialhistorisk studie*, Lund, 1962.

Englund, Peter, *Det hotade huset. Adliga föreställningar om samhället under stormaktstiden*, Stockholm, 1989.

Fahlbeck, Erik, "Studier öfver frihetstidens politiska idéer", *Statsvetenskaplig Tidskrift*, vol. 18 (1915); vol. 19 (1916).

Frängsmyr, Tore, *Svensk idéhistoria. Bildning och vetenskap under tusen år. Del I: 1000–1809*, Stockholm, 2004.

Garnsey, Peter & Richard Saller, *The Roman Empire: Economy, Society and Culture*, London, 1987.

Gordon, Daniel, *Citizens Without Sovereignty. Equality and Sociability in French Thought, 1670–1789*, Princeton, 1994.

Görlitz, Walter, *Die Junker. Adel und Bauer im deutschen Osten. Geschichtliche Bilanz von 7 Jahrhunderten*, Limburg an der Lahn, 1964.

Greśkowiak-Krwawicz, Anna, "Anti-monarchism in Polish Republicanism in the Seventeenth and Eighteenth Centuries", in *Republicanism. A Shared European Heritage*, vol. 1: *Republicanism and Constitutionalism in Early Modern Europe*, ed. by Martin van Gelderen & Quentin Skinner, Cambridge, 2002.

Hallberg, Peter, *Ages of Liberty. Social Upheaval, History Writing, and the New Public Sphere in Sweden, 1740–1792*, Stockholm, 2003.

Hammar, Elisabet, « *La Française* ». *Mille et une façons d'apprendre le français en Suède avant 1802*, Uppsala, 1991.

Hammar, Elisabet, *L'enseignement du français en Suède jusqu'en 1807. Méthodes et manuels*, Stockholm, 1980.

Hazard, Paul, *La crise de la conscience européenne 1680–1715*, Paris, 1961.

Hennings, Beth, *Gustav III som kronprins*, Stockholm, 1935.

Hessler, Carl Arvid, "Aristokratfördömandet. En riktning i svensk historieskrivning", *Scandia* 15 (1943:2).

Hours, Bernard, *Louis XV et sa Cour. Le roi, l'étiquette et le courtisan*, Paris, 2002.

Hylland Eriksen, Thomas, *Ethnicity and Nationalism: Anthropological Perspectives*, London, 1993.

Hyvärinen, Matti & Jussi Kurunmäki, Kari Palonen, Tuija Pulkkinen & Henrik Stenius (toim.), *Käsitteet liikkeessä. Suomen poliittisen kulttuurin käsitehistoria*, Tampere, 2003.

Ihalainen, Pasi, *Agents of the People*, Leiden & New York, 2009, forthcoming.

Ihalainen, Pasi, "I vilken mån talades det om folksuveränitet och representativ demokrati på den svenska riksdagen 1771–1772?", *Historisk Tidskrift för Finland*, vol. 93 (2008:2).

Ihalainen, Pasi, "Lutherska drag i den svenska politiska kulturen i slutet av frihetstiden. En begreppsanalytisk undersökning av fyra riksdagspredikningar", in *Riksdag, kaffehus och predikstol. Frihetstidens politiska kultur 1766–1772*, red. Marie-Christine Skuncke & Henrika Tandefelt, Stockholm, 2003.

Ihalainen, Pasi, "Parlamentspredikningarna som medium för officiell politisk teori i England, Holland och Sverige på 1700-talet", *Historisk Tidskrift för Finland*, vol. 88 (2003:2).

Ihalainen, Pasi, *Protestant Nations Redefined. Changing Perceptions of National Identity in the Rhetoric of the English, Dutch and Swedish Public Churches, 1685–1772*, Boston & Leiden, 2005.

Ihalainen, Pasi, *The Discourse on Political Pluralism in Early Eighteenth-Century England. A Conceptual Study with Special Reference to Terminology of Religious Origin*, Helsinki, 1999.

Ihalainen, Pasi, "The Sanctification and Democratisation of 'the Nation' and 'the People' in late Eighteenth-Century Northwestern Europe: Proposing a Comparative Conceptual History", *Contributions to the History of Concepts*, vol. 3 (2007:2).

Ilmakunnas, Johanna, *Aristokraattinen elämäntapa ja sen rahoitus 1700-luvun Ruotsissa. Carl ja Axel von Fersenin tulot, varallisuus ja kulutustottumukset*, Helsingin yliopisto, 2004 (unpublished thesis).

Jouanna, Arlette, *Le devoir de révolte. La noblesse française et la gestation de l'État moderne, 1559–1661*, Paris, 1989.

Jussila, Osmo, *Suomen historian suuret myytit*, Helsinki, 2007.

Jägerskiöld, Olof, *Hovet och författningsfrågan 1760–1766*, Uppsala, 1943.

Jägerskiöld, Stig, "Tyrannmord och motståndsrätt 1792–1809. En studie kring J. J. Anckarström", *Scandia* 28 (1962).

Kaitaro, Timo, "Klandestin filosofisk litteratur. Upplysande allusioner och nätverk", *Historisk Tidskrift för Finland*, vol. 88 (2003:2).

Kantorowicz, Ernst H., *The King's Two Bodies. A Study in Mediaeval Political Theology*, Princeton, 1957.

Karlsson-Sjögren, Åsa, *Männen, kvinnorna och rösträtten. Medborgarskap och representation 1723–1866*, Stockholm, 2006.

131

Karonen, Petri, *Pohjoinen suurvalta. Ruotsi ja Suomi 1521–1809*, Helsinki, 1999.

Kjellin, Gunnar, *Rikshistoriografen Anders Schönberg. Studier i riksdagarnas och de politiska tänkesättens historia 1760–1809*, Lund, 1952.

Klinge, Matti, "Télémaques budskap i Sverige", *Det roliga börjar hela tiden. Bokförläggare Kjell Peterson 60 år den 20 december 1996*, Stockholm, 1996.

Korkman, Petter, *Jean Barbeyrac and natural law*, diss., Åbo Akademi, 2001.

Koselleck, Reinhart, *Preußen zwischen Reform und Revolution. Allgemeines Landrecht, Verwaltung und soziale Bewegung von 1791 bis 1848*, Stuttgart, 1967.

Koselleck, Reinhart, *Vergangene Zukunft. Zur Semantik geschichtlicher Zeiten*, Frankfurt am Main, 1979.

Lagerroth, Fredrik, "En frihetstida lärobok i gällande statsrätt", *Statsvetenskaplig Tidskrift för politik – statistik – ekonomi. Ny följd*, vol. 40 (1937).

Lagerroth, Fredrik, *Frihetstidens författning. En studie i den svenska konstitutionalismens historia*, Stockholm, 1915.

Lagerroth, Fredrik, *Sveriges riksdag. Historisk och statsvetenskaplig framställning*, vol. 6, *Frihetstidens maktägande stander 1719–1772*, Stockholm, 1934.

Lappalainen, Mirkka, *Suku, valta, suurvalta. Creutzit 1600-luvun Ruotsissa ja Suomessa*, Helsinki, 2005.

Lesch, Bruno, *Jan Anders Jägerhorn. Patriot och världsmedborgare, separatist och emigrant*, Helsingfors, 1941.

Lindberg, Bo, *Den antika skevheten. Politiska ord och begrepp i det tidig-moderna Sverige*, Stockholm, 2006.

Lindberg, Bo, "Latein und Grossmacht. Das Latein im Schweden des 17. Jahrhunderts", in *Germania latina – Latinitas teutonica*, hrsg. Eckhard Kessler & Heinrich C. Kuhn, München, 2003.

Lindkvist, Thomas & Maria Sjöberg, Susanna Hedenborg & Lars Kvarnström, *Det svenska samhället*, Lund, 2006 (2 vols).

Lindroth, Sten, *Svensk lärdomshistoria. Frihetstiden*, Stockholm, 1978.

Linton, Marisa, *The Politics of Virtue in Enlightenment France*, Basingstoke, 2001.

Lönnroth, Erik, *Den stora rollen. Kung Gustaf III spelad av honom själv*, Stockholm, 1986.

MacIntyre, Alasdair, *After Virtue: a Study in Moral Theory*, London, 1985 (1981).

Malmström, Carl Gustaf, *Sveriges politiska historia från K. Carl XII:s död till statshvälfningen 1772*, 6 vols, Stockholm, 1855–1877.

Mandrou, Robert, *L'Europe « absolutiste ». Raison et raison d'État 1649–1775*, Paris, Fayard, 1977.

Manninen, Juha, *Valistus ja kansallinen identiteetti. Aatehistoriallinen tutkimus 1700-luvun Pohjolasta*, Helsinki, 2000.

Mattsson, Annie, "Kvinnliga tidsfördriv och manliga mätresser. Kön och sexualitet i smädandet av Gustaf III", *Historisk Tidskrift för Finland*, vol. 92 (2007:4).

Maza, Sarah, *The Myth of the French Bourgeoisie. An Essay on Social Imaginary, 1750–1850*, Cambridge, Mass., 2003.

Melkersson, Martin, *Staten, ordningen och friheten. En studie av den styrande elitens syn på statens roll mellan stormaktstiden och 1800-talet*, Uppsala, 1997.

Merisalo, Outi, "The *Querelle des Anciens et des Modernes* at the Academia Aboensis in the Eighteenth Century", in *Germania latina –Latinitas teutonica*, hrsg. Eckhard Kessler & Heinrich C. Kuhn, München, 2003.

Miller, Fred D., *Nature, Justice and Rights in Aristotle's Politics*, Oxford, 1995.

Motley, Mark, *Becoming a French aristocrat. The education of the court nobility 1580–1715*, Princeton, 1990.

Nicolet, Claude, *Le métier de citoyen dans la Rome républicaine*, Paris, 1976.

Nilsén, Per, *Att "stoppa munnen till på bespottare". Den akademiska undervisningen i svensk statsrätt under frihetstiden*, Lund, 2001.

Nordin, Jonas, "Anders Johan von Höpken. 'Sveriges Tacitus'", *Drottning Lovisa Ulrika och Vitterhetsakademien*, red. Sten Åke Nilsson, Stockholm, 2003.

Nordin, Jonas, *Ett fattigt men fritt folk. Nationell och politisk självbild i Sverige från sen stormaktstid till slutet av frihetstiden*, Stockholm/Stehag, 2000.

Nordin, Jonas, "Frihetstidens radikalism", in *Riksdag, kaffehus och predikstol. Frihetstidens politiska kultur 1766–1772*, red. Marie-Christine Skuncke & Henrika Tandefelt, Stockholm & Helsingfors, 2003.

Nordin, Jonas, "I broderlig samdräkt? Förhållandet Sverige–Finland under 1700-talet och Anthony D. Smiths *ethnie*-begrepp", *Scandia* 64 (1998: 2).

Nurmiainen, Jouko, *Edistys ja yhteinen hyvä vapaudenajan ruotsalaisessa poliittisessa kielessä*, Helsinki, 2009, forthcoming.

Nurmiainen, Jouko, "Frågan om 'etnisk nationalism', nationell självbild och 1700-talets Sverige", *Historisk Tidskrift för Finland*, vol. 88 (2003:3).

Nurmiainen, Jouko, "Gemensamma privilegier för ett odalstånd. Alexander Kepplerus som borgmästare och samhällstänkare", in *Riksdag, kaffehus och predikstol. Frihetstidens politiska kultur 1766–1772*, red. Marie-Christine Skuncke & Henrika Tandefelt, Stockholm & Helsingfors, 2003.

Nurmiainen, Jouko, "Particular interest and the common good in Swedish mid-18th-century diet politics: the 'Finnish' perspective", *Scandinavian Journal of History*, vol. 32 (2007:4).

Nyman, Elmar, *Indragningsmakt och tryckfrihet 1785–1810*, Stockholm, 1963.

Pakkasvirta, Jussi & Pasi Saukkonen (toim.), *Nationalismit*, Helsinki, 2005.

Parland-von Essen, Jessica, *Behagets betydelser. Döttrarnas edukation i det sena 1700-talets adelskultur*, Hedemora, 2005.

Pocock, J. G. A., *Barbarism and Religion*, vol. 3: *The First Decline and Fall*, Cambridge, 2003.

Pocock, J. G. A., *The Machiavellian Moment. Florentine Political Thought and the Atlantic Republican Tradition*, Princeton, 2003 (1975).

Pocock, J. G. A., *Virtue, Commerce, and History. Essays on Political Thought and History, Chiefly in the Eighteenth* Century, Cambridge, 1985.

Proschwitz, Gunnar von, *Gustave III de Suède et la langue française : recherches sur la correspondance d'un roi*, Göteborg, 1962.

Reichardt, Rolf & Eberhard Schmitt, *Handbuch politisch-sozialer Grundbegriffe in Frankreich 1680–1820*, München, 1985–.

Richter, Melvin, *The History of Political and Social Concepts*, Oxford, 1995.

Roberts, Michael, *The Age of Liberty. Sweden 1719–1772*, Cambridge, 1986.

Rosenberg, Hans, *Bureaucracy, Aristocracy, and Autocracy: The Prussian Experience, 1660–1815*, Cambridge, Mass., 1958.

Runeby, Nils, *Monarchia mixta. Maktfördelningsdebatt i Sverige under den tidigare stormaktstiden*, Uppsala, 1962.

Runefelt, Leif, *Dygden som välståndets grund. Dygd, nytta och egennytta i frihetstidens ekonomiska tänkande*, Stockholm, 2005.

Saastamoinen, Kari, "Johdatus poliittisiin käsitteisiin uuden ajan alun Ruotsissa", in *Käsitteet liikkeessä. Suomen poliittisen kulttuurin käsitehistoria*, toim. Matti Hyvärinen, Jussi Kurunmäki, Kari Palonen, Tuija Pulkkinen & Henrik Stenius, Tampere, 2003.

Sandström, Allan, *Officerarna som fick nog. Anjalamännen och Gustaf III:s ryska krig 1788–1790*, Örebro, 1996.

Sarkamo, Ville, "Karolinernas akillesval. Krigaräran inom den karolinska armén under stora nordiska kriget (1700–1721)", *Historisk Tidskrift för Finland*, vol. 90 (2005:4).

Saussure, Ferdinand de, *Cours de linguistique générale*, Paris, 1916.

Schieder, Theodor, *Friedrich der Grosse. Ein Königtum der Widersprüche*, München, 1983.

Schilling, Heinz, *Höfe und Allianzen. Deutschland 1648–1763*, Berlin, 1994.

Schulze, Hagen, *Staat und Nation in der europäische Geschichte*, München, 1994.

Sennefelt, Karin, *Den politiska sjukan. Dalupproret 1743 och frihetstida politisk kultur*, Hedemora, 2001.

Skinner, Quentin, *Liberty before Liberalism*, Cambridge, 1998.

Skinner, Quentin, "Motives, Intentions and the Interpretation of Texts", *New Literary History* 3 (1972).

Skinner, Quentin, "States and the freedom of citizens", in *States & Citizens. History, Theory, Prospects*, ed. by Quentin Skinner & Bo Stråth, Cambridge, 2003.

133

Skinner, Quentin, *The Foundations of Modern Political Thought. Volume 1: The Renaissance*, Cambridge, 1978.

Skinner, Quentin, *The Foundations of Modern Political Thought. Volume 2: The Age of Reformation*, Cambridge, 1978.

Skinner, Quentin & Bo Stråth (eds), *States and Citizens History, Theory, Prospects*, Cambridge, 2003.

Skuncke, Marie-Christine, *Gustaf III – Det offentliga barnet. En prins retoriska och politiska fostran*, Stockholm, 1993.

Skuncke, Marie-Christine, "La liberté dans la culture politique suédoise au XVIIIe siècle", *Liberté : Héritage du passé ou idée des Lumières ?*, éd. Anna Grześkowiak-Krwawicz et Izabella Zatorska, Krakow/Warszawa 2003.

Skuncke, Marie-Christine, "Medier, mutor och nätverk", in *Riksdag, kaffehus och predikstol. Frihetstidens politiska kultur, 1766–1772*, red. Marie-Christine Skuncke & Henrika Tandefelt, Stockholm & Helsingfors, 2003.

Skuncke, Marie-Christine & Henrika Tandefelt (red.), *Riksdag, kaffehus och predikstol. Frihetstidens politiska kultur, 1766–1772*, Stockholm & Helsingfors, 2003.

Smith, Jay M., *Nobility Reimagined. The Patriotic Nation in Eighteenth-Century France*, Ithaca, 2005.

Stenius, Henrik, *Frivilligt, jämlikt, samfälligt. Föreningsväsendets utveckling i Finland fram till 1900-talets början med speciell hänsyn till massorganisationsprincipens genombrott*, Helsingfors, 1987.

Svedjedal, Johan, "Textkritisk litteraturteori. Några linjer i svensk och anglosaxisk textkritisk debatt", in *Textkritik. Teori och praktik vid edering av litterära texter. Föredrag vid Svenska Vitterhetssamfundets symposium 10–11 september 1990*, red. Lars Burman & Barbro Ståhle Sjönell, Stockholm, 1991.

Tandefelt, Henrika, *Konsten att härska. Gustaf III inför sina undersåtar*, Helsingfors, 2008.

Tocqueville, Alexis de, *L'ancien régime et la Révolution*. Préface, notes, bibliographie, chronologie par Françoise Mélonio, Paris, 1988.

Valentin, Hugo, *Frihetstidens riddarhus. Några bidrag till dess karakteristik*, Stockholm, 1915.

Van Gelderen, Martin, "The state and its rivals in early-modern Europe", in *States and Citizens History, Theory, Prospects*, ed. by Quentin Skinner & Bo Stråth , Cambridge, 2003.

Van Gelderen, Martin & Quentin Skinner (eds), *Republicanism. A Shared European Heritage*, Cambridge, 2002, 2 vols.

Williams, E. N., *The Ancien Régime in Europe. Government and Society in the Major States 1648–1789*, London, 1999 (1970).

Winton, Patrik, *Frihetstidens politiska praktik. Nätverk och offentlighet 1746–1766*, Uppsala, 2006.

Wolff, Charlotta, "Aristocratic republicanism and the hate of sovereignty in 18-century Sweden", *Scandinavian Journal of History*, vol. 32 (2007:4).

Wolff, Charlotta, "Kabal och kärlek. Vänskapen som alternativ sociabilitet i 1700-talets hovsamhällen", *Historisk Tidskrift för Finland*, vol. 89 (2004:2).

Wolff, Charlotta, "Pro Patria et Libertate. Frihetsbegreppet i 1700-talets svenska politiska språk", *Historisk Tidskrift för Finland*, vol. 92 (2007:1).

Wolff, Charlotta, *Vänskap och makt. Den svenska politiska eliten och upplysningstidens Frankrike*, Helsingfors, 2005.

Index

www.ingramcontent.com/pod-product-compliance
Lightning Source LLC
Chambersburg PA
CBHW081740270326
41932CB00020B/3351